For Nancy,
whose love and encouragement was the lighthouse in my life when I was ready to crash onto the rocks; and Susan and Mike, who helped with the move, but more importantly, introduced me to the best thing that ever happened to me.

—*J.H.*

For my late mother—a gentle, sweet soul of a woman—who passed away in 1990. There is a hollow place in my heart ever since she left to take her place with the angels, but of course, she was always an angel—I just didn't realize it at the time.

—*"Doc"*

PATRICK STEWART

James Hatfield
and George "Doc" Burt

PINNACLE BOOKS
KENSINGTON PUBLISHING CORP.

PINNACLE BOOKS are published by

Kensington Publishing Corp.
850 Third Avenue
New York, NY 10022

First Printing: September, 1996
10 9 8 7 6 5 4 3 2 1

Printed in the United States of America

He is brilliant and stubborn, warm and prickly, insecure and dominating. He made bald sexy and captured women's hearts with a commanding "Make it so." He is Patrick Stewart, and this is his story.

Patrick Stewart reveals everything you want to know about the intriguing man behind Captain Picard, from his tragic childhood to his rise from obscurity to TV immortality . . . along with the last word on the raging debate over who is the better captain, Picard or Kirk. (Here are some hints:

* Picard's *Enterprise* has windows.

* Picard can tell the difference between a real woman and a mirage.

* Kirk was captured and held prisoner on every third mission.

* Picard didn't have to cheat at the *Kobayashi Maru* scenario at Starfleet Academy.

* Two words: No toupee!)

I have truly loved what I've done in my life.
I think I've been blessed, very fortunate,
to have had the experiences I've had for 30 years. . . .
My only unfulfilled ambition:
I want to live forever

—Patrick Stewart, 1994

Table of Contents

Authors' Note and Acknowledgments

Patrick Stewart is an extraordinarily complex individual. He closely guards his personal life but understands the global interest in everything about him and his career. Although Stewart declined to assist personally in the writing of this biography, he certainly did not make any public or private attempt to dissuade his friends and colleagues from cooperating. For that we are grateful.

We are indebted to so many people who helped make this book possible. First and foremost is Tracy Bernstein, our long-suffering editor at Kensington, who battled the Kirk vs. Picard forces at the publishing company to even pitch the idea of a Stewart biography and who graciously allowed us a thirty-day extension when we bit off more than we could chew.

To research our subject as thoroughly as possible, we began trying to read everything ever written about Patrick Stewart, an enormous task considering an acting career that spans two continents and forty years of theater, television and motion picture performances. For assistance in combing through the mass of print, audio, video and online reviews, articles and interviews of Stewart, we are beholden to P.S.N. member Sally K. Dickson in the U.S. and Michelle Merrick in the U.K. Without sounding too melodramatic, there obviously would not have been a book without their combined efforts.

Sue Harke, *Star Trek* archivist, consultant and fan extraordinaire, deserves many thanks for her endless sources and connections, prodigious memory and tireless efforts to make this book happen. Her assistance, especially during the last quarter of this project, was invaluable.

Our special thanks to Rose W. Clark, senior editorial assistant at a national newspaper (which shall go nameless at her request), who dealt admirably with the research problems imposed by a tight production schedule, and provided us with a treasure chest of previously published (but difficult to obtain) articles, interviews and photographs; and where would we have been without those walking-and-talking human *Trek* encyclopedias Larry Nemecek (*The Next Generation Companion*), Treksperts Mark Altman (*Sci-Fi Universe*) and Edward Gross (*Cinescape*), *Inside Trek* columnist and freelance writer Ian Spelling, and *Warp 10* and *Subspace Chatter* online editor Ruben Macias.

We are especially grateful for the kindness and continued friendship of Ed Echols, who took the time on the night before his wedding to dig through stacks and stacks of back-issue *Playboys* to find the one with the Stewart interview. The authors really believe he was using the search as an excuse to take one last bachelor's stroll down memory lane before the wedding bells rang the next afternoon.

A specialized group of Trekkers who were of great help with research, fact documentation, and photographs and are due many thanks are members of the International Fans of Patrick Stewart; the Patrick Stewart Estrogen Brigade (*especially* Karen A. Droms); the Patrick Stewart Network; and the Patrick Stewart Appreciation Society in the U.K. (Margaret Rainey and Anita Van-

Gelder in particular). All of these ladies were dedicated in their intentions to make absolutely sure that what we wrote would clear up several inaccuracies previously written about Mr. Stewart in other publications.

Jake Dakota, our research assistant, spent months gathering *Trek* books, magazine articles, newspaper clippings, radio and TV interviews, and online information—all of which he diligently filed and cross-referenced, while trying occasionally to give the office some semblance of order. While the authors worked on the book, he chased leads, pored over microfilm, chased out-of-print newspaper articles, convinced reluctant people to talk, and always somehow opened slammed doors. J.D. can now take that much needed vacation with our hearty thanks and, of course, our advance against royalties.

We are forever indebted to Pat Remington, C.J. Holland and, especially J.V.H., who were exceptionally helpful with their time, information, recollections, and insightful perspectives into Stewart's persona.

Other sources are still associated in some official capacity with the *Star Trek* franchise and/or Paramount Studios and because of their positions, cannot be thanked publicly. They have asked for anonymity and we have respected their wishes, but we are grateful for their enormous assistance nonetheless.

And, finally, to author Ruby Jean Jensen, who cleared the way through the wilderness; Marcia Amsterdam, our literary agent, but more importantly, our friend; and Nancy Bledsoe, for her continuing faith and support and grace under pressure.

—James Hatfield & George "Doc" Burt

Prologue

All Good Things . . .

He's made me a little more thoughtful. A little less impulsive. I hope, more patient. I was very short on patience and tolerance once.

> —Patrick Stewart, responding to a *TV Guide* interview when asked, 'How has playing Captain Picard changed you?'

In 1987, Patrick Stewart, an accomplished Shakespearean actor with finely sculptured features, prominent nose, highly polished crown, and resounding voice, walked into his *Star Trek* audition at Paramount Studios, assumed an air of unassailable authority, and walked away with the starring role. For the next seven years, as Captain Picard, Stewart repeatedly delivered memorable performances as he skillfully guided his crew on countless grand adventures through the galaxy of *The Next Generation*. Stewart's Picard was the epitome of leadership: strong, forceful, and forever dutiful to his purpose, exuding authority and presence, honor, and intellect.

By the end of the series, however, Stewart was over-extended, doing far more than just portraying Picard. He noted that the producers allowed him to do his critically acclaimed one-man show, *A Christmas Carol*, in London during the Christmas season. After returning to the *Next Generation* set for the last half of the final season, the producers kept him busy with very complex episodes, as well as one final directorial turn.

Once pressed about the rigor and tumult of the final season, Stewart admitted that the months leading up to the end of the series were some of the most trying of his career. "This is the toughest job I've ever done, except maybe when I worked on a building site unloading cement blocks. That was marginally more difficult. And the last three months have been especially tough, culminating with this epic special. In the final two hours, I was in every single scene of the episode and shifting between time periods. There were moments when I thought I wouldn't be able to finish the episode," he confessed. "I was so tired. And yes, it did lead to some outbursts like the one [with *Entertainment Tonight*], for which I apologized personally to everyone concerned. It was turning into a three-ring circus with the press on the set every day." Stewart, who had usually been accessible to interviewers in the past, had stomped about the Paramount sound stage during the finale's filming, screaming at the top of his lungs, "Get that bloody camera out of my face!" to an *Entertainment Tonight* crew that had been assigned to tape a segment on the bridge of the starship *Enterprise*.

Stewart, self-cast as the *enfant terrible*, had been for the past seven years the ruler of the roost: some days comical and engaging, and just as often boorish, moody, and manic. *Next Generation* directors, producers, writers, and the actor's co-stars during the series's long run on TV were in agreement when they collectively described Stewart as "very focused, rather passionate and given to occasional speechifying. But he's also gregarious, a delightful storyteller and pleased to laugh at himself."

Stewart, however, wasn't the only cast member acting strangely during the filming of the show's much ballyhooed final episode. Of course, some backstage strain was inevitable whenever a hugely successful series such as *The Next Generation* came to the end of its television life. Amid a blaze of worldwide media scrutiny, a crew already exhausted by the long, ambitious season, and a cast mindful of both the onrushing *Star Trek Generations* movie and their pending unemployment for the first time in seven years, you could practically cut the tension on the set with a type-3 phaser rifle.

Jonathan Frakes, one of Stewart's closest friends and the actor who portrayed Commander William Riker, the captain's first officer, acknowledged that he didn't want the series to end. "I think we were having a classic psychological reaction to having our jobs taken away from us. Speaking for myself, and a couple of others, we were acting out our frustration and disappointment. Instead of being in touch with our emotions as we would like to be, I think we were unsure what this meant. We had grown so close and so intimate and to see the end of the road created a very strange energy in all of us."

"We're a family in crisis," added LeVar Burton, the actor who played the blind *Enterprise* engineer, Geordi La Forge. "You can't end something like this without pushing people's buttons. It's going to bring up strong emotions, and everybody's going to handle it differently."

Aiming to make series finale *The Next Generation*'s best-ever segment, director Winrich Kolbe came to feel the project was taking a backseat to various unrelated distractions: the actors' ongoing contract negotiations for the upcoming *Trek* movie, their blaming of Stewart for the cancellation of the show, their fear about less-than-stellar roles post-*Next Generation,* and a revision to the already complex production schedule so Gates McFadden, who played Dr. Beverly Crusher, could leave long enough to shoot *Mystery Dance,* pilot for ABC.

"It was the end of the season, everybody was basically tired and worn out, and tempers were short," Kolbe explained. "It came to blows about halfway through. We had a big argument, which led to a couple of run-ins with camera crews by an exhausted Stewart, who never liked to be filmed while rehearsing anyway."

Why was *The Next Generation* being canceled at the height of its popularity, particularly peculiar since most of the cast had another year remaining on their contracts? Reportedly, Stewart, the most famous bald superstar since Telly Savalas, was becoming more and more concerned about being sucked into the career black hole that had seemingly swallowed some other *Trek* veterans. Also, Stewart had supposedly refused to loop segments of the last episode on weekends and reports were being leaked from the *Next Generation* set that the other cast members were getting fed up with his supercharged ego and Prima Donna attitude.

Stewart, an intelligent, articulate man with the deep, crisp, and clear voice of a person twice his size, offered his own interpretation on the end of the highest-rated syndicated drama in the history of television. "I was nervous, yes! I had seen it happen to others. I looked at *Star Trek* as a very luxurious albatross. I was ready to move on for a quite a while. For me, the timing is perfect. I had been increasingly feeling that I'd given the best of my work on the series. The last two years especially have found me feeling an intense restlessness. I needed to go on to something else. I wanted to find work that would dynamite the captain Picard image."

When the final scene for *The Next Generation*'s series ending episode, *All Good Things* . . . was finally completed and the cameras were shut off for good on Paramount's Stage 18, Stewart stood on the scaffold above the fatigued production crew and delivered a surprise farewell address:

"I've been cleaning out my trailer and I found a piece of paper," he told the crowd in his ever-commanding and familiar British baritone. "It's a quote that I read at Gene Roddenberry's [the late *Star Trek* creator's] memorial, and it suddenly seemed really appropriate.

" 'To walk,' " he majestically quoted from the writings of British psychotherapist Robin Skynner, " 'we have to lean forward, lose our balance, and begin to fall. We let go constantly of the previous stability, falling all the time, trusting that we will find a succession of new stabilities with each step. The fullest living is a constant dying of the past, enjoying the present fully, but holding it lightly; letting it go without clinging and moving freely into new experiences. Our experience of the past, and of those dear to us, is not lost at all, but remains richly within us.' "

So there was no official farewell, no-last-time-before-an-audience lovefest like the cast of *Cheers* had (nor, mercifully, would there be any drunken revelry on *The Tonight Show* with Jay Leno). Instead, production came to an end with Stewart fittingly recalling the tribute prose he had delivered at the creator of *Star Trek*'s memorial service. Truly, all good things must end.

As the tears subsided, Jonathan Frakes took a chair and began to hum *The Next Generation* theme music. A moment later, Brent Spiner, who played the golden-skinned android, Data, joined in. So, then did Michael Dorn, who portrayed the surly Klingon Worf. And then Burton. And then Stewart. Eventually it was a glorious chorus of swaying, arm-waving *Enterprise* officers booming out round after round after round.

"Since this is our last day, there's something I've been meaning to tell you all," Stewart said as he put his arm romantically around a burly, mustachioed stagehand. Ever since he had ended his twenty-five-year marriage in 1990 and broke off an engagement with another woman four years later, there had been whispered rumors circulating around Hollywood that Stewart was gay. He even found "something quite flattering" in the suggestions of others that he was not a conventionally heterosexual male.

For a brief moment, but what seemed like eons, the cast and crew were frozen in time, their faces aghast as they collectively wondered if Stewart had chosen this moment to publicly acknowledge his alleged homosexuality. But when his face broke out into a smile, everyone on the set realized that he was simply unwinding from the relentless stress of the past few months and was honoring a promise the cast had made to each other seven years earlier: during some seventeen- or eighteen-hour days on the set, one of them would "always be responsible for one big belly laugh a day."

However, as the cast and crew took Stewart's lead and became more determined to turn the atmosphere buoyant, the moody actor abruptly retreated back to his set chair and seemed preoccupied with his thoughts as he sipped tea (Tetley's, not Earl Grey) and played a round of Tetris on the Nintendo Game Boy his two children had given him as a Christmas present. Occasionally, he would set the teacup and video pastime aside and stare blankly off into the distance.

Looking like a lost orphan in the middle of the cavernous sound stage, Stewart perhaps had the distinct feeling that he, too, was slipping back through three different time periods—the present, the future, and back to the past—just as his character, Captain Picard, had done in the two-hour series finale that they had just completed filming.

In his mind, Stewart could visualize the history-making scene he would soon film for *Generations*, when William Shatner's legendary Captain James T. Kirk would die in his arms and the *Star Trek* torch would be passed on to *The Next Generation;* Stewart may have felt slight pangs of regret and guilt in the present time as he watched his fellow cast members crying and hugging and realized that he had all the affection in the world for these people and because of his reluctance to continue working on the series, they were now out of regular work; and, finally, Stewart's mind might have travelled back to the past—back in time to the beginning of *The Next Generation,* when he was so sure he was going to get fired that he didn't unpack his bags for six weeks. Back farther to his years with the Royal Shakespeare Company. Back farther to his roots. Back to the British town of Mirfield. Back to a violent childhood and an alcoholic father that made his life a living hell . . .

One

Yesterday's Nightmares, Tomorrow's Dreams

Lord we know what we are, but know not what we may be.

—Shakespeare, *Hamlet,* 4:5

Patrick Stewart was born on July 13, 1940, in Mirfield, a small town of 12,000 in Yorkshire, the largest county in England. His father, Alfred, was a housepainter, active trade unionist, and highly decorated career soldier who served in World War II as a sergeant major in a British Army parachute regiment. Patrick's mother, Gladys (Barraclough), helped make ends meet as a factory weaver. His childhood memories of her dead-end work in the cotton mill were bleak: "[She] operated an enormous, terrifying machine in a huge, drafty weaving shed along with two hundred other women. She was merely a cog in the wheel of the local industry, making heavy woolen blankets."

Young Patrick was brought up in what he later described as "a poor working class family in a house that had one room downstairs and one room upstairs. My much older brothers, Geoffrey and Trevor, and I shared a double bed in my parents' bedroom." The family, far from being a haven of peace and happiness, was an emotional and physical battleground. It was that classic dysfunctional family setting that first exposed Patrick to physical violence, and also the setting that established the emotional context and meaning of violence. True, there existed some degree of love and happiness, but they were canceled out by the brutality and humiliation of emotional and physical abuse.

A child's notions about love and trust, right and wrong, are formed by his parents' words and deeds. In Patrick's family, unintended consequences began to develop early on. A confused Patrick began to believe that when something was really important it justified the use of physical force. A rambunctious, hell-raising young Patrick became increasingly involved in brawls with other kids at school and was on the verge of being expelled several times.

Alfred was celebrated as a hero when he came home to Mirfield after the war ended, but he couldn't cope with civilian life afterward. The transition from reserved and disciplined soldier to common, unskilled laborer created feelings of frustration and inadequacy, which, when fueled by alcohol, festered into rage and violence, especially against his family.

Patrick's memories of his childhood were frequently frightening, a period in which, he recalled, "the *threat* of violence was always present . . . the bogeyman was real flesh and blood in my life. I never knew what would happen next, and I spent a large part of my childhood afraid." Alfred's abuse did not immediately start with physical violence, but rather with a steady and prolonged barrage of verbal fault-finding and denigrating insults, which unlike physical abuse, left scars that were less obvious. Like most children his age, Patrick was impressionable, sensitive to his environment and very fragile. And Alfred made it very clear that Patrick would never live up to his expectations: his frail physique wasn't "manly enough," and although the boy was considered to be an exceptional soccer player in school, he didn't perform in sports to the level his father had predetermined. Even worse he was interested in "that bloody, make-believe world of acting," occasionally performing in plays at the local church.

All children need to feel worthy and loved, but Alfred had effectively shattered Patrick's self-confidence and self-esteem. His father's constant belittling convinced him that he was somehow inferior and created emotional problems that affected him for many years to come. In an interview in 1995 he said that for much of his life he had used acting to help him embrace parts of his own personality that he had found hard to reconcile because of his violent childhood—qualities like vulnerability, vengefulness, and fear.

Stewart also readily admitted that because of the abuse by his father, he developed something of an obsession with playing authority figures, everyone from Henry V to Titus Andronicus to Captain Picard. "It's difficult to know what came first, whether others saw these things in me and therefore gave me these power roles or if I would have assumed them anyway. I do know that for many years as an actor, I had difficulty expressing certain emotions because I think I had conditioned myself for so many years not to let them out. I'm sure I did that because it just wasn't safe to let them out." When asked which emotions he was the most concerned about showing, he answered, "Anger—that's one of them. Any truly intense feelings of love and happiness were also difficult."

Slowly Alfred's relentless psychological abuse of young Patrick began to shift more from the verbal and emotional to the physical. In the name of discipline, he moved from corporal punishment to violence. "Mine was a violent childhood due to a father who drank, couldn't hold his liquor and took it out on my mother, my two brothers and me," Stewart recalled almost forty years later. "Ugly scenes still haunt me to this day—blood splattered everywhere on the walls and floor, broken skin, cuts, bruises, black eyes. A living hell."

"Just to look at him [Alfred] was reason to get hit," Stewart's brother, Geoffrey, revealed in a candid interview in 1992. "He beat our mother and us. He ruled the family with an iron fist and we lived in fear of him coming home. During the war it was a comfort to the family that he was away. We used to pray for him *not* to come back. Patrick was eventually the only one to stand up to him. He was fourteen and no one in the family will ever forget it. One day Dad came home, found some of Patrick's pals there and ordered him, 'Get rid of those buggers!' Patrick said, 'Drop dead!' The world stood still with everyone thinking, 'Dad is going to kill him.' But suddenly, Dad turned away. He didn't say a word."

It didn't stop the physical abuse, though. Stewart's older brothers left home while still in their teens and Patrick was left to try to protect his mother, who usually received the worst of Alfred's beatings. "I led a strange life as a child," Stewart later said. "Mondays through Fridays were usually quiet and peaceful. But on the weekends my father drank heavily with his working buddies at neighborhood pubs and when he came home it was frightening. He would begin arguing with my mother and I'd hear them from my upstairs bed. Soon my father would be screaming and my mother would be crying. Finally, I'd run downstairs and stand in front of my mother to protect her. Sometimes it helped, but other times my father would hit me and then shove me out of the way and begin beating my mother. He beat her so badly that the doctors, paramedics and ambulance had to be called."

Remarkably, young Patrick kept his "house of pain" well hidden from most of his friends and neighbors. His English teacher at Mirfield Secondary Modern School, Cecil Dormand, was "stunned" to learn years later that Stewart had grown up in fear, terrorized by a brutal father who beat his wife and sons. Even Joan Oxley, who lived in the house across the street from the Stewarts, said, "Patrick must have been a brave lad, keeping his hurt inside." But one of Stewart's boyhood friends remembered Alfred as a cruel tyrant who never allowed his sons to have friends in the house and dished out physical punishment for the slightest misbehavior. "Once in gym class, Patrick took off his shirt and I saw a horrifying bruise on his arm. He said he'd fallen but I saw tears in his eyes. That bruise was obviously caused by fingers digging into his skin."

Stewart continually vacillated about publicly admitting that in his youth he had been the recurrent victim of merciless beatings at the hands of his father. Although he always acknowledged that he was raised in a "violent childhood" where he was "afraid all the time," he told an entertainment magazine "I wasn't beaten, but there was violence in the house. My father would get very angry. He would lose control." In an interview with *The Advocate* in August 1995, Stewart seemed to be easing himself out of denial. "It was mostly a childhood where the *threat* of violence was always present, but I was not beaten on a regular basis. It's just that there was violence in the air, and that created a certain sense of chaos in one's life, because nothing was ever really certain."

Typical of most victims of physical abuse, Stewart has always made excuses for his father's violent behavior. "I came across a photograph," he recalled recently. "I'm sitting on a beach, in a deck chair, and my father is tickling me. And I'm squirming with laughter. I must have been about 6 years old. If anybody had asked me, 'Did your father ever make you laugh?' I'd have said, absolutely not. He made me feel a lot of things, but he never made me laugh. And yet there it was. And I looked at the photograph and I could remember it. I knew what his fingers felt like in my ribs. I'd forgotten that my father made me laugh. And that's as important a memory to record as that he occasionally lost control of himself."

Stewart has also stated publicly that his father was "a very impressive individual, and he gave me and my two brothers many excellent qualities, certainly in terms of perseverance, discipline, stamina. And in some respects a certain code of ethics—which, of course, was not *consistent* unfortunately, but nevertheless it existed.

"I remember two or three years ago my eldest brother showing me my father's army pay book. When a military man leaves the service, on the last page of the book there are areas in which the commanding officer will comment on how the soldier has performed. And when my brother showed me this, it was like we were looking at a design. Because there were dozens of these areas, and opposite every one was written the word *exemplary.* Exemplary, exemplary, exemplary. I've so often wondered just what kind of strain it must have put him under to live like that—in his public life, anyway."

In 1993, Stewart finally revealed that psychological counseling, hypnotherapy, and medication had helped him "come to grips" with his violent past and rescued him from a lifetime of mental scars. "I lived with my emotional pain for a long time, unable to share it. But I found the courage to seek professional help in 1990 and thanks to therapy, I now realize that hearing my father's powerful voice is the reason I've never been able to tolerate loud, abusive voices throughout my life. Even today, if someone shouts at me or I hear a parent snapping at his child on the street, it triggers feelings of terror in me and I often feel like running away. My understanding and emotional growth is continuing, and I'm grateful for that. But I have the feeling this learning and readjusting process will be going on for the rest of my life."

The Great Escape

Educated at Mirfield Secondary Modern School, Stewart had set his heart on a stage career and participated in a drama course when he was twelve years old. Amazingly, Mirfield with its population of just 12,000, supported a dozen or so amateur theater clubs. He found that the world of acting provided an escape for him in a multitude of ways, including having a legitimate excuse to get away from his father at night when he had to go to rehearsal. Reflecting back years later on why he chose acting, he responded, "It is very personal and quite complicated. I was pretty unhappy as a child due to my upbringing and background and, in a nutshell, I suppose it can be summed up as an attempt to escape from the real world into a much more com-

fortable, imaginary world. . . . It cauterized the fear
and the hurt and the pain. Being able to go somewhere
else and say, 'What if?' or 'Once upon a time' was comforting. But even more than that, it introduced me to
a world where there was stability and politeness, generosity and humor. The escape of the theater saved my
life. If that sounds too dramatic, I can safely say it saved
my sanity."

Stewart's earliest childhood heroes were actors: comedian Danny Kaye, whose work he admired enormously, English performers Alec Guiness, Ralph
Richardson, and especially the young Peter O'Toole,
whom he had seen working in provincial repertory.
Even after he became an international star himself,
Stewart once said that O'Toole remained "the most
charismatic actor I've ever seen on stage. He would
actually burn with an extraordinary light when he was
performing. I took a lot of inspiration from him."

In 1953, when he was thirteen, Stewart, an obsessive
movie-goer, saw Elia Kazan's film, *On the Waterfront,* the
one motion picture that had the greatest impact on his
life. Although it was set in faraway Brooklyn and dealt
with shipyard workers and union men, the tough and
gritty social conditions in the movie were something
Stewart very much recognized and identified with—being poor, coming from a pretty rough neighborhood,
not being better educated, having holes in his clothes,
speaking with a heavy accent. "On a Monday night I
went to see a film I'd never heard of," he later recalled,
"I'd been utterly seduced by Technicolor, and I remember when the titles came up feeling irritably disappointed to see that the film was in black and white.
Until then I had imagined myself in a world populated
by people like Debbie Reynolds and Doris Day. My
friends would be Tab Hunter and Rock Hudson. All the
lawns were green and freshly mowed. All the houses

were painted white, everybody looked wholesome and nice and everybody had a car and a telephone—and then *bang*. Everything changed from that moment on, partly because I saw that people made movies about *me*. . . . I saw that movie four times in the week that it was on, even taking my poor mother to see it, who didn't understand what the hell was going on. Marlon Brando was, and still is, a role model as a performer. I'm extremely proud that, over the years, I have gotten to meet Karl Malden and Eva Saint who came into my dressing room in Stratford many years ago. They knocked on the door after a performance to say hello. That was an extraordinary thrill. My knees went weak! I even got to work very briefly with Rod Steiger in my first feature film called *Hennessy*."

Stewart began his acting career with a mind reading act. Wearing an ancient tuxedo jacket and an oversized top hat borrowed from a local undertaker, he and two friends put together an act for a revue at their high school in Yorkshire. At the start of the performance, Stewart greeted the audience and introduced his pal Alan Thompson as The Great Mesmo, "the most incredible mind reader of all time." Then Stewart tightly blindfolded Thompson and went out into the audience.

"He'd ask someone to hand him something—anything," Thompson later recalled. "It would perhaps be a pack of cigarettes and he would hold it up and say, 'Great Mesmo, tell me what I am holding in my hand?' I'd pretend to concentrate for a few moments, then I'd say, 'A pack of cigarettes!' The audience gasped. What they didn't know was that there was a third member of the 'Great Mesmo' team hidden behind the stage curtains. He'd peep through a crack in the curtain, spot what Patrick was holding up and whisper to me what it was. That was the secret of our success."

Stewart's English teacher, Cecil Dormand, was quite often in attendance when he performed, and Stewart later admitted that he owed Dormand a personal debt of gratitude for convincing him to pursue an acting career. "It was Cecil who cornered me in the old school hall in my last year of school and asked me whether I'd ever thought of becoming a professional actor," Stewart said. "Of course I hadn't. It was a ludicrous idea. I didn't know anyone who had ever become a professional actor. Even though I loved what I did, I didn't allow myself that fantasy because it wasn't a remote possibility. Cecil Dormand had first put a copy of Shakespeare in my hand and said, 'Don't read it to yourself, read it aloud so we can all hear.' "

In 1955, at the age of fifteen years and two days, Stewart dropped out of school after having completed the minimum education that the state required at the time, to become a $7.50 a week junior reporter for the local newspaper, *The Mirfield Reporter,* but his heart was not in it. With the help of one of his former teachers, he developed a flair for language but only worked at the paper for two years. The job interfered with his play rehearsals and when his boss made him decide between a career in journalism or acting, Stewart followed his dream.

"I was always faced with either covering an assignment or attending an important rehearsal or performance," he explained. "I would try to cover events in advance or afterward by making phone calls. I used to get my colleagues to cover for me, but often I would just make up a decent story. Finally, of course, I was found out. I had a terrific row with the editor who said, 'Either you decide to be a journalist, in which case you give up all of this absurd amateur theatricals, or you get off my paper.' I was seventeen, and I packed up my typewriter with the sticky keys and left out of spite. I objected to being told how I should lead my life."

Stewart went home and told his parents he'd quit his job, and his father responded with his characteristic psychological abuse, threatening to beat "some sense into the boy." The cruel, demeaning words of "loser," "no count," "worthless piece of shit," repeated themselves in Stewart's head many years after they were spoken.

Stewart chose acting, "because it provided periods of absolute joy and delight that I had never experienced before," but he still had to work other jobs to earn a living. For almost a year he worked as a salesman in a furniture shop in the nearby town of Dewsbury, and as an acting exercise, he would become whatever kind of salesman he thought the customer was expecting. "I was better at selling furniture than I was at journalism," he later admitted.

Stewart was determined to be a professional actor. When not working at selling furniture or attending the multitude of drama courses he had enrolled in, the seventeen-year-old would hang out with other young aspiring actors at their family's homes, listening to Walton's music for Lawrence Olivier's film of *Henry V,* and acting out various Shakespearean scenes. Stewart seemed more mature than his young colleagues, but they nevertheless loved his company.

One of his closest friends at the time was Brian Blessed, who would later become a renowned and beloved star of British stage and screen. Blessed once described the young Stewart as a "shy, self-effacing young man" who possessed "genuine humility and grace." He also said that the future *Enterprise* captain was "reserved, serious, introverted" and "smiled and laughed rarely."

At the Blessed home, Stewart watched in bewilderment when his friend wrestled with his father on the floor of the sitting room and became even more astonished when Blessed's mother, roaring with laughter, stopped the boisterous roughhouse play by threatening to hit them both with a frying pan. When Blessed visited Stewart in his home, obviously the atmosphere was formal and tense and there was no open display of affection.

Stewart was an intensely private young man and spent a great deal of time alone, reading, listening to BBC radio broadcasts, and exploring Yorkshire's historic landscapes of moors and dales, where the people were "warm, generous and kind" and the villages were straight out of *Wuthering Heights*. Sometimes on Saturdays, he would buy a ticket from Mirfield to York, where the great tower of York Minster, one of the finest Gothic cathedrals in Europe, dominated the entire countryside. "As a very romantic youth, which is what I'm afraid I was," Stewart recalled, "I felt that in this superb building I could feel the past all around me and if I half closed my eyes I could hear it and almost see it."

On other weekends, Stewart escaped from his father's brutality by riding his bicycle to the Yorkshire Dales, a vast expanse of rural hill country in the northwestern section of the county. For Stewart, one of the most delightful and moving experiences was to sit and watch the light change on a dales hillside.

When asked once what was the best setting in Yorkshire for love, Stewart answered, "In terms of any real romance, it should be any dales hilltop in August, when the heather is in full bloom. And then, if you're with a loved one, you can [say to] them Kathy's famous phrase to Heathcliff in *Wuthering Heights*, just before she died, 'Fill my arms with heather, Heathcliff.' But for me, one of the most romantic spots will always be the ruined abbey at Whitby, where there on a school trip I found a quiet and secluded corner and first kissed Barbara Sydon," his boyhood crush.

In the Company of Shakespeare

Stewart's strikingly powerful face, slightly oriental-looking eyes, and obvious acting ability and dedication on the stage eventually caught the attention of the right people. In 1957, he was awarded a two-year drama scholarship to the Bristol Old Vic Theatre School, the school on which he had set his heart and one of the country's most respected professional academies, where he would receive formal drama training and the opportunity to bring his skills up to the level of his enthusiasm. Even more importantly, he would be living hundreds of miles away from his father as he took up residence near the "Old Vic," which was a large, rambling estate in the country. For Stewart, acting had literally provided a means of escape from Alfred's constant abuse.

On the eve of his departure, he was summoned by his eighty-year-old grandmother, who wished to share a deep, dark family secret. She told him about William Stewart, his paternal grandfather who had deserted her many years before, leaving her with four small children.

"After sending my mother out of the room, she told me about him," Stewart remembered. "As I already suspected, he was an actor and the last time anyone had ever heard of him was when the police paid him a visit at the old Elephant & Castle Theatre in London regarding nonpayment of family maintenance. It was in the middle of a play and William evidently per-

suaded the police to let him finish the performance.
While the police waited in the wings, William did his
part and exited through a side door and was never
seen again. But it is believed that he changed his
name and left for the U.S. The man was obviously a
swine." It was for this reason that Stewart's family, especially his father, was strongly against him becoming
an actor.

Nevertheless, Stewart continued to endure the relentless emotional abuse of his father (but only when
he came home to visit, which was rather infrequent)
and spent two years at "Old Vic," honing his natural
acting abilities and losing his thick northern accent
with the assistance of the great movement teacher,
Rudi Shelley. Speaking slowly and clearly, with a Continental accent, Shelley's voice was bass-baritone with
a delivery that was an object lesson in the meaning
of grace: the maximum effect with the minimum of
effort. Stewart's theatrical English accent, combined
with his own bedroom baritone, would make a lasting
impression years later when it would take on an unmistakable air of authority in Shakespeare, *Star Trek:
The Next Generation*, and in voice-overs selling Pontiacs,
RCA satellite dishes, and MasterCards. Stewart has
never hesitated to credit his former teacher Shelley,
with fine-tuning his vocal cords and creating that famous stentorian voice.

Shelley's air of tremendous authority also extended
to the way he dressed. The slim teacher with dark,
searing eyes, a long, gaunt face with a strong nose,
and a lion's mane of wavy, brown hair, usually wore
elegant, black, flared trousers, a green cowboy-style
shirt, darker green waistcoat and a large burgundy, silk
handkerchief around his neck, held in place by a ring
of leather. Stewart was an impressionable young man,
starving for attention at the time, and was immediately

enamored of his flamboyant, authoritative mentor. Shelley, likewise, realized that his young protégé had tremendous potential and he knew without a doubt that his dedication and talent would take him far.

The teacher and his serious, but sensitive, student spent many long hours together after school at Old Vic. They went to the cinema together, took long walks in the English countryside, listened to Samuel Barber's *Adagio for Strings* and the Mozart piano concertos while sipping wine at Shelley's flat, and Shelley continued to develop Stewart's deep, resonant baritone by reading long passages aloud from Shakespeare, the Bible, Charles Dickens, and Lewis Carroll. Some of Stewart's friends at school questioned Shelley's special interest in his star pupil and the hours they shared together when school was not in session, but most realized that Stewart had simply found a father figure in Shelley, someone to love, respect, and admire. Someone very much unlike his father.

It was also at this young age that Stewart experienced the trauma of losing almost all of his thick, brown hair within a few months. He looked around at other young men with hair and saw that women found them considerably more appealing. "I did a number of things to prevent it and then, when I saw it was unpreventable, to hide it," he readily admitted. But while he initially tried to disguise his baldness with hairpieces, he found them increasingly uncomfortable. "When I was younger, I used to think in terms of how I could disguise myself in roles. Now I want my work to say something about me, contain more of my experiences of the world." On stage, Stewart's exploration of personalities and characteristics eventually gave way to self-expression.

In 1959, Stewart, an exemplary (although self-described "obsessive") acting student, graduated in the top of his class at Bristol Old Vic and was awarded with his first public stage performance, playing the part of the pirate Morgan, in an adaptation of Robert Louis Stevenson's *Treasure Island* at the Theatre Royal in Lincoln, England. After only a month, he moved over to the Playhouse Theatre in Sheffield, where he assumed a variety of roles in repertory from 1959 until 1961. When he was twenty-one he joined the touring company of the Bristol Old Vic and traveled to Australia, New Zealand, and South America, appearing in Shakespeare's *Twelfth Night* and Alexandre Dumas' *Lady of the Camelias*. During his tour, he worked with the noted British actress Vivien Leigh, who in 1939 had starred as Scarlett O'Hara in the classic American film, *Gone with the Wind*.

While on tour with the Old Vic in Australia, Stewart experienced a memorable, life-threatening incident when he went bodysurfing, and was hit by a rapid series of three successive waves. When the undertow dragged him along the ocean bottom he was sure he was going to drown. Finally when his head bobbed up to the surface, he was only three to four feet away from another man on a surfboard, who asked, "Are you all right?" Stewart replied, "I'm fine, really." Then he went under again. He shed some light on the incident in an interview years later, "I meant him to understand *I'm drowning. Please help me.* But I could not say those words. I expected and hoped he would understand my rather complex code. I've lived a lot of my life like that—sending out codes most people couldn't possibly decipher." Stewart admitted, however, that his need to hide his true self stemmed from the intimidation of his childhood. "I worked obsessively and managed successfully to suppress my feelings until I wasn't feeling anything at all."

Stewart always enjoyed the stimulating change of working with a different ensemble company every few months, sometimes weeks. Partly because he was an intern acting student and partly because he preferred the constant variation of different repertory groups and ensemble companies, Stewart was always moving from one theater to another and from one play to another. In 1962, he returned to the stage company in Sheffield, but remained only six weeks. Then from 1962 through 1963, he performed at the Library in Manchester, England. From there he went to Liverpool and acted on the stage at the Playhouse into 1964. Finally, he returned to his beloved Bristol Old Vic company, where his assignments included such major characters as Shylock in Shakespeare's *The Merchant of Venice* and the title characters in the Bard's *Henry V* and in Bertolt Brecht's *The Life of Galileo*.

"For me, to have had all those years in the theater in England," Stewart once said, "and to have done years of rep, a different play every week as I moved up to better and better companies, play after play, role after role after role after role, late nights just spent cramming lines for the next day, no sleep, going in to work and doing a show . . . that was such a fine time."

In 1964, Stewart was scheduled to head to Spain with a touring company and wanted to go to a pub with a friend from Old Vic to relax and drink a few beers before departing in the next few days. "Unfortunately, I drank too much, sang too loud and began acting stupid," Stewart recalled. "My friend and I took the stage in the pub and put on an impromptu performance which undoubtedly was not one of my finest."

In the audience was a director who had previously worked with Stewart, and seated next to him was choreographer Sheila Falconer. The two had just come from the theater where they had been auditioning actors and actresses for roles in a planned musical production. As Stewart stumbled about the pub's small stage drunkenly, singing off-key at the top of his lungs, his director friend turned to Falconer and said almost apologetically, "He's much younger than he looks and much older than he's acting."

An apparently not amused Falconer replied, "Obviously."

Stewart viewed himself as unattractive with "a big nose and a weird-shaped face" and was surprised and confused if any woman showed interest in him. But amazingly, "After we were introduced, Sheila seemed like she enjoyed my company and wanted to see me again."

Their relationship was slow going at first as the typically guarded and intensely private Stewart refused to express his true feelings for her. Like pulling teeth, she finally got him to reveal his love for her and then the relationship took the fast track.

Two

From Shakespeare to
Star Trek

You must NOT do this. This is a terrible mistake. You'll ruin your career."

—A colleague on Patrick Stewart's accepting
the role of Captain Picard

When Stewart spoke, people listened. He had finally lost the thick accent he'd grown up with and now spoke Elizabethan English as if it were his mother's tongue, causing many theatergoers to lend an ear to what he was saying on stage. One critic said that his voice "makes you want to applaud at the end of each sentence."

Stewart's natural ability to captivate an audience and leave them totally satisfied found its perfect setting when in 1966 he realized the fulfillment of his dreams

and became a member of the internationally renowned Royal Shakespeare Company (RSC).

"I have arrived. I have *finally* arrived," he cried on
the telephone to his former teacher and mentor, Rudi
Shelley. "It is the culmination of everything I ever
wanted to do. I never want to leave the British stage.
Never!"

Considered by critics and fellow performers alike to
be one of England's leading theater talents, Stewart
made his RSC debut in February 1966 at the Aldwych
and in the following month he married Sheila, whom
he had dated off and on for the past two years while
touring with the Old Vic.

During those financially difficult years as a young
married couple, she was very resourceful. A cheap
soupbone or a bag of beans went a long way in their
house, and they always had enough to eat. "You
should act as much as you can and that is the only
way you can learn the skill," she would tell Stewart.
"Don't worry too much how much money you're making. Doing the work is what counts."

Stewart was gone a considerable amount of time,
either at the theater performing matinee and evening
shows or with a road tour, but when he was home they
enjoyed each other's company. Before they could afford a television, they listened to their favorite shows
on the BBC radio and read a lot of books aloud to
each other. They were determined to make their relationship work and start a family in spite of the fact
that they were financially strapped and barely able to
make ends meet each month.

"When our first child, Daniel, was born," Stewart
proudly remembered, "I don't think I had ever been
happier in my life. We really couldn't afford a child
and I was traveling way too much, which wasn't fair
to either his mother or him. But I have to admit, he

was certainly worth the sacrifices we had to make. And then a few years later, even though we still couldn't afford another child, Sheila gave birth to a beautiful girl, Sophie. If you keep waiting to have children when you can afford them, then you will never have a family."

"A Good, Solid Actor"

One of Stewart's first RSC performances, at the Stratford upon Avon theater was in the role of Hippolito, one of the few noble characters in the blood-drenched Jacobean drama *The Revenger's Tragedy,* by Cyril Tourneur. Cast mostly with newcomers to the RSC and directed by Trevor Nunn, who was to become the RSC's artistic director in 1968, the landmark production was hailed by critics as one of the greatest presentations of the decade.

Stewart also had roles in *Hamlet* and in *Henry V,* the production in which he met Malcolm McDowell, who would portray the villainous Dr. Tolian Soran opposite Stewart's Captain Picard almost thirty years later in the seventh *Star Trek* motion picture, *Generations.* Though McDowell left the acting troupe after little more than a year to pursue a career on British television, he said in a 1994 interview, "Patrick went on to do very well there. He was exactly the same as he is now—bald as a coot—and he could have played any old man at twenty-two. He's always been a good, solid actor, a wonderful company man and I think he was a wonderful leader of the company of *Star Trek Generations.*"

In 1967, at the end of his first season with the RSC, Stewart was offered a three-year contract to stay on. From a phone booth he called Sheila and said, "It's happened. I'm just going to stay forever." No longer an intern performer Stewart became an associate artist with the RSC and went on to portray Grumio in *The Taming of the Shrew,* Worthy in *The Relapse,* and Duke Senior in *As You Like It* in Stratford and in London and on its 1967-68 American tour. For the 1968-69 season, he appeared in four Shakespeare productions, both in England and on tour across the United States.

During the American tour, Stewart had a small part in *King Lear.* In fact, he really only had one line: "Ho la! What trumpet that?" which he was supposed to say right after a trumpet blared offstage. Unfortunately, during a matinee he had not been paying attention to the dialogue and suddenly there was a long pause on stage. Stewart, thinking that he'd missed his cue, shouted out his line with great gusto and typical Shakespearean panache, only to discover that the actor playing King Lear had been pausing dramatically in the middle of a very emotional speech. So when the trumpet actually did sound, Stewart had to improvise quickly, saying "Ho la! What trumpet *THAT?*" Obviously, the lead actor was furious and Stewart apologized to him afterward, promising never to screw up his lines like that again. But during the evening performance, Stewart repeated the same mistake. This time, all the other actors in minor roles on-stage were finding it extremely difficult not to burst out laughing and the lead actor looked at Stewart as if he were going to skin him alive after the performance.

As part of the RSC's so-called "light brigade," which was comprised of the less established members of the company, among them Helen Mirren and Ben Kingsley (who would years later win an Academy Award for the title role in *Gandhi*), Stewart played a mix of Shakespearean and non-Shakespearean roles in 1969. He returned to the Stratford in the following year, with substantial Shakespearean parts including the title role in *King John*. Ronald Bryden of the London *Observer* applauded Stewart's "remarkable performance" as the "grinning, shambling clown-king playing with power like firecrackers, half-enchanted, half-terrified by the bangs. . . . It's a glittering, original achievement."

In the early 1970s, while working for the company in Stratford upon Avon, Stewart would come home from the Globe Theatre on Saturday afternoons between the matinee and the evening performance of *King Lear* or *Macbeth* and have tea with his young family. Stowing his sword in the entryway and hitching up his tights, the weary actor would feign interest as he watched whatever was on television with his two children, Daniel and Sophie, and very often it would be the original *Star Trek* series in its initial run.

"I do recall quite intense actors snapping at each other very briskly," he recalled in an interview some twenty years later. "I don't think I saw an episode all the way through because I had to drive back to the theater for the evening show. But I remember thinking that it was interesting and odd and out of the ordinary. My children—who adored the show—would act out every scene for me in the morning. Ironically, the very first time they came to visit me on *The Next Generation* set we were doing one of those famous moments on the *Enterprise* where we're under attack and the crew is thrown about in their seats. The premier thing they ever saw me do was what they had illustrated for me so many times before."

Beginning in the early seventies, Stewart was consistently chosen for major roles in the RSC's Shakespeare productions. In his article for *Players of Shakespeare 1*, he described his preparation for such an assignment: "My homework begins with reading the play—contriving an innocence if the play is familiar—setting my imagination free to react intuitively and simply to whatever the reading suggests. After a long rehearsal period, when the play has been so dismantled and probed that the simple elements, such as the storyline, or the bold outlines of a character or of a relationship, have become blurred or submerged with elaboration and detail, it is valuable to remind oneself of those first uncomplicated responses."

In addition to authoring articles on Shakespeare, Stewart founded and became an active participant in the Alliance for Creative Theater, Education & Research (ACTER), which revolutionized the understanding and teaching of Shakespeare by involving RSC actors such as himself with college teachers and students by interpreting and performing the plays. That year through ACTER, Stewart began traveling quite often to American campuses, especially in California, where he taught classes and workshops, and performed in Shakespearean productions either in person or on video.

In the RSC's 1972 cycle of Shakespeare's four Roman plays, *Coriolanus, Julius Caesar, Antony and Cleopatra,* and *Titus Andronicus,* Stewart essayed the parts of Aufidius, Cassius, Enobarbus, and Bassianus (and, in London, Aaron). In his review of the four plays after their transfer to the RSC's London venue, Robert Cushman of the London *Observer* complained that, as Cassius, Stewart was "given to stressful pauses, often before perfectly innocuous words," but the critic applauded the actor's "gleeful golliwog Aaron" as "his best performance." Stewart also won applause for his portrayal of the world-weary soldier Enobarbus in *Antony and Cleopatra,* which was televised in Britain in 1974 and in the United States in 1975. To each character, Stewart brought prodigious memory, precise articulation matching precise textual understanding, and a musical ear and voice for verse. Great intelligence, emotion, discipline, and power marked his every Shakespearean performance.

Stewart next appeared as the eccentric and idealistic Dr. Astrov in the RSC's 1974 production of Anton Chekhov's *Uncle Vanya,* which subsequently toured the United States, Canada, and Australia. The following year he played the part of Eilbert Lovborg, Hedda's former lover, in the company's staging of Henrik Ibsen's *Hedda Gabler,* starring Glenda Jackson. The actors later reprised their roles for *Hedda,* a screen adaptation of the play written and directed by Trevor Nunn. Although critics could not agree on the merits of either the stage production or the film version, they were mostly unanimous in their opinion that Glenda Jackson overshadowed her supporting cast. Frank Rich, in his review for the *New York Post,* felt that Stewart alone had delivered a performance to match Jackson's: "With the exception of Miss Jackson and Patrick Stewart as Lovborg, the performances were awful."

At this time in his life, Stewart was missing the challenge of the early years in the theater in England, the years of repertory. Also, the strain of being a talented, hardworking actor in the RSC, yet struggling to support a wife and two children on the contemptibly slight amount of $400 a week was beginning to take its toll.

Stewart's wife, Sheila, was wearing second hand clothes and Daniel and Sophie also needed new clothes and supplies for school; their house needed repairs and bills from just normal day-to-day living expenses were beginning to pile up. Stewart knew he would suffer the scorn and slings and arrows from his RSC colleagues, some of whom he expected to look down their long noses at him, but he was determined to find additional work and extra income, either in television commercials or with minor film roles, to make ends meet and provide more for his children than had been provided for him when he was growing up in Yorkshire.

Through the mid- to late 1970s, Stewart increasingly accepted parts in television and film. His earliest television work included roles for the BBC as Lenin in *Fall of Eagles* (1973), Joseph Conrad in *Conrad* (1974), and the British Labour Party leader Clement Attlee in a film about Winston Churchill entitled *A Walk With Destiny* (1974). In 1975 he appeared as the Inventor in a BBC series called *Eleventh Hour*, and in the same year he was first seen on film, in a minor part in the suspense drama *Hennessy.* Stewart donned a hairpiece to play the cunning, guilt-ridden Sejanus in *I, Claudius* (1976), the BBC's much-praised miniseries about the first eighty years of the Roman Empire, which aired in the United States, thus making Stewart's work familiar to American television audiences as well. He also performed in the title role of the BBC's 1976 production of *Oedipus Rex.* In 1979 he was cast as Sergey Tolstoy, the famous novelist's son, in *Tolstoy: A Question of Faith,* and in his most notable part, Karla, the chief of Soviet espionage, in the highly-touted BBC miniseries *Tinker, Tailor, Soldier, Spy.*

Meanwhile, Stewart continued to act in both classical and contemporary works staged by the RSC. He won distinction for his portrayal of the embittered ex-militant Larry Slade in a powerful 1976 production of Eugene O'Neill's pessimistic barroom drama *The Iceman Cometh,* and during the following season, when the company ventured to mount a new production of *A Midsummer Night's Dream,* Stewart took the part of Oberon. Bernard Levin, reviewing the performance of *Dream* for the London *Sunday Times,* questioned the decision by the director to turn Oberon "into a Red Indian, clad only in a loincloth and going berserk from time to time," but he concluded nonetheless that "Patrick Stewart's Oberon, despite the handicap of his get-up, is virile and ethereal at the same time." Robert Cushman of the London *Observer* also cheered Stewart's performance. "In a mainly young and untried company, the experienced Patrick Stewart stands alone. Generally thought a dour, plain actor, he has in fact a considerable flair for the exotic."

Stewart also played in a 1977 production of *Bingo*, a purported biographical portrait of Shakespeare by Edward Bond, presenting the playwright as a traitor to the working class who puts an end to his guilt and misery by committing suicide. The London *Sunday Times* applauded Stewart's portrayal of Shakespeare as "a trim, rugged man on the brink of disintegration, his body held together by constant physical effort. . . . You can almost see his tendons and sinews stiffen. . . . His mouth and chin, rigid with all the terror that an egomaniac can feel, send out ripples of palpable anxiety."

Reprising the role of the cynical then transfigured Enobarbus in the 1978 staging of *Antony and Cleopatra*, Stewart won the 1979 Society of West End Theatre (SWET) Award for best supporting actor. Stewart was also nominated for a SWET Award in the category of best actor, for his interpretation of the smoldering, vengeful Shylock in *The Merchant of Venice*. Initially unenthusiastic about the prospect of playing for the second time what he saw as a one-dimensional role, Stewart was eventually won over by the character's complexity. "The role took me by surprise and I learned again the important lesson on the foolishness of coming to Shakespeare with preconceived ideas," he wrote in *Players of Shakespeare 1*. "This was a perfect instance of that rare and blessed identification with a character, which an actor cannot manufacture, but which will, at the most unexpected moment, pounce, grab him by the throat and invade his heart." Bernard Levin of the *Sunday Times* agreed, "Patrick Stewart's Shylock takes all the chances given, and they are many; it is a portrait etched with a master's vigor."

That production of *The Merchant of Venice* was the last time Alfred Stewart saw his son perform before dying in 1980 at the age of seventy-six. Stewart had always said that acting saved his life by letting him escape from his drunken father's rages, and he found it ironic that in the past few years his proud father had boasted to his friends about his son's success as a renowned actor with the RSC. Alfred had severely beaten his son after learning from his drunken friends at the pub that twelve-year-old Patrick had been standing on Mirfield street corners impersonating Laurence Olivier, but in his old age "he'd come to worship Patrick as an actor," Geoffrey Stewart acknowledged.

Stewart's style of acting had undergone transformation over the years, particularly when he read the play *The Winter's Tale* soon after his father's death. "For the first time I was prepared to directly draw on my own experiences and feelings and instincts in a role," he later admitted. "I played Leontes, a monstrously unhappy individual in a play of great beauty and emotional power and I understood it. I think it was that empathy that enabled me to find something deeper and richer than I found in my work before, and to not be afraid to let my own feelings infect the play. For years, I didn't. For years, I assumed that acting was putting on something from the outside rather than discovering it within you. I want to see an actor show me himself as much as I want to see the role in the play. I'm not interested in fancy tricks or technical fireworks—that's very boring. I want to be touched by something else."

The RSC celebrated the long-awaited opening of its new London theater, the Barbican, in 1982, with Trevor Nunn's production of both parts of Shakespeare's *Henry IV,* with Stewart in the title role. "Stewart plays [Henry] from behind a saintly mask," the London *Times* observed, "consciously cultivating a mildly benevolent manner that is repeatedly torn aside by eruptions of rage (as where he counsels Hal to adopt 'humility,' shrieking the word at the top of his voice)." *Henry IV* was Stewart's last major assignment with the RSC, as he increasingly turned his attention to television and film work.

Who's Afraid of Patrick Stewart?

Stewart's film roles were largely minor, whether in ambitious features, such as Leondegrance in the dream-like King Arthur rendition *Excalibur* (1981), David Lynch's adaptation of the 1984 science-fiction epic *Dune* (admittedly not his best effort), and the costume drama *Lady Jane* (1986); and in motion pictures better soon forgotten, such as *Code Name: Emerald* (1984), *The Doctor and the Devils* (1985), the dreadful *Wild Geese II* (which Stewart considered his most embarrassing job, but took it to pay for new windows in his house in 1985), and *Lifeforce,* a horror thriller about life-draining extraterrestrials.

In *Dune,* Stewart played the character Gurney Halleck, warmaster to the duke Leto Atreides (Jurgen Prochnow) and one of the teachers of his son Paul (Kyle MacLachlan). In Frank Herbert's *Dune,* one of the recognized classics of science-fiction literature, Gurney Halleck is an important character. But in the

David Lynch version, Halleck's role is somewhat diminished. "The role was never as important or as significant in the film as in the book," Stewart reluctantly admitted in a magazine interview almost a decade later. "Halleck is a musician, poet *and* warrior. Well, all you really saw of him was the warrior side. David Lynch *did* shoot the book, but it just didn't get on the screen. It's a good film, but I suspect there's an even better film in all that David shot. I don't think David Lynch's work was seen at its best in *Dune.*"

The actor also took up the blade in a world of swashbuckling fantasy, albeit in the grim, muddy, and bloody Camelot of *Excalibur.* "It has some of the finest images I've seen on the screen," Stewart said. "At that time, I found the director, John Boorman, a little remote, very, very preoccupied with images and the look of the film. But those were the early days of filming for me and I was probably a little timid."

Stewart's other venture in science fiction came as Dr. Armstrong in *Lifeforce,* directed by Tobe Hooper, who had previously sat in the director's chair for *The Texas Chainsaw Massacre* and *Poltergeist.* "I have to say, of all the [science fiction/fantasy] movies I've done," Stewart recalled, "Tobe Hooper was the director to whom I got the closest. I liked him very much and I admired his work. As compared to my experiences with David Lynch and John Boorman, Tobe was much more accessible. And even though my part was not large, he spent a lot of time with me. He was a very good listener and he would incorporate the actor's ideas."

On television, Stewart reprised his role of the Soviet spymaster, Karla, in the BBC miniseries *Smiley's People* (1982), the Polish Communist Party secretary Wladyslaw Gomulka in the CBS made-for-TV movie *Pope John Paul II* (1984), and the jealous composer Antonio

Salieri in the BBC production *The Mozart Inquest* (1985), a mock trial to determine whether Mozart's death was the result of foul play.

Noteworthy among his stage performances in the 1980s was his portrayal of the biblical King David, and, later, the title role in Peter Shaffer's play *Yonadab* at the National Theatre of Great Britain. But the role Stewart coveted the most was one he never got—that of Falstaff. "For me, everything universal in Shakespeare is contained in that character," he once said. "He is simultaneously funny, unspeakable and tragic. He is the ultimate creation of Shakespeare—a monstrous, selfish, wicked, devilishly comic, damned, sad man—and I've always been very moved by him."

However, when an interviewer once asked Stewart which role had been his favorite to play during his long and successful career as an actor, he chose George, the aging, eloquent, emotionally bruised professor, from a heralded 1987 production of Edward Albee's stinging marital drama *Who's Afraid of Virginia Woolf?* for which Stewart earned the 1987 London Fringe Award for Best Actor. "I had never played a leading role in a modern American play before nor in one that was as emotionally demanding. It's a very long play, about three and a half hours, and it requires an enormous amount of stamina—physically and emotionally."

Singling out Stewart for special praise, the London *Sunday Times* raved, "Patrick Stewart plays George with a gaunt body and a face blasted by suffering and self-knowledge. It is simply spellbinding to see this compact, bull-like actor transformed into a battered victim of life: the final scene, when he turns on Martha, his gray and ravaged face is etched on my memory with the painful sharpness of acid." John Vidal, writing for the *Guardian*, concurred, "The key to the production is Patrick Stewart's virtuoso performance as George. . . . There is a reserve, a restraint in his acting which allows room for reflection. By not rising to Martha's bait he can defuse or direct the passions and by imploding rather than exploding his torment appears the greater. Watch his hands, too. He taps his fingers, he fiddles with his laces, he grasps at the chairs, and when he stands, swaying slightly as he tears another strip off his wife's composure, his hands are perfectly still by his side. They speak volumes."

The Big Risk

The production of *Who's Afraid of Virginia Woolf?* was a huge success and was in the process of transferring to the West End (London's equivalent of Broadway) when Stewart was offered the plum role of the noble and disciplined Captain Jean-Luc Picard on *Star Trek: The Next Generation,* the sequel to the cult classic 1960s television show that he used to watch with Daniel and Sophie when they were young.

After three decades of stage work, Stewart now had to choose between his first love—live theater—and the potential to achieve on a television series the kind of success that he had always craved. Working with the RSC for twenty years was a rarefied experience that provided immense enrichment and creative satisfaction, but every actor in the company knew that there was a larger world outside Stratford upon Avon every time they picked up their small paychecks.

Despite its stature, RSC's efforts appealed to a minority taste. It seemed incredible to the actor that tens of millions of viewers were expected to watch *The Next Generation,* which was certainly more people than had ever seen him on stage in his whole career. Stewart also felt it was past time to earn a very good living for his family after thirty years of struggling financially as an actor. As a classical stage actor for most of his life, he had achieved a great deal of artistic and spiritual fulfillment but very little in terms of *real* money, and he had no doubts that this new incarnation of *Star Trek* would be very successful.

Even though Stewart had absolutely no interest in science fiction, there was something slightly classical, almost Shakespearean, in *Star Trek*'s dramatic, archetypal storytelling. The show had always had its literary pretensions; allusions to Shakespeare abounded, and it had often been compared to *The Odyssey*. "There was something heroic and epic to the underlying themes," Stewart explained. "In terms of ambition, the stage on which it was set was Homeric. *Star Trek* is epic in nature as has been a lot of classical work that I've done. *Star Trek* is drawn on a very big canvas."

Unfortunately, there was also the innate possibility that he would become *too* associated with his *Trek* persona. He was very aware of how closely identified William Shatner, Leonard Nimoy, and the other cast members had become with the characters they played on the show. Despite the universal popularity of the original series in syndication and the box office success of the theatrical movies, none of the actors had warped to stardom on anything other than *Star Trek*.

Stewart had a genuine fear that the Captain Picard role would become an albatross and there was also the distinct possibility that he would be associated with a show that was going to trash the original series and be nothing more than a shallow, money-making rip-off. Yet, every aspect of the new *Trek* series—working in Hollywood, being in a TV series, the challenge of topping something that had been successful before—was irresistible and attracted Stewart to the part.

The role of Captain Jean-Luc Picard would represent a major change in the style of Stewart's career, and he had always been an actor who had found contrast, especially *violent* contrast in his work, to be appealing. He wanted to do something that was unusual, unexpected, and outside his range of experience. The prospect of doing an American television series was intriguing, particularly one that was dedicated to dealing with *ideas* as well as the usual formula of relationships, plot, and regular characters. "You must NOT do this," one of Stewart's friends and a senior colleague at the RSC, warned him. "This is a terrible mistake. You'll ruin your career."

About halfway through his formal training as an actor at Bristol Old Vic, the principal of the school, Duncan Ross, had pulled Stewart aside and given him the best advice that the actor would ever receive. "Patrick, you will never achieve success by insuring against failure." It took the difficult choice between a life on his beloved British stage or possible stardom in an American TV series to make Stewart realize what Ross meant. For years he had played it safe, never taking that big risk that could see him fall and utterly fail.

He knew now that if he didn't take the risk, he would never succeed.

Three

Promotion to Captain

I wouldn't know a space/time continuum or warp core breach if they got in bed with me.

—Patrick Stewart on *Star Trek*'s unique "language"

In America, the burning question was, Could the magic of the original *Star Trek* series be duplicated? Could they catch lightning in a bottle again? "The speculation is over," announced Mel Harris, then president of Paramount Television Group, during a studio press conference on Friday, October 10, 1986. "The answer is yes. *Star Trek* lives. Starting next fall, beginning with a two hour telefilm followed by twenty-four one-hour episodes, *Star Trek* will return to television in the form of a new series. Although this is a new starship *Enterprise*, a new cast and new stories, the man at the helm is still the same. Twenty years ago, the genius of one man brought to television a program that has transcended the medium," Harris said. "We are enormously pleased that that man, the creator of *Star Trek*, Gene

Roddenberry, is going to do it again. Just as public de-
mand kept the original series on the air, this new series
is also a result of grass roots support for Gene and his
vision. And we're proud to have him once again supervising all aspects of the production."

Why a new series? Independent stations had be-
sieged Paramount with requests for new, first-run episodes, studio executives said at the time of the initial
announcement. In reality, though, there was deep concern that the original series was losing ground in syndication as well as beginning to look extremely
antiquated as television became more sophisticated
with computer-generated graphics and special effects.
Regardless of the fans' devotion, their fervor for
watching the same seventy-nine episodes over and over
again was beginning to dissipate. With a near-geriatric
and exorbitantly priced original cast of William Shatner and Company, an all new-new cast and setting
would provide fresh, less costly, and longer-lived actors
to take advantage of the seemingly endless appeal of
the *Star Trek* phenomenon.

In the beginning, the new series didn't even have a
name. In an October 24 memo, series producer Bob
Justman proposed forty-four titles. *Star Trek: The Next
Generation* was not on the list, although two came close:
"The New Generation" and "The Second Generation." The first-draft series bible of November 26 carried the *Star Trek: The Next Generation* monicker, but
another Justman memo, dated December 15, suggested nineteen more possible titles. Earlier, on October 31, he had even suggested just keeping the title
Star Trek and letting the "obvious differences between
the two shows clear up any confusion."

Ironically, *Trek* fans weren't enthusiastic when Paramount revealed plans to produce the syndicated spin-
off. "Some people were afraid of the new *Star Trek*

because the old people wouldn't be in it," Justman said. "It was a threat to them. But I don't think that will last very long. You form new relationships all through life. Sometimes the old relationships are the best, sometimes they're not. But there's room in this world for diversity. People resist change for various reasons."

"Many fans of the original had a jealous, possessive resistance to the very *idea,*" Stewart himself later recalled. And it didn't help that William Shatner and Leonard Nimoy, stars of the original series, publicly voiced their dissatisfaction in media interviews and at *Trek* conventions around the country.

"It's a mistake," said Shatner prior to *The Next Generation*'s debut. "Taking the familiar crew in new areas is fine, but with a totally new cast, it would be a misnomer to call it *Star Trek.*" Nimoy, still standing by his former captain's side, echoed Shatner's remarks. "The chemistry of that [original] group of characters was unique," he warned. "And there will be constant comparisons with the old series and with the four movies."

However, in creating the new *Enterprise* crew, Roddenberry, Justman, and the others on the production team continued to distance *The Next Generation* from its forebear by striving to shed the familiar and dominating duality of the Kirk-Spock relationship. Roddenberry's hopes for the original series, before the casting of Shatner and Nimoy turned the show into a star vehicle, was to create an ensemble cast and not a star cast. This time they chose to divide the attributes of that dynamic pair among the new characters so that they could assemble an ensemble cast in the style of *Hill Street Blues, M*A*S*H,* and *L.A. Law.*

The first casting call went out to talent agencies on December 10, 1986:

TO: ALL TALENT AGENCIES
RE: PARAMOUNT "STAR TREK: THE NEXT
    GENERATION"
1-HR. SERIES FOR SYNDICATION
2-HR. TV MOVIE TO START END OF MARCH
24 1-HR. EPISODES TO START END OF MAY
Exec. Producer: Gene Roddenberry
Supv. Producer: Eddie Milkis
Producer: Bob Justman
Director: TBA
Casting Director: Helen Mossler
Casting Assistant: Gail Helm
WRITTEN SUBMISSIONS—ONLY—TO: HELEN
    MOSSLER, PARAMOUNT, BLUDHRON 128,
    5555 MELROSE AVE., LOS ANGELES, CA
    90038
PLEASE BE ADVISED THAT WE DO NOT
    HAVE A SCRIPT YET AND ARE JUST IN
    THE PRELIMINARY CASTING STAGES.

SEEKING THE FOLLOWING SERIES REGU-
    LARS:
CAPT. JULIEN PICARD—A Caucasian man in his
    50s who is very youthful and in prime physical
    condition. Born in Paris, his Gallic accent ap-
    pears when deep emotions are triggered. He is
    definitely a 'romantic' and believes strongly in
    concepts like honor and duty. Capt. Picard com-
    mands the Enterprise. He should have a mid-
    Atlantic accent, and a wonderfully rich
    speaking voice . . .

The initial description of the Captain Picard character, including the first name of Julien (and the nick-
name of Luke), would undergo further revisions as the
new production team exchanged ideas and, later, when

actors began auditioning for the role. "Kirk came out of an earlier time in my life when I was pretending to be part of my macho southern background, and [the character] reflects some of that," Roddenberry later admitted to an interviewer. "Macho feelings about women, and so on. But in twenty-five years, my feelings have changed enormously about those things and I think Picard represents that. He's more mature."

As preliminary casting began in March 1987, one of the earliest of the unavoidable staff shakedowns occurred, one that would have long-term implications for the new series: producer Eddie Milkis was replaced by Rick Berman, who would become the prime force responsible for transforming the series into a bonafide success story in its own right.

Ironically, Berman hadn't sought to run the series and was only handed the producing reins when the division he presided over, "longform and special projects"—miniseries and TV movies—was phased out by the studio. Having begun in the fall of 1986 as Paramount's liaison between the studio and *The Next Generation*, Berman came aboard in 1987 to take over for Milkis, who had decided to check out early on his one-year contract. "By that time I'd decided I had to get back to my other commitments," Milkis said. "But it was a very, very easy transition. Rick was very up-to-the-minute; he was in total sync with us."

"I had been Paramount's 'studio guy' for the series for about two weeks when Gene Roddenberry asked me to lunch, and it was love at first sight," Berman remembered. "He went to the studio and said, 'Can I have him?' and they said yeah." And that he added warmly, was the beginning of a relationship with Roddenberry that was "very special," although when he was offered the chance to steer the new *Star Trek*, he took it despite being advised against it by friends and associates in the entertainment business.

"I had a lot of people who told me I was nuts," Berman said later. "But I had a feeling it was going to work and I decided it was worth the risk of leaving a well-paying job at a movie studio to work on a science-fiction sequel syndicated television series." His track record for quality work and most recognizable production credits prior to *Star Trek* were the award-winning PBS special *The Primal Mind* and as the Emmy-winning executive producer of the children's educational show *The Big Blue Marble* from 1977 to 1982.

"He was just perfect," Justman recalled in an interview in 1992. "We couldn't have found someone better to do the show. He's a perfect executive producer, and a perfect hands-on producer at the same time."

So now it was the new production team of Berman, Justman, and veteran casting director Junie Lowry, who embarked on a massive search to bring the new *Trek* characters to life and cast the permanent ensemble cast, screening their choices with Paramount casting agents before presenting them for Roddenberry's approval and eventually final authorization from the studio.

Berman, Justman, and Lowry sat in a conference room in *Star Trek*'s modest production-office trailer and assessed the performances of more than fifty actors and actresses, selected in advance by Lowry, who paraded in, one by one, and eagerly read for them. Berman and Justman were unhappy with almost everyone they saw. They were courteous and full of praise after each actor read, but once the actor departed and the door was closed, it was a different story. "Too boring," "too ugly," "too handsome," "bad actor," were some of the more frequent comments.

Only weeks into the show's development, Justman and his wife attended a dramatic reading at UCLA on "The Changing Face of Comedy" in which Stewart participated. On one of his annual California trips on behalf of ACTER, Stewart was contacted by a professor friend at the university and asked to help illustrate a lecture by reading selected passages from Oscar Wilde, Noel Coward and, of course, Shakespeare. Inspired by Stewart's moving performance, Justman suddenly turned to his wife and said, "I think we have just found our captain!" Later the *Trek* producer would admit, "I'd never thought of him before, but once I saw him, that was the captain in my mind. I couldn't shake it. I've never been so sure of anything as I was with that."

Still, Roddenberry had his heart set on *Cagney & Lacey*'s Stephen Macht for the role of the *Enterprise*'s captain. An excellent actor with a craggy face who projected real strength and masculinity, Macht was called back three times to read for the part of Picard. "As far as the other characters, they were far more the selection of Bob Justman and mine than they were of anybody else," Berman said. "Gene basically approved, like the studio did, the people that Bob and I chose, and he was not all that involved in it. He was very stubborn about who he wanted to be Picard."

Justman set up a meeting among Stewart, Berman, and Roddenberry soon after "discovering" the British actor, urging that he be included in the cast somehow—and even wrote in an October 17 memo that Stewart at least be considered for the part of Data, the android.

"I got Patrick Stewart's picture and I looked at it, astonished," Roddenberry recalled. "And I said, 'I'm not going to have a bald Englishman for a captain.' Almost everybody had that reaction. But then I became aware of Stewart's acting ability. And I saw a lot of things. The more I saw him, the better I liked him."

A few days later Stewart was called to audition for *The Next Generation*. Initially he didn't realize he was reading for the part of Captain Picard, but believed that his would be a modest role on the series. "I consider myself fortunate not to have known more about the *Star Trek* phenomenon or that I was considered for the Picard role, otherwise I might have been intimidated," Stewart confessed in an interview years later. "I just assumed that I would be a token Brit on the intergalactic crew relegated to beaming people up and down from God knows where."

When no commitment was made, Stewart returned to his native England and back to the stage. "[Paramount's interest] was not something that I took seriously for one moment," he said. "For every thirty interviews you go for, one of them might turn into an offer. I had no expectations whatsoever." But soon Stewart was called back to Hollywood for a second audition. "And they just said, 'Thank you again,' and I left."

The actor returned to England and then he was summoned back *again*. But this time they wanted him to read for the part wearing a hairpiece. "I discovered there are things that you can do if you try hard enough," Stewart later said. "Sunday morning, my wife drove my hairpiece—he's known as 'George,' this hairpiece [after the role of George in *Who's Afraid of Virginia Woolf*, for which he first donned it]—to Heathrow, and put it in an envelope into somebody's hand who took it on the plane and took it off. And that afternoon I drove to a little shed somewhere out in the fringes of the Los Angeles airport and picked up George. I remember thinking, 'My God, they better offer me this job after what its cost me!'"

"The minute we looked at [the toupee], we realized it was wrong," Roddenberry told one reporter. "That wasn't the Patrick we wanted. He looked like a drapery clerk."

"The final reading I did for *Star Trek* actually turned into an offer," Stewart said. "And it happened so quickly I couldn't be found. After my reading . . . I went off and had a very, very long breakfast and I read the British newspapers. You know, I felt about the audition that, well, there it is, I've done it. It's now behind me and I've done my best. So I spent a long time . . . over a long leisurely breakfast while my agent and other people were scouring the town looking for me to tell me I got the role. Then, I think, was the most difficult period of thinking hard about the job and thinking about whether it was something I should do."

"I was very involved with the original casting on *Star Trek* and if I could pride myself on any casting coup it had to do with Patrick Stewart," Berman said years later. "Bob [Justman] discovered Patrick Stewart and brought him to the attention of Gene Roddenberry and Roddenberry said no. I met Patrick Stewart and said to Bob Justman, 'We have to convince Gene to use this guy,' and Bob said to me, 'We can't, it's a waste of time. When Gene makes up his mind it's a waste of time to try and change his mind.' But in my case, ignorance was bliss. I didn't believe that and I was the guy who basically bugged Gene into realizing that Patrick was the best Picard."

Finally at the end Roddenberry relented and said, "Well, let's go with Patrick. He's our best choice." Stewart didn't really fit his concept, but once he decided that Stewart was the character, he wrote the character for Stewart.

On May 15, 1987, Paramount announced the cast of largely unknown actors who would become *Star Trek: The Next Generation*. Most news accounts emphasized LeVar Burton in the role of Geordi La Forge, thanks to his acclaimed role in the landmark television miniseries *Roots*. The new captain, it was simply noted, would be played by a longtime member of the Royal Shakespeare Company and occasional movie actor, Patrick H. Stewart.*

"As we often say with a stage play, it is very often the role that is the attraction," Stewart explained in an interview on why he accepted the part of Captain Picard. "Therefore, the leader in the 24th century was especially interesting. Actually, I knew what *Star Trek* was. I had watched it with my children. But I wasn't aware of the significance that *Star Trek* had played in the culture of the second half of the 20th century in America.

"I was utterly unaware of the millions of people around the world whose lives had been touched by the original show and by the great affection and fondness it was held with," Stewart recalled, almost in awe. "I didn't know that day-to-day philosophies had been built around the fundamental outlook of *Star Trek*. I didn't know the significance of sitting in the captain's chair. This was first made clear to me in the week that I accepted the part. A friend of mine in Los Angeles asked, 'Patrick, how does it feel, to be going to play an American icon?' I didn't know that what I was get-

---

* Stewart added an 'H' as a middle initial when he applied to the Screen Actors Guild because there was already another actor with the name Patrick Stewart. After conferring with his family he later chose 'Heweh,' the Scottish equivalent to Hugh, as a second name.

ting involved in was so subtly, deeply, profoundly interwoven into American culture. . . . I didn't know that I was sailing into history with this."

Almost as soon as Stewart was signed, the comparisons to William Shatner and legendary Starfleet Captain James T. Kirk began. "For a long time, people would say to me, 'Oh, you're the next William Shatner'—a phrase that used to irritate me at times. . . . I *never* had a problem with Captain Kirk," Stewart told one interviewer. "Many other people tried to *impose* a problem on me. I was uneasy about that. Until our show aired, every meeting, every interview, every contact on the street was always, 'How is your show going to be different? How are you going to compare? Are you the new Captain Kirk?' Those were impossible questions to answer. I knew what we were doing had a totally different personality. With *Star Trek: The Next Generation,* we are not replacing anyone; we are simply what we are. What had been before is still there. Nothing has been taken away; it will always be there.

"For twenty-five years, I played roles in Shakespeare that actors had been playing for four hundred years before me and that will be played by actors long after I'm dead. So what is there to get upset about?"

"We're Not Here to Have Fun!"

"I was a pain in the ass when I first came to America. I was pompous and altogether too full of myself," remembered Stewart years later. "My very first shot for *Next Generation* was in the middle of the second day of filming. I didn't work the first day because it was a location day with Brent Spiner [Data] and Wil Wheaton [Wesley Crusher] and Jonathan Frakes [Commander Riker]."

The first scene Stewart had to film was of Captain Picard walking along the corridor of the *Enterprise,* when the holodeck door opened, and out came young Wesley Crusher and Commander Riker. "The scene had something to do with the throwing of a snowball," Stewart remembered. "My first time on camera was a reaction shot, of me looking at the two of them. So the shot was set up, they rolled camera, and I looked at them, did my reaction, and the director called, 'Cut.' Jonathan says, 'Huh! So I see, *that's* what they call British face acting, eh!' I said to him at that moment that it wouldn't be an easy ride for me to do the series. I was mocked and made fun of all the time. Everybody in the cast seemed to think it's funny to imitate the way I talk.

"I was fortunate enough to work with a group of people who I think liked me enough to not want me to go on being a pompous ass," Stewart continued. "I do remember a company meeting I called during the first season. Denise Crosby was still on the show and I said that I felt that the set was much too undisciplined and that we should all exhibit much more self-control. I remember Denise saying, 'Come on, Patrick, it's just fun.' I said, very adamantly, 'We're not here to have fun!' Well, they wore me down. They wouldn't do the things I wanted them to do." He paused for a moment. "They just laughed at me and wouldn't let me take myself too seriously. I'm grateful for that now. It's one of the things that literally changed my life."

If Stewart appeared aloof and formidable at first, he turned out to be disarmingly charming (after his self-proclaimed "Americanization") and soon won the wildly enthusiastic respect of the other cast members. "One of the reasons this show didn't take the dive we all feared it would in the back of our minds in comparison to the old show," Jonathan Frakes pointed out, "is because they cast the characters so well. They hired actors who like to act instead of hiring movie stars or models. For virtually all of us, this was the biggest job of our career and we're so happy about that. It was an ensemble and I think it was a good ensemble."

A New Captain on the Bridge

In the two-hour premiere, which debuted the week of September 28, 1987, the maiden voyage of the USS *Enterprise* introduced the television audience to the new *Star Trek* crew that would begin the next "ongoing" mission. Captain Picard is sent by Starfleet to investigate how the low-tech Bandi race could have built the gleaming new Farpoint Station, a staging planet deemed vital to the interests of the Federation.

En route the *Enterprise* is almost sidetracked permanently by the all-powerful Q, who considers humanity too barbarous to expand further and contaminate space. To prove his point, he tries Picard and his senior crew members and sentences them to death in a kangaroo court. Picard is able to save their lives only by offering to prove humanity's worth during his ship's upcoming mission to Farpoint. An intrigued Q agrees and the *Enterprise* arrives at the station, where the crew can find no explanation for the Bandi's mysterious new technology until a vast alien ship appears and opens fire on the old Bandi city. Q tries to goad Picard into firing on the newcomer, but the *Enterprise* away team finds that the attacker is actually a life-form trying to free its mate from the Bandi clutches. Farpoint Station, it is discovered, was built entirely by this enslaved creature. As the freed aliens leave the planet, a disappointed Q vows he'll be back to test humanity yet again.

"The first episode really felt like two stories, two pieces of a jigsaw puzzle forced together," recalled Stewart. "I feel that the later episodes were better, if for no reason than that the company was better and knew their characters better and were less worried finding out if the show would succeed. There was so much riding on our shoulders on this show. As captain of the new *Enterprise,* I was expected to guide Paramount's immensely profitable *Star Trek* franchise into the future. . . . I didn't unpack my suitcase for a whole month. I had a conviction that one morning they would all simultaneously wake up and say, 'What have we done? We have cast this middle-aged, bald, Shakespearean actor as the captain of the *Enterprise.* We must have been insane!'

"I watched the pilot with my hands over my eyes," Stewart continued, assessing his performance in the series's premiere. "I didn't feel it was working. I got some really good feedback from people, but personally, knowing what I can do as an actor and what was up there, I wasn't really happy."

But for all the pressure, long hours, and dissatisfaction by Stewart and the rest of the cast, the result seemed to please most critics. Ed Bark of *The Dallas Morning News,* writing for the Knight-Ridder-Tribune service, thought the pilot "soared with the spirit of the original," coming off as a "fine redefining of a classic and a considerable breakthrough for non-network syndicated television." Don Merrill in *TV Guide* proclaimed that *The Next Generation* "is a worthy successor" to the original and said "the new *Enterprise* captain, played by English Shakespearean actor Patrick Stewart, is terrific. As Captain Jean-Luc Picard, he heads a capable ensemble, all of whom understand the secret of acting in a science-fiction show—believe the story, no matter how wild or unbelievable it may seem in script form. When the story calls for Stewart to become angry, his voice takes on that rich, fruity, resonant sound that good English actors produce so well."

But the most important critical response was from the audience. "We needed the core group of Trekkers to validate our efforts," said John Pike, Paramount's president of network television. "The one thing we didn't want to do was fracture the *Star Trek* franchise."

Thanks to the huge fan following of the original series, the heavy advance promotional campaign, and a surprising and poignant cameo appearance by original cast member DeForest "Dr. McCoy" Kelly (which was specifically engineered to smooth ruffled feathers), *The Next Generation*'s high-class, high-tech, high-budget premiere episode beat its prime-time network competition in Los Angeles, Dallas, Seattle, Miami, and Denver, a boast that the original *Star Trek* series could never lay claim to.

Although Stewart was very vocal around the set concerning his personal disappointment with the premiere two-hour movie, Jonathan Frakes, who often kept his co-star well-grounded in reality, reminded Stewart that during the week that the pilot aired, more people saw the former Shakespearean actor perform than had in the previous twenty-seven years of his career combined.

Four

Power Struggle

The King is not bound to answer the particular endings of his soldiers.

—Shakespeare, *Henry V* 4.1.84-157

After working together a few weeks, Stewart and the other cast members all liked each other enormously. They were unified, in large part, by the newness of their venture and by the relative lack of luxury of their accommodations. Because the series needed time to prove itself a long-term ratings success, the cast was working at lower salaries than actors on established shows, and their tiny, no-frills trailers reflected their first-year status. The women had tried to create a cheery patio outside their group of trailers by borrowing furniture from the prop department: a white wicker umbrella table and chairs, a fake cactus, and a small inflatable raft that Denise Crosby (Lt. Tasha Yar) had thrown over a permanent puddle of water near her trailer.

Outside his trailer, Stewart had posted a sign reading, BEWARE, UNKNOWN BRITISH SHAKESPEAREAN ACTOR. Initially he missed acting on the British stage, but as the series progressed, he found himself believing more and more in it as a piece of quality work. "People ask, 'All those years as a classical actor, twenty-five years with the Royal Shakespeare Company, don't you feel that doing *Star Trek* is a comedown?' They perpetually suggest to me that I might be slumming or selling out by coming to Hollywood to do this television series, that in some way, I was betraying my Royal Shakespeare Company past. . . . I was an actor looking for work, interesting work, and consider myself fortunate to have landed this job. You know, all the time I spent sitting around on the thrones of England as various Shakespearean kings was nothing but a preparation for sitting in the captain's chair on the *Enterprise*. Like Shakespeare, *Star Trek* is truly a heroic series and I mean that quite seriously in the Pyrrhic sense of heroic. The style of our language is not absolutely naturalistic language: it's somewhat heightened. *Star Trek* has always had that quality about it. Its dialogue isn't like ordinary dialogue. It doesn't sound like *Hill Street Blues* or *thirtysomething*. The Bridge of the *Enterprise* is very much like a classical stage: it is dramatically organized, and I often feel it when I walk the Bridge. And being accustomed to years and years of wearing tights without pockets in them, the Starfleet uniform has come as second nature. You have nowhere to put your hands."

On the set, Stewart was preoccupied with memorizing his lines during every spare second. He had never had any difficulties learning and remembering lines but the technobabble of *Star Trek* was a challenge. When he first memorized his lines, he would learn them almost mechanically. "The advantages to that and being in front of the cameras, is not to know the line real well thus creating some spontaneity," he once told an acting student.

Stewart also spent time on the set figuring out ways to improve the script whenever possible and didn't hesitate to speak with the director of each episode. The directors were generally receptive to his ideas, and the two would make several phone calls to Berman and Justman throughout the filming. Often the production duo would call back to say, "Gene wants it done the way it's written." Roddenberry, the show's creator and executive producer, had gone over the scripts with a fine-tooth comb, and ultimately it was his vision that prevailed.

As good as the original *Star Trek* series had been, even the most devout Trekker had to admit it was light years away from perfection in both execution and concept. Even as Roddenberry faced the challenge of making *The Next Generation* click, he was aware that few creators ever got a chance to improve on their earlier successes. He might have escaped the problems of prime-time scheduling, effects budgets that part only for rubber monsters and cardboard walls, and network censorship, but how could he improve the series itself?

Word traveled fast around Hollywood that the new series would have all new scripts but that episodes would be little morality plays much like the old series. "*Star Trek* deals with heroes on a very big scale," Stewart said in an interview during the first season. "It's part morality play. Yet I feel that we have not really addressed certain issues as controversially as we might. I would like to see aspects of the political world of the Federation in the 24th century addressed from a much less utopian point of view. Political life is ambivalent and filled with gray areas. I always felt the show could be more radical politically. But it's Gene's vision," Stewart added, obviously not pleased. "We're showing a unified, compassionate Earth—one that has removed poverty, violence, and suffering. We are caught up in and embracing that vision and expanding it, but it belongs to Gene."

Leonard Nimoy, famous for his portrayal of the legendary Mr. Spock, shed some light on Roddenberry's optimistic, but hypocritical, futuristic vision while promoting his *Star Trek* memoirs, *I Am Spock*, in 1995. "Gene had this concept that humankind would improve gradually, that it was greatly capable. There would come a day, he believed, when diversity would become acceptable. But that doesn't necessarily mean he would practice that in his own daily life.

"Gene was anti-Semitic, clearly. This may have been a universe Jews could feel comfortable in. But rest assured—he didn't create it to make Jews comfortable. . . . Bill [Shatner] and I were both Jewish. So was Robert Justman, one of the key members of his production staff. So it wasn't as if Gene was denying Jews access. To be fair, Roddenberry was anti-religion. And apart from being a racial-cultural entity, Jews, to him, were a religious group. But he was certainly anti-Semitic. I saw examples not only of him practicing anti-Semitism, but of him being callous about other peoples' differences as well. His attitude toward women, for instance. Gene was a big chauvinist. The early women on *Trek* were mini-skirted, big-boobed sex objects—toys for guys. He cleaned up that act gradually only because people pointed it out to him. . . . Indeed, he saw the response [to *Trek*] and only then did he become what he modestly called 'a philosopher, junior grade.' "

In fact, it was Roddenberry's idealistic and utopian view of the future that created the infamous revolving door of *The Next Generation*'s writing staff the first year.

A myriad of veteran original *Trek* writers such as D. C. Fontana (*Journey to Babel*) and David Gerrold (*The Trouble with Tribbles*) joined the show only to be fired or leave several weeks—sometimes days—later. One such writer described the show as "like Vietnam, you didn't want to get too close to them because you knew they wouldn't be there very long; Johnny Dawkin, Sandy Fries. . . . They'd be given a script to write and direction and before they could learn what the show was about they'd be torn apart by the staff and thrown to the wolves or Gene would just say I hate them and they'd be out the door. You suspended your own feelings and your own beliefs and you got with Gene's wacky doodle, hope-filled future vision—or got rewritten or fired. It was strange."

Producer Berman was the first to admit that while he was at the forefront of staying true to Roddenberry's optimistic ethos, it was not a vision of the future he personally shared. "The writers were being rewritten by Gene, and there was a lot of tumult because people didn't know where they stood. We had to develop stories that were entertaining and thought-provoking while staying true to Gene's unique unifying vision of *Trek*. The most frustrating thing for writers was his ban on interpersonal conflicts among the crew, based on his belief that such petty and ego-driven problems would be a thing of the past by the 24th century.

"There were some things that existed with Roddenberry that were frustrating to us," Berman continued. "Not to have conflict among your characters makes it very difficult, because all the conflict has to come from outside."

Classically trained in plays about the kings of England, full of quarrels and treachery and kinfolk at each other's throats, Stewart was especially adamant about developing Shakespearean-style conflicts between the characters. He also wanted Roddenberry to be more broad-minded about the firmly established fundamentals of Captain Picard's character and permit the actor to expand and explore the darker, more elemental and more mysterious sides of the *Enterprise*'s Gallic commander. Stewart knew there would be many facets to Picard and wanted to show fans that the captain had a sense of humor, that he had all kinds of passions and enthusiasms for curious, unexpected things. Would he be vulnerable and let his guard down? Would he have any romantic relationships?

"It was always my intention *not* to set out to create a perfect hero," Stewart admitted later. "I think the best heroes are the ones with flaws." And Stewart wanted badly to find the flaws of Jean-Luc Picard.

Roddenberry had never liked the idea of beaming a starship captain right into the middle of the unknown, possibly dangerous situations week after week but lost that battle on the original series. With the new *Star Trek* series, he was adamant in his insistence that First Officer Will Riker lead most landing parties while Picard stayed aboard. Stewart unsuccessfully argued the point that his character, whom he considered an explorer, would miss out on all the action and drama of exploring strange, new worlds and new civilizations and boldly going where no one had gone before. As always, Roddenberry had the final say in the matter, which was almost always a veto, unless he liked the idea and then he usually took the credit while burying the contributions of those who made it a reality.

Head-to-Head Battles

During *The Next Generation*'s first season, lines were often being rewritten on stage and sometimes overdubbed in postproduction to try to make sense of confusing storylines. Why so many story problems? The most obvious reason was the sheer enormity of developing stories that were entertaining and thought-provoking while staying true to Roddenberry's notion of future collegiality and his distaste for warfare.

"Everyone always wants me to do space battles," Roddenberry once remarked. "Well, screw them. That's not what *Star Trek* is about."

The first hour-long episode, *The Naked Now*, was criticized for being nothing more than a remake of the original series' first season episode, *The Naked Time*, and sparked the first fan outcries that many *Next Generation* plots were being lifted from the original *Star Trek*. "It was an homage, not a copy," Berman said of the episode. "We even mentioned the old *Enterprise* and its remedy, which doesn't help our crew after all."

Except for proving that the new ensemble could interact and establishing the underlying Picard-Beverly sexual tension (which would go unresolved until the sixth season), Stewart didn't much care for the episode. Like the fans, Stewart was asking the writers, "Don't you have any new ideas?"

Despite Stewart and others who complained of a copycat format and episodes, ratings began to rise as soon as the series hit the air. *The Naked Now*, the first regular installment, would continue the pilot's success by taking its time slot in Boston, Denver, and Houston, according to A. C. Nielsen. *TV Guide* reported on December 26 that thirteen ABC affiliates and two with CBS had dumped their network programming to carry *The Next Generation* in prime time, and perennial sixth-place Chicago station WPWR-TV jumped to number two in that time slot—a 1,100 percent ratings increase.

In the second episode, *Code of Honor*, a planet's plague sends the *Enterprise* to Ligon II, where Tasha

Yar is kidnapped by the planet's chief ruler (who is black and wears an African-like headdress and costume). To secure Yar's return, Captain Picard must abide by the Prime Directive and the Ligonians' code of honor, while hoping that his security officer can survive a fight to the death with the ruler's "First One" wife.

Stewart, a longtime staunch supporter of liberal causes, vehemently objected to the installment's "1940s tribal Africa" view of blacks. "If you had turned on your television in the middle of the episode and didn't see the *Enterprise,* you would have thought the show was a *National Geographic* special about African tribes," commented Stewart. In addition, he was very dissatisfied with the fight scene's virtual re-enactment of the win-or-die battle from the classic *Amok Time* episode.

Also tried in *Code of Honor* (and once more in the first season's *The Last Outpost* before being scrapped) was the building of Picard's extreme pride in his Gallic heritage to the point of humorous defensiveness. Roddenberry felt the scene fondly echoed back to the original *Trek's* recurring "Russian joke" with Chekov, who believed his motherland was the birthplace of almost all inventions and discoveries. "It just wasn't working," Stewart later said. "Even worse, Picard was almost becoming a caricature and I didn't find anything amusing about that."

The script for *Justice,* as it aired, bore only a slight resemblance to the story of terrorism and anarchy as screenwriter John D. F. Black originally pitched it. "*Justice* is about the human answer to what you do when violence in the streets becomes rampant," he explained. "How do you stop it? And once you've stopped it, what happens next? Let's say that what we do is kill everybody who is a terrorist or suspected of being a terrorist. Now the people who have killed everybody, what do they do? We're talking about a society dealing with some aspect of itself."

Stewart, a vocal opponent of capital punishment and the United States' "primitive animal urge to smell blood," was enamored of Black's first draft, but major rewrites by Roddenberry added the planet's machine-god and the culture's preoccupation with sex. "I really liked the original concept of the episode," Stewart later remarked. "It effectively dealt with the idea of vengeance. Should the government take a life for a life? Then we should rape rapists, beat up violent husbands, and castrate child molesters, chop off the right hands of thieves. That, too, would be just. . . . But if we respond to that urge, what are we and where are we going? Not forward, that's for certain. If there is a sanctity on human life, there is a sanctity on human life. There are no clauses, no exceptions. No ifs, no buts, no special cases." An obviously disappointed Stewart added, "The initial concept for *Justice* met this issue of society's need for vengeance head on, [but Roddenberry's rewrites] got too fanciful, sexual and there was an innocence that was missing."

The Battle was Stewart's favorite episode to date and, in his second directorial outing, Rob Bowman (who would later go on to fame as a director and producer of *The X-Files*) particularly enjoyed working with the actor, who had the stage all to himself during filming of the ghostly *Stargazer* battle scenes. The director used a Steadicam in those sequences (the first such use on *The Next Generation*) to evoke an unsteadiness not just of the derelict *Stargazer* but of the mind-controlled Picard as well.

"It was a little bit intimidating when I first got the script," Bowman admitted. "I was going to be dealing with Patrick Stewart, whose knowledge is unending, and I really wanted to tap that; I really wanted to get in there and make that man work. At the same time, I was concerned I didn't have enough notches on my belt to bring the best out of him. I think what I ended up doing was making my own little version of that movie, while not letting Patrick do his version of it. The only thing I could be comfortable with was my version, so I'd say, 'This is what I want in this scene,' and Patrick just gave it to you."

Writing producer Maurice Hurley wrote the script for *Hide and Q* but after Roddenberry rewrote it extensively, Hurley used the pen name C. J. Holland. "That's where Gene and I had our little talk about the future," Hurley said, setting the stage for the inevitable power struggle to wrestle the creative control of the series from Roddenberry. "Mine was more action-oriented and less philosophical, if I can say that. It was a matter of procedure of how the show was being done. It had nothing to do with who's right and who's wrong, because that's a subjective call. When you have people on a show who are your staff writers, you don't take work away from them. You get them to modify it closer to what you want, rather than just do a rewrite."

It is in this episode during the battle of wits between Picard and Q in the ready room, that the title of the captain's prized display book can be read: *The Globe Illustrated Shakespeare.* What isn't so clearly visible is that the book, as usual, is opened to Act III, Scene 2, of *A Midsummer Night's Dream,* one of Stewart's favorites. Stewart had finally won a long hard battle with Roddenberry in an attempt to "fill in the picture" and "add details" to Picard's personality, and hopefully lay a foundation for the captain's character.

"Picard is a visionary, a dreamer, an adventurer and a compassionate man," Stewart explained in an interview with a British magazine. "He is a literate, cultured man who still reads books and listens to classical music. He has a large library, when reading has become something of an oddity in the 24th century and Picard is perfectly comfortable quoting some of his favorite authors, including William Shakespeare, Charles Dickens and Lewis Carroll."

Stewart wanted to move his character from one point at the beginning of the season to another at the end of the season, and one of the problems with Roddenberry's script rewrites and influence on the series was that the characters never changed.

"With each episode, I tried with the writers to work in something new about Picard, something that expands the audience's knowledge of who this man is," Stewart said. "I don't know much more about him than they do. If I'm doing my job properly, the audience will know things about Picard that I *don't* know and never will know. If acting is the endeavor it should be, it *must* be open to the possibilities for the audience to have insight into the character. The audience can see things that are *not* planned to be there."

Stewart often commented that if you looked at the original series and saw all the incredible adventures the characters went through, you couldn't help but notice that they were still the same characters at the end as they were at the beginning. Stewart strongly believed that was not the way life truly was and wanted to arc Captain Picard through the first season, but Roddenberry's constant rewrites of the scripts and vetoes of Stewart's character suggestions was a major disappointment to the actor.

For the first time in his professional life, Stewart was not in full command of his character.

"Changes are Coming"

During the second half of the first season, as Roddenberry continued to assiduously rewrite nearly every script to conform to his vision of the future, Stewart began to ally himself with *Next Generation* producer and former Paramount vice-president, Rick Berman. "Rick was a little more liberal and tolerant about what I was permitted to explore as a character," Stewart later told a *Time* magazine interviewer.

Berman confided in Stewart one of the best-kept secrets of the *Star Trek* franchise: From *The Next Generation*'s conception, Roddenberry was only third on Paramount's list of potential producers for the new series. First the studio had approached the father and son team of Sam and Greg Strangis (who went on to produce Paramount's *War of the Worlds)*, whose take on *The Next Generation* (a show dealing primarily with Starfleet Academy and space cadets) was not what the studio brass was looking for. Leonard Nimoy, whose astonishing evolution from the original series's Mr. Spock to the fiscally frugal director of two very successful *Star Trek* movies had earned him the respect and admiration of Paramount's executive board, was approached next. He rejected their offer because he did not want to get bogged down with the unyielding strictness of a weekly TV series when his successful non-*Trek* directorial career *(Three Men and a Baby)* was finally separating him from the umbilical cord of the Spock character. Out of options and choices, Paramount turned to Roddenberry.

Their reluctance was understandable after the way Roddenberry badmouthed the studio's executives throughout the '70s, blaming them for the failure to revive the original series as a weekly show once again. After the success of *Star Wars* and *Close Encounters of the Third Kind,* Paramount Studios, in the form of its chairman, Barry Diller, president Michael Eisner, and a very young and naive executive by the name of Jeffrey Katzenberg, gave Roddenberry $45 million (which included about $20 million in carried-over expenses from the failed development of a new weekly series) to make a *Star Trek* movie, hoping that he would film one of the greatest science fiction epics ever made. Instead, Paramount got *Star Trek: The Motion Picture,* a production nightmare and big-budgeted creative disaster.

The studio hoped that Roddenberry would be contained for *The Next Generation,* despite the fact that they had been forced to cede full creative control to obtain his cooperation. But as writers continued to come and go like Tribbles, Paramount decided that their salvation would eventually be their former vice-president, Rick Berman, who they believed would ultimately become the real winner in the power struggle involving the studio, Roddenberry and a cadre of writers.

"I went through a rather strenuous apprenticeship," recalled Berman. "I learned what was *Star Trek* and what wasn't. I learned all the nomenclature, all the rules and regulations. I learned the difference between shields and deflectors—that was a day right there. Slowly, Gene began to trust my judgment and also to trust that I would adhere to the rules, that I would not be someone who would want to change *Star Trek.* "

However, Paramount had sent down the word from the executive offices: Find a way to sail the *Enterprise* between the Scylla of Roddenberry's own "prime directive"—a stricture against any conflict among members of Starfleet—and the Charybdis of mass-market appeal. And somehow find a way to appease Stewart, the series's frustrated lead actor. The *last* thing in the world Paramount wanted was for their *Enterprise* captain to storm off the set after less than a year, citing "creative differences."

A few days later, Berman met with Stewart and told him to "Be patient. Changes are coming." A sympathetic Berman said that he knew the actor was used to discussing dialogue and character with directors, but that American television was an entirely different world than the Royal Shakespeare Company or BBC TV productions. They discussed the pace of the show, the long hours, the messengers who rang Stewart's doorbell at nine o'clock at night with Roddenberry's rewrites, and the directors who changed with every episode.

Berman promised Stewart that future episodes would concentrate more on the development not only of Picard, but the other major characters. Berman ended the long conversation by telling Stewart, "If you have a problem with Roddenberry in the future, come directly to me." A few weeks later, the show's staff was restructured and Berman received the title of co-executive producer.

Shaking hands through tentative smiles, Stewart and Roddenberry espoused a new spirit of cooperation, promising to work together without the artistic clashes of the first half of the season.

Signs of Character Development

In an episode halfway through the first season, Stewart was able to display his rarely used comedic talents. In *The Big Goodbye,* Captain Picard attempted to relieve the stress of an upcoming diplomatic mission by role-playing in his favorite holodeck program, a 1940s hard-boiled detective named Dixon Hill. Some *film noir* references, including Redblock and Leech as echoes of the Sydney Greenstreet and Peter Lorre

characters from one of Stewart's favorite childhood
movies *The Maltese Falcon,* made their way into the
script after suggestions from the lead actor. Even
Dixon Hill's office was identical to Bogart's, right
down to the window and the venetian blinds.

The Big Goodbye was "jeered" by *TV Guide* as too derivative of an original-series episode, *A Piece of the Action,* a comic turn that featured a planet's culture
based on 1930s gangland Chicago. Stewart and most
of the *Trek* fans disagreed. He felt the comparison was
based merely on the appearance of "trench coats and
three-piece suits." Eventually, those suits were good
enough to help earn the series an Emmy award for
costuming, and the episode was chosen by the George
Foster Peabody Award Board for its "best of the best"
award—the first for an hour-long first run drama.

Better known as the "Pulitzer Prize" for broadcasting, the prestigious Peabody Award is designed to rec-
ognize distinguished achievement and meritorious
public service by radio and television networks, local
stations, cable TV organizations, and individuals.
Widely considered the symbol of excellence in broadcasting, it is the most competitive of the many entertainment awards. Since 1940, more than 30,000
programs, personalities, and institutions have been
nominated, with fewer than 1,000 Peabody Awards
eventually presented. To be the recipient has become
the highest goal to which performers and creators of
programming can aspire.

Writing producer Hurley was also very defensive of
the award-winning episode. "I thought it was just
great. It was a use of the holodeck, it was a use of the
cast, a use of the ensemble. I thought the acting in it
was exceptional, the direction was wonderful and so
was the lighting. It was like a breath of fresh air. It's
got humor and life to it. The thing is that *Star Trek*

can't brood. If it broods, it gets self-important and self-indulgent and preachy, like it has a tendency to do if it's not careful."

Hurley and Berman worked closely together to write the Klingon "information episode," *Heart of Glory*, which closely examined the warrior race and, notably, the character of Worf. "It gave you everything you wanted to know about what happened with the Klingons," explained Michael Dorn, the actor who portrays Worf. "Why did they become allies? Why is Worf there? How did he get there?"

Hurley, credited with writing the episode, stated, "That episode was where Rick Berman and I were hitting our stride; that's where we were locked at the hip in putting these shows together. When I had a problem, I could go in and we could sit there, close the door, yell and scream. I'd pace, he'd make suggestions. The two of us made stories work in that room that had to be shot in a couple of days. We were under enormous time pressure, and we were working hand in glove. We had a wonderful time, on that show especially." Finally, it appeared that Berman's promise to Stewart that the show's characters would begin showing signs of development was coming true.

The following episode, *The Arsenal of Freedom*, was initially scripted as a Picard-Crusher love story, and Stewart was excited about the prospect of showing Picard's passionate, romantic side. "It started out as a vastly different episode," said writer and former *Next Generation* producer Robert Lewin. "It was originally going to be a love story in which Picard was dying and Beverly [Crusher] was going to reveal how she really felt about him. I tried to deal with that in a very sensitive and moving way, but it gradually changed because of Gene [Roddenberry]. He did not want to do a love story." To Stewart's disappointment, Roddenberry opted instead for the final product, which was an extremely ambitious action-adventure episode about arms merchants.

Beverly's diminished role in the final draft of *The Arsenal of Freedom* underscored the absence of meaty roles for Gates McFadden, Marina Sirtis, and especially Denise Crosby. Long before *Skin of Evil* was filmed, rumors were flying at warp speed about the manner of Crosby's departure as a regular cast member on the series and the reasons for it. Thanks to media reports, it became widely known that she was dissatisfied with the Uhura-like sparseness of her role as Security Chief Tasha Yar and had asked to be released from her contract on friendly terms so that she could pursue a film career. Ironically, during the first half of the season Marina Sirtis, who played Counselor Deanna Troi, almost left the show, too, after her character went unused in four episodes.

Hannah Louise Shearer, who rewrote the original draft by *Outer Limits* veteran Joseph Stefano, said the in-house debate on the nature of Yar's exit finally went the way Roddenberry wanted, with a "senseless" but typical sudden death befitting a security chief. Originally, Yar's demise came much earlier in the episode and the focus was more on the evil creature that killed her than on the crew's reactions to their comrade's death.

Jonathan Frakes (Commander Riker) cites *Skin of Evil* as one of his favorite episodes. "I think we took greater chances then than we did later."

Director Joseph Scanlan offered his own view on the episode. "When you read the script, it has a wonderful intellectual quality to it, forgetting the complications of creating the creature. This entity had such an ironic quality. I thought his dialogue was extremely interesting and found his one-on-one with Picard to be the ultimate face-off."

If the sadness of the final holographic memorial scene looked tearfully real, it was. Yar's death and Crosby's departure were sad for the actors as well as for the characters. Marina Sirtis (Deanna Troi) began sobbing during reaction takes as her friend cued her from off-camera, leading Stewart and the others into one of the most emotional scenes shot for the young series.

"In the funeral scene, everybody played their parts wonderfully," recalled Michael Dorn, who plays Worf, the Klingon officer. "And they showed Patrick on camera and you *didn't know* what he was going to do. Is he going to cry? That's the edge. That's what got me. Only very seldom have I seen this work. I would have to have Patrick's ability because he *does* move people."

In the episode *We'll Always Have Paris,* writer Hannah Louis Shearer "wanted something that was utterly romantic [and] that explored the character of Picard, [giving] some insight into why he was who he was." If this story doesn't quite come off as another *Casablanca* (the source for the episode's title), it's not surprising. Shearer and her co-writer, Deborah Dean Davis, wrote the script on five days' notice, but Shearer said the final product was "toned down seventy-five percent."

As late as the final draft, Picard and Jenice Manheim (played by former *Mamas and Papas* Michelle Phillips) actually spent the night together, and Troi confronted Beverly about her feelings for the captain, which she had not yet sorted out. "It's very uncomfortable," Shearer said. "I think that was true on staff as well. The women in the office loved it, they loved the idea of Picard being in love and wanted him to make love to this woman, which was in our original draft. The men backed off from it very powerfully. It was not an easy show to write."

After getting bogged down with a romance episode for Picard, the series' writers wanted to bounce back the following week with a gritty, literally down-to-earth episode involving a conspiritorial plot against Starfleet.

Stewart actually believed that the episode *Conspiracy* was going to be a hard-edged story about treachery and betrayal. Originally it was a *Seven Days in May* kind of script about a coup inside Starfleet, by officers—all Picard's friends—who felt the Prime Directive was too restrictive and that the Federation was getting soft and complacent. Predictably Roddenberry rejected the plot, ruling against a conspiracy within his beloved Starfleet. Berman became directly involved and managed to keep "ninety-five percent of the original hard edge," but the conspirators were changed from members of a faction of Starfleet to intelligent alien parasites who invaded the officers' bodies and used them as hosts to take over Starfleet Command.

Episode writer Tracy Tormé explained, "I really felt that although the show had improved a great deal, that we were still too comfortable and weren't pushing the limits of what we could do. I wrote *Conspiracy* with the idea of doing something different; something with an unhappy ending, a harder edge." The result was the first moody episode of the series and one of its darkest ever.

In yet another tell-tale sign that Roddenberry's control over the show was slowly diminishing, the final episode of the first season reintroduced the familiar *Trek* villains, the Romulans. Their boasts to Picard that "We're back" in the episode's final scenes, reinstated them as a primary source of conflict for the Federation despite Roddenberry's vows at the beginning of the season that these alien antagonists would not be part of his *Next Generation*.

"Just a Better Captain's Chair"

Its shakedown year over, *The Next Generation* finished the season on May 16, 1988, with a 10.6 rating—or about 9.4 million households watching from 210 local stations—and ranked first among eighteen- to forty-nine-year-olds, the prime demographic group sought by advertisers. Not only was it a worthy successor to its namesake but also a commercial hit, ending its debut year as the number one first-run series in syndication and the number three syndicated show over all, behind Merv Griffin's game show kings *Jeopardy!* and *Wheel of Fortune.* Beyond North America, in eight European and Asian countries where first-run airing was initially restricted, the series picked up a direct $2 million in videocassette sales by its first summer hiatus.

Though comparisons to the original *Star Trek* series persisted, by season's end *The Next Generation* had developed an identity of its own. *TV Guide* writer Gary D. Christenson compared their differences with those in his generation of Americans: *"Star Trek* depicted us in reckless youth, with a starship captain who tamed space as vigorously as we laid claim to the future. . . . *Star Trek: The Next Generation* reveals the child grown— a little more polished, but also more complacent. And if there's a bit of gray and a wrinkle or two, so much the better."

At the end of the season, Stewart finally answered the critics who complained that the new *Enterprise* captain was no James T. Kirk. "One of Picard's characteristics as opposed to Captain Kirk's is that he continually says to people, 'Tell me what you think—I want to hear your views.' He is generous with his time, eager to learn new concepts. Less of a shoot-from-the-hip cowboy and more of a diplomat, he is a leader who leads from the front, but at the same time sees himself as part of the group."

Once again, Berman met with Stewart and promised him that by the time filming began for the second season Roddenberry would be forced out of power and that *The Next Generation* would soar despite him, not because of him. Other than having more input into the character development of Captain Picard, Berman asked Stewart if there was anything else he wanted on his "wish list" for the following year.

"Just a better captain's chair," Stewart fired back. "One that fits *my* body and NOT some set designer's. After all, it is the captain's chair and the last time I checked, *I* was the ship's captain."

Five

A Piece of the Action

I don't want to be the star of the show like William Shatner was on the original Star Trek. *I simply want a piece of the action because it seems to me that Riker and Data are getting all the attention.*

—Patrick Stewart's complaint to Rick Berman
at the end of the second season

As Rick Berman had promised Stewart at the end of *The Next Generation*'s first year on the air, Gene Roddenberry, whose contract forbade banishment from the set, was "kicked upstairs" and given a largely ceremonial title at the beginning of the second season in November 1988. Paid handsomely and allowed to comment on every story idea and scripted draft of the episodes, Roddenberry abruptly came to realize that for all intents and purposes, he'd actually been removed from the driver's seat. With Roddenberry assuming the role of figurehead and the departure of Robert Justman as Supervising Producer, due to health reasons, Rick Berman took over as "Admiral" of Paramount's coveted *Star Trek* franchise. It would not be a smooth transition of power, however, and before long Berman would have to accept the fact that a proud and determined Roddenberry would "kick and fight all the way down to the mat," essentially making the second year nothing more than a slugfest worthy of a Las Vegas heavyweight fight.

Filling the void on the story side was Maurice Hurley, who came aboard early in the first season and quickly rose up the ladder to fill the power vacuum in Roddenberry's absence. At the beginning of *The Next Generation*'s sophomore year, Hurley was the head writer and with the combined efforts of Berman the series took on a darker tone. Although adhering to the strictures of Roddenberry's universe governing the interpersonal relationships of the characters, they were quick to point out that space was not always a happy and cheerful place to be.

Many changes were made for the show during its second year. Longtime *Star Trek* fan Whoopi Goldberg was added to the cast as Guinan, a recurring regular who tended bar in the new Ten-Forward lounge. At the same time, Gates McFadden, who portrayed Dr. Beverly Crusher, was unceremoniously fired by Roddenberry in an attempt to prove to Berman that he could still wield some power on the set.

At a *Star Trek* convention in Los Angeles during the summer hiatus in 1988, Roddenberry's secretary, Susan Sackett, for whatever reason, let it be known that McFadden would not be back for the second season. When Roddenberry was introduced and walked out onto the stage, there were several chants of "BRING BACK GATES!" During the question-and-answer section, he was asked about bringing the actress back to the series.

"I like Gates McFadden, too," Roddenberry answered. "I think she's a charming lady and a good actress. However . . . there's no way any amount of talk about Gates McFadden will do anything more than the fact she is liked will already do for us. As far as it being a vote, are we going to have Gates McFadden [back?], you all move 'For' and I say 'Nay.' The Nays have it. You have to accept that because if I were to listen to your voice, I could have listened to the network voices and other people saying, 'Do this. Do that.' *Star Trek* would have been about shit. Really. There is such a thing as telling the artist what you want and like and then leave it up to him to do what he does. That's the only way it can be."

"There were those who believed at the end of the first season that they didn't like the way the character was developing because of Gates' performance, and managed to convince Mr. Roddenberry of that," Berman said years later, adding, "I was not a fan of that decision."

By way of contrast, the new doctor, Kate Pulaski, was created somewhat in the image of the crusty country doctor, "Bones" McCoy, from the original series. But while the sparks she brought were welcome to Stewart and many other cast members, most of them resented the handling of McFadden's departure and the fact that Diana Muldaur, the actress that would play Dr. Pulaski, was a good friend of Roddenberry's. Berman's choice for the role was Christina Pickles, a regular on the NBC medical drama *St. Elsewhere*.

The highly touted ensemble cast was reduced in the second season to a triumvirate clearly reminiscent of the original *Star Trek*'s Kirk, Spock, and McCoy. This time Picard, Riker, and Data shared the spotlight as the gang of three that would dominate the stories throughout year two, while characters such as Worf,

La Forge, Troi, Wesley, and the newly added Dr. Pulaski were relegated to supporting status.

True to his word, Berman also presented Stewart with a more distinctive command chair on the bridge of the *Enterprise,* one that better fit the actor's body with armrest panels permanently mounted open instead of hinged. "It's ergometrically designed for Patrick Stewart's butt," commented Jonathan Frakes. The captain's chair during the first season had been all leather, but it squeaked when Stewart moved around. The new one was made of a comfortable combination of leather and fabric and Stewart didn't look too kindly on others sitting in his seat.

"I've seen people leap out of it when he walks on to the set," said Richard James, the show's production designer. "He's the only one allowed to sit in it."

However, on one occasion, Jason Davis, a young terminally ill boy was allowed to visit the set of *The Next Generation* courtesy of the Starlight Foundation and Stewart, tears welling up in his eyes, allowed the boy to sit in his captain's chair and pose for photographs with the rest of the cast.

After Jason died, his mother contacted Stewart via an online interview: "I know that seeing you increased my son's life. He so loved to tell everyone how he got to meet you and what you're really like. Meeting you and the cast was more important than when he met the President of the United States. . . . The trip was so nice. He loved the ship and my favorite picture is of Jason sitting in the chair. . . . I can't put into words what the trip did for my son. You are his hero and he got to visit with you. It was like giving my son the moon. . . . Thank you for giving a dying young man his dream."

Stewart replied: "I'm so happy to hear from you but also so very sad to hear Jason died. I and all of *The Next Generation* cast will never forget his visit to the set. Although it seems to you we were giving him so much, in fact, the opposite was more true. With his cheerfulness, sense of fun, mischievousness and delight in everything around him (despite the severe handicap of this illness), he touched all of us so deeply. And I have not forgotten nor will ever forget the short time he spent with us. Thank you for letting us share for a few moments in Jason's beautiful personality."

And in This Corner . . .

Stewart initially felt that the writing staff on the series hit their stride during the second season, even though they constantly battled with Roddenberry and a strike by the Writer's Guild went unsettled for six months. "They seemed to find a direction," Stewart later said. "There suddenly seemed to be this climate of discussion among the writers and the cast about what we wanted to do with the show. This was a new phenomenon. We were a little bit more on the same wavelength."

However, the euphoria lasted only until the third episode when the Roddenberry-Berman-Paramount power struggle came full circle once again and, as usual, took the edge off a really creative and well-written script. In *Elementary, Dear Data,* La Forge persuades Sherlock Holmes fan Data to play the role of the detective on the holodeck with the engineer as Watson. But Holmes' original cases are no challenge to Data's memory, so Dr. Pulaski—who has yet to accept the android as anything more than a machine—challenges him to solve a new computer-generated case.

Stewart was extremely satisfied with the developing Pulaski-Data friction and the verbal opposition between the two characters. More importantly, the British actor was enamored with the episode's wondrous Victorian London set of carriages and gas-lit back alleys, which was built in just three days. Stewart felt like he was back on the stage in England again and he absolutely shone with a new energy and spirit, until Roddenberry axed the original ending for the episode.

"We had a large fight about it," Maurice Hurley admitted. "In that ending, Picard knew how to defeat Moriarty. He tricked him. He knew all along that Moriarty could leave the holodeck whenever he wanted to, and he knew because when Data came out and showed him a drawing of the *Enterprise,* if that piece of paper could leave the holodeck, that means that the fail-safe had broken down. When he knew the paper had left the holodeck, he knew that Moriarty could as well, so he lied to him. The doctor says, 'How could you lie to Moriarty?' Picard basically says, 'Well, after all, it is Moriarty, and until we know whether he is saying what he's saying because that's how he really feels or if it's more of his guile and deceit, it's best to be very safe.' Hurley, Stewart and the writers thought it made the captain look clever, but Gene thought it made Picard look deceitful, dishonest and it hurt the character."

In a bizarre turn of events in the *Time Squared* episode, Picard is confronted by his own double from six hours in the future, incoherent and disoriented after being recovered from a shuttlecraft that has recorded the *Enterprise's* destruction in a vast energy whirlpool. As the time of the ship's destruction nears, the Picard from the future begins to revive, while the *Enterprise* captain of the present grows more and more uncertain for fear of endangering the starship and repeating the steps his future self made, thus resulting in the ship's end.

This story, originally titled *Time to the Second,* began as the first of what Maurice Hurley, who wrote the script, had planned as two linked episodes, with *Time to the Second* a prelude to the upcoming *Q Who?* But Roddenberry once again scrapped the idea just to prove to Berman, Hurley, and Stewart that he could. The result was a confusing ending to the episode.

"It doesn't make any sense," Hurley said. "But it does if Q is pulling the strings. Then the whole thing works. Those two [episodes] were supposed to be tied together. What we were left with was a bullshit ending."

Even though *The Icarus Factor* was primarily about Riker's estranged father returning and Worf's Klingon Age of Ascension ceremony on the holodeck, Stewart was encouraged that the episode was "an emotional piece, a character piece between two people."

"The father has deserted Riker for 25 years, then he comes back and they have this confrontation," Director Robert Iscove explained. "Well, according to Roddenberry, by the 24th century we've all kind of resolved those feelings of anger. So it's very hard to play. If you're not going to serve the resentment and anger . . . you can't get into any real human drama.

"The future *isn't* perfect," he added. "But every time you push against it, the immediate people—Berman, Stewart and all of them—agree with you, but then it goes to Roddenberry, the ultimate voice, who says you can't do that. I was supposed to do some more of them, but I said, 'Thank you very much, but I can't.' There's just no place to go with it. If you can't deal with the emotion, what's the point?"

In *Q Who?*, the mischievous superbeing returns, commandeering Picard in a shuttlecraft. Warning the captain of human complacency, the omnipotent alien transports the *Enterprise* to the deepest recesses of the galaxy. There they encounter the unstoppable, cybernetic super race known as the Borg, who slowly begin to disassemble the Federation starship with their superior technology.

This episode, which was an attempt by Hurley to create some new jeopardy and a new villain, was Stewart's favorite of the second season. "The Borg are a variation of an insect mentality. They don't care. They have no mercy nor any feelings. They have their own agenda and that's it. If all of them die in the process, they don't care. They are truly relentless."

Observed episode director Rob Bowman, "We didn't know day to day if we were making a stinker or a winner. It was just too weird. When I saw the final print with the effects and the music, I thought, 'Wow, Maurice was right. It really is disturbing.' I don't know how he got it past Roddenberry. Maurice was adamant about this. He championed this thing through with a fervor which couldn't be stopped and he was, basically, like a bull in a ring. Everybody got out of his way and a lot of people thought he was dead wrong.

"There were some arguments about this show," Bowman continued. "It was an incredibly difficult episode. Patrick even got a little bit hostile that the rest of us were not taking it seriously enough, we were a little bit too jokester and he was right. . . . We wanted to make a great episode. The script was very unusual and the Borg were, we thought, really quite threatening and we wanted to get that across."

In the following episode, *Samaritan Snare,* the *Enterprise* encounters an apparently dimwitted race of beings, who recruit Geordi's help to fix their malfunctioning drive unit and threaten him with violence unless he stays aboard to assist them with their technological incompetence. At the same time, Picard is escorted by Wesley via shuttle for a life-saving heart transplant. According to Stewart, the episode was "the most wretched piece of *Star Trek* ever filmed, an insult to the intelligence of the people who watched the show faithfully.

"For instance, before Geordi beams over, Worf says explicitly to Riker, 'Do we have to send them our chief engineer because they have a little problem?' and it's never answered. On the trip over to the starbase . . . Wesley asks why would anyone use a defective heart transplant. A valid point, Mr. Crusher. A major piece of idiotic plotting is they send Picard to a medical facility where . . . no one was qualified to handle the operation if it went at all wrong. Then they have to call the *Enterprise* to bring Dr. Pulaski over to do the operation. . . . None of the plot could have happened if all of the characters hadn't suddenly become morons that week."

Manhunt was conceived as a sequel to *The Big Goodbye* and *Haven*, in which Picard's Dixon Hill and Majel Barrett's Lwaxana Troi made their first season appearances. *"Manhunt* was designed as a starring vehicle for Roddenberry's wife, Majel," remembered Rob Bowman, director of the episode. "I was asked to make sure that she does her best, so everyday that's what we worked on. There's really no story tie between her want, which is a mate, and Picard going to Dixon Hill. It was just a way for us to get to the old stuff. There's no reason for him to particularly go there. We had a great time doing the '40s stuff. I'd looked forward to that since *The Big Goodbye*. . . . They changed it a great deal to accommodate Majel and sacrificed what I thought were some of the *film noir* to the show. The emphasis was shifted from the *noir* to Majel, the boss's wife."

The episode also turned out to be the swan song for one of the series's more popular writers, Tracy Tormé, whose second season scripts *The Royale* and *Manhunt* had—according to the writer—been so mutilated that he had to use a pseudonym on both works. Tormé, who had served as a Creative Consultant in year two and had once been groomed to take over the reins of the show under Berman, was not prepared for the "take no prisoners" power struggle and to suffer through the endless divisive rewrites by Roddenberry that had characterized the show for two seasons.

Maurice Hurley, the series's head writer, who had also grown tired of the infighting at the show, gave notice that he, too, would be leaving through the infamous revolving door. The mass exodus continued with producers John Mason, Mike Grey, Burton Armus, Leonard Mlodinow, and Scott Rubenstein. Collectively, they claimed of Roddenberry, "It's ironic that *Star Trek*'s Writer's Guide is referred to as 'The Bible' since his 'thou shalt nots' abound and those who violate his commandments are either struck down or leave the show of their own volition."

Berman informed the Paramount brass that there were always "producers and writers who were standing in line to work on the series," but Patrick Stewart, the show's main star, was not just complaining anymore. He was threatening to quit if Roddenberry was allowed to continue to interfere with the production of the series. Berman told the studio executives that in the original series, William Shatner had asserted the predominance of his character, excluding his supporting cast from most seminal dramatic scenes and episodes, but Stewart simply wanted a "piece of the action," pointing out that Roddenberry's rewrites of the scripts always placed Riker and Data in positions where it seemed that they received the most attention.

When Stewart complained that Picard did nothing but talk, a petty Roddenberry made sure the captain was left on the bridge while his subordinates got the call to action via an away team. "Watching Picard is like visiting a social worker," concurred science-fiction writer Ben Bova in a magazine review of *The Next Generation*.

Berman met with Stewart during the break between the seasons and asked Stewart what he wanted for the next year. "New uniforms," the actor quickly answered. "You and the other creative people are of the mind-set that our characters must look unruffled at all times— even during action sequences. Well, forget it. *You* try saving various galaxies and coming out without a wrinkle. The costumes are a couple of sizes too small, Rick, because you want them to be as tight and smooth as possible. The material pulls on every part of the body and my chiropractor has told me to tell the studio that either you take me out of the costume or I'm going to sue them for damage it's doing to my body."

Berman promised his temperamental lead actor that the Starfleet duty uniforms would be changed from a stretch fabric to a two-piece, wool-blend costume by the time filming began for the third season.

During the summer hiatus, Paramount let Roddenberry know that they couldn't stomach the idea of his horrid mismanagement and interference in the successful series any longer. The message was transmitted in a way that Roddenberry and his lawyers couldn't misconstrue its meaning: "We're happy to use your name and your creation, but don't call us, we'll call you."

Six

Dissatisfaction Guaranteed

I like the stimulation of fresh work. I always enjoyed . . . between a matinee and evening performance, the play would change, the costume would change, the sets would change, indeed the character would change.

—Patrick Stewart explaining why he wanted to quit *The Next Generation* after only three years

Stewart has often said that he considers *Star Trek: The Next Generation*'s third season as its finest year because it signaled a dramatic change from the policies and dramatic tone of the first two seasons. Without Roddenberry's impediment and constant rewriting of the scripts, Stewart was finally allowed to fully explore the dimensions of his character through stories that he found to be "well-written, thought-provoking and entertaining." The show's success could be measured in more concrete ways as well, as throughout the 1989-90 season the series built on its opening 10.8 viewer rating and added to its affiliation of 235 stations, already the highest among syndicated shows.

Much of the credit for the show's newfound confidence went to the new head of the writing staff, Michael Piller. When Maurice Hurley announced at the close of the second season that he was leaving the show, Rick Berman brought aboard a science-fiction veteran, Michael Wagner, who had headed the writing staff on the short-lived ABC series *Probe*. Wagner came aboard in hopes of charting a new, smoother course for the starship *Enterprise*. But three weeks after joining the staff as an executive producer, he was off the show, citing "creative differences."

Before leaving, Wagner recommended Piller, his *Probe* series associate, as his replacement on *The Next Generation*. Fresh from a four-year tour-of-duty on *Simon & Simon*, Piller arrived already a fan of the show, and embraced the idea of rejuvenating the sputtering *Enterprise*. More importantly, he ranked Stewart as the best actor on television and considered it an honor and a challenge to create scripts that better defined the Jean-Luc Picard character.

Helping to ease the transition were former executive script consultants Hans Beimler and Richard Manning, who had worked on the series the first season but had left over creative altercations with Roddenberry; Ronald D. Moore, a talented fan whose dream came true when his spec script for *The Bonding* got him hired as story editor; Ira Steven Behr as a writing producer; Richard Danus as executive story editor; and story editor Melinda Snodgrass, who had been honored with a Writer's Guild nomination for her *The Measure of a Man* script (one of Stewart's favorite from the second season in which he dramatically argued Data's rights as a sentient being in a courtroom).

Stewart, along with Whoopi Goldberg, who played the advice-dispensing bartender Guinan, also began frequently rewriting some of the third season episodes to make them more controversial. "Gene [Roddenberry] resisted any political labeling whatsoever," Stewart once said. "For me, I've been interested in politics of the people of the world since my childhood, when at the age of eight or nine I performed a political candidate's campaign song on the street corner. With the active and very enthusiastic support of the producers and writers, we did go much more on the nose with political issues. I always thought that was terrific! And I think it gave our show a lot more substance."

With Maurice Hurley's departure and Roddenberry effectively eased away from hands-on duty, Berman also involved himself more with the writing, bringing Piller under his administrative and creative protection. Unlike Roddenberry, however, *Star Trek*'s new "Great Bird of the Galaxy" asserted his authority as chief of day-to-day operations subtly and diplomatically. Berman was seeking a new and more distinct look to the series. Piller, meanwhile, complemented Berman with his eye for strong script material and although they had their differences occasionally, they combined their efforts with Stewart to boldly take the series where the original *Trek* had never gone.

The two producers inevitably directed their attention to casting. The year-long letter-writing campaign to return Gates McFadden to the show was not directly mentioned when Berman lured her back to reprise her role as Dr. Beverly Crusher, citing Diana Muldaur's "lack of chemistry" with the rest of the cast. The actress's portrayal of Dr. Pulaski had earned her share of disdain from fans who rejected the acerbic doctor mainly because she continually admonished the innocent android Data in much the same way McCoy belittled Spock in the original series. But while Spock could easily defend himself and often got the last logical and unemotional word, Data was like a child being abused by some evil stepmother. In addition, many of the fans wrote Paramount complaining that they sorely missed the underlying sexual tension between Crusher and Picard, which had been established early on in the first season of the series.

"Obviously, our dedicated viewers strongly believed that Gates' departure from *The Next Generation* left a vacuum," Stewart concurred. "There was something special, a bond, between Beverly and the Captain and when she left to go back to Starfleet Medical, it fractured that unique relationship and, of course, our astute fans sensed the hole in Picard's soul. Dr. Pulaski not only reminded them of what was missing, it put more salt on the wound."

"Diana Muldaur is a marvelous actress and it's obvious that I think so because I've used her many times," Roddenberry said, as one of many of his executive decisions from the first two seasons were rescinded by Berman and the creative staff. "But it's all just chemistry. Beverly had that little something. . . . Somehow the way the captain bounces off her works well. It works with Muldaur, too, but it just seems to work a little more with Crusher." And then in an attempt to save face, Roddenberry added, "It was always our intention to leave the door open for her return to the show."* Muldaur

* A persistent rumor circulating in Trekdom (which has never been denied nor confirmed by all parties involved) is that a *Next Generation* producer made sexual advances toward Gates McFadden during the first season and, when she refused, he asked Roddenberry to write her out of the series. At the end of season two, Stewart went to Rick Berman and reportedly demanded that McFadden be hired back. When asked at *Trek* conventions about the alleged sexual harassment, the actress's standard reply is that Stewart "sounded me out, NOT felt me out" about being reinstated to the cast ensemble at the beginning of the third season.

went on to create the similarly acerbic, though ill-fated role, of Rosalind Shayes on NBC's *L.A. Law*

Piller recalled that the transformation of *The Next Generation* wasn't easy. "That was a panic-driven season—we were 'riding the rims,' as we called it," he said. "I can't claim full credit for [the success]; we had a lot of good writers here. I will claim credit for my contribution, which is that I just have an idea for what I think makes a good dramatic story."

"We did have a lot of chaos in the first and second seasons," Stewart later said. "We had a lot of turnover among the staff. Then Rick and Michael took over the helm and things settled down. And, thanks to them, Picard was finally becoming a character with some character."

Boy's Club

Booby Trap, the sixth episode of the third season, was the first *Next Generation* episode to be directed by a woman, Gabrielle Beaumont. Stewart, who had complained publicly that he felt "much discomfort" about *Star Trek's* treatment of women, was elated to see the show finally evolving from "Roddenberry's Jurassic Period."

"There is a kind of boys' club about *Star Trek,*" the actor once said in an interview. "It's in the air all around the show, in the producers, in the front office, in the writers' building. I felt that that they could not escape from their own essential rigidity in their attitudes to women. Our actresses were not finding sympathetic ears for the things they had to say, and I think at times they simply got exhausted by the battle. They were continually featured as sexual objects, as softer, weaker, and therefore—it always seemed to me—second-class individuals. And because I believed and still do that the show represents what our underlying philosophies are, it doubly irritated me that in that area I thought we were failing."

In the original series, rarely were women self-respected. More often than not, Roddenberry scripted them to be good-time playthings and obsequious helpmates. Women existed primarily as a foil for Captain Kirk's rampaging libido. Stewart always liked to point out to *Next Generation* writers that the most widely admired of all the original *Trek* episodes was anchored by a strong and self-assured female guest star, Joan Collins. In the time-traveling *City on the Edge of Forever,* she played a 1930s social worker who held the promise of a world leadership role that could change the course of World War II and the entire 20th century.

Roddenberry, who apparently fancied himself quite the playboy, evidently slept through the women's liberation movement because the women of *Star Trek* didn't change much between the '60s and the '80s. There was Nurse Chapel, who was made to pine embarrassingly after the stone-cold Mr. Spock, and Counselor Troi's first season miniskirts; Yeoman Janice Rand, who was Captain Kirk's mostly silent girl Friday, and the limited role of Security Chief Tasha Yar; Lieutenant Uhura's groundbreaking status as the only woman on the bridge and Beverly Crusher's single-parenthood, both hardly explored. Stewart challenged the third season writers to break away from Roddenberry's male chauvinistic universe.

"Even after Denise Crosby's departure from the series, there are three self-possessed women [Troi, Crusher, and Guinan] among the *Enterprise* crew who can hold their own in the male bastion of Starfleet," Stewart lectured the writing staff. "It's no longer 'where no man has gone before,' but 'where no *one* has gone before.' Troi's role in the first two seasons consisted mostly of emotional barometer readings and getting impregnated by an alien, as if the writers couldn't figure out what to do with her and the others that wasn't some 'female' thing. The stereotyping of female behavior in our series, and the male attitude toward females, still remains where it was thirty years ago. I think it stinks."

Stewart requested the show's writing staff to really delve into the rich possibilities of gender-specific concerns and, more specifically, to pen scripts which would have Dr. Crusher sometimes challenge Captain Picard's orders. "The fans of the second *Trek* series are ready for the show to take a warp-speed leap in a new direction for women's roles."

Boredom Sets In

In *The Vengeance Factor*, Picard mediates a dispute between a pirate band and the leader of their homeworld, in order to allow the renegades to return under a grant of amnesty. The murder of one of the band's clansman is perpetrated by Yuta, Commander Riker's latest romantic fling who's seeking vengeance for the destruction of her clan.

The episode had a decidedly dark tone, particularly the teaser (the pre-credit sequence) in which Riker leads an investigating away team that comes across numerous corpses. The conclusion of the show was somewhat controversial for two reasons: first, that Riker is forced to kill Yuta and, second, that Picard has no reaction whatsoever to this action.

"They [the producers] *were* worried about the ending and the idea of Riker doing something like that," concurred Timothy Bond, a veteran *Next Generation* director, who helmed the episode. "Regarding Picard,

I'm afraid there is a reason for his lack of reaction: opticals. He couldn't move for that one period where she gets vaporized. In retrospect, . . . it was . . . a mistake. . . . I just had this idea that it would be really neat that when she's vaporized, Picard was there, in the shot. That meant putting several layers of elements into the shot and in order for it to work properly, Picard had to stand still. Not a good reason. When I saw it, I actually regretted the decision, but by then the ship had sailed. Believe me, Patrick noticed too. He even asked, 'I'm just supposed to sit here and do nothing?' The other problem is what *could* he do? We knew Riker had to kill the girl and we didn't want to get Picard shot by the phaser. In retrospect, what I should have done is what you usually do—don't have him in the shot. If he's not, then the audience doesn't think, 'Why doesn't Picard react?' We had a lot of rationales at the time, but we were wrong and, believe me, we got an earful from Patrick."

The Defector episode, one of Stewart's favorite of the series, concerned Romulan Sub-lieutenant Setal's warning to the Federation that a Romulan incursion in the Neutral Zone would set the stage for a massive invasion. A planned pre-credits teaser on the holodeck with Data as Sherlock Holmes was cut just two days before filming began due to a lawsuit by the estate of Arthur Conan Doyle after the *Elementary, Dear Data* episode.

"We sat down a day or two before we started shooting to figure out what we were going to do," recalled Michael Piller. "Someone suggested a Shakespeare teaser, so I went to Patrick, who's obviously our company scholar, and asked, 'What would be a good Shakespearean play that would echo the script?' Actually there was a Shakespearean play called *The Defector*, but it was too unknown for our purposes. So he came back with *Henry V,* and he picked out the scene and section and we condensed it to use it as an echo, with Data and Picard acting in the play on the holodeck.

"If you watch the episode," Piller continued, "there's a scene where Picard and Data are talking about how the crew is holding up, and then Picard says a line or two that echoes the play. Then, in the confrontation with the Romulans, there are suggestions of *Henry V* in Picard's stance, bravery and decisions, and what the argument is about. If you are a musician, as I am, it is a trick that you throw into arrangements to echo other songs and play on a melody that reminds you of something else. I was very proud of that. I also liked the tension, the decision making, lonely at the top. It almost became Picard's show as a result of adding King Henry to the mix. Patrick and all of us were very pleased with it."

Stewart's campaign to give Picard's character more action and romance began to bear fruit in *The High Ground.* The normally stoic captain belts a terrorist on the bridge of the *Enterprise,* foreshadowing his encounter later on in the season with the Borg. The story also provided the third season's version of the ongoing tease of Beverly almost confiding her feelings to Picard, begun in *Arsenal of Freedom.*

Written in response to the producers' request for another action-adventure script, Beverly Crusher is kidnapped by a band of terrorists who are demanding independence for their territory, and believe the Federation has allied themselves with the government. Originally conceived as a parallel to the American Revolution, the rebels' cause was changed to resemble that of Northern Ireland, according to episode writer Melinda Snodgrass. "I felt it made our people look incredibly stupid," she said. "I wanted it with Picard as Cornwallis and the Romulans would have been the

French, who were in our revolution, trying to break this planet away."

Stewart had his own take on the episode. "The writers didn't have anything interesting to say about terrorism except that it's bad and Beverly gets kidnapped. Big deal! . . . We get to have pulpit-pounding speeches about terrorism and freedom, fighting and security forces versus society. It was like a Roddenberry script with its attempts to deal with social issues. Too preachy."

Although Stewart thoroughly enjoyed the continuing battle of wits between the chameleon-like Q and Captain Picard in *Deja Q,* the actor was once again unhappy with his role on the series and threatening to quit in February 1990. Stewart felt that the writers and producers were simply making sporadic attempts every few episodes to either turn him into a "talking head or an action figure," while in other shows "the cardboard Picard just said, 'engage' or 'make it so' or 'status report, Number One.' " His continued grievance was that Captain Picard's character was not being *consistently* developed and this time Stewart chose Michael Piller to be the sounding board for his complaints.

"Patrick came to me in the middle of the season and said, 'I'm bored, you haven't given me anything interesting to do,' and he was very unhappy about that," revealed Piller. "He was upset with the way Picard was being treated and he had every right to be, but third season we basically were just trying to keep our head above water because we didn't have anything in development." Although a number of scripts and stories had been purchased by the writing staff as a result of their open script submission policy, the third season had begun with only a few ideas in the conceptual stage.

Stewart offered his own interpretation for that period of dissatisfaction a few years later. "All my life I've been a working actor who has moved through all the media accepting a variety of different jobs all around the world. And I've relished that. I've thought myself very fortunate to have so many different opportunities. I've never been in a long run of a single play but I've always felt that it's something that would become difficult for me after a while.

"I like the stimulation of fresh work," Stewart explained. "I always enjoyed, for example, working on repertoire with the Royal Shakespearean Company when, between a matinee and evening performance, the play would change, the costume would change, the sets would change, indeed the character would change."

Stewart had quietly made up his mind that if his character didn't undergo some drastic changes by year's end, he would give Berman and Paramount Studios notice that they could expect the fourth season of *The Next Generation* to commence with a new captain on the bridge of the USS *Enterprise*.

Not only was Stewart bored with his role on the series, he had also come to the sad conclusion that his personal life was in a dull rut. With Sheila electing to remain in England while his daughter, Sophia, continued her education, his wife's occasional visits to the States were few and far between. He was a wearied and lonely middle-aged TV star living in the Hollywood Hills section of Los Angeles, which was certainly not a state of mind conducive to marital stability and loyalty.

When he was not working seventeen to eighteen hours a day on the set of *The Next Generation*, Stewart spent his off-hours with his "best buddies" from the show, especially co-star Jonathan Frakes, whose devil-may-care, live-life-to-the-fullest attitude Stewart particularly relished. Stewart also enjoyed the company of several teachers and professors from UCLA, whom he had known through his ACTER organization for the past several years.

Stewart's closest male companion, though, was actor Ben Kingsley. "We have been friends for twenty-five years," he told one TV interviewer. "We were bit part players in the Royal Shakespeare Company when we first came here in 1968, and I see him whenever he's in town."

As the two men grew older they began to look more like brothers with their similarly shaped bald heads. When Stewart was a guest on Arsenio Hall's talk show, he was asked if people ever confused them. "[Kingsley] was here two or three weeks ago, and I went to pick him up at his hotel," the actor said, relating a story he told more than once on the talk show circuit. "I have a convertible, and the top was down. He was waiting for me on the sidewalk, he got in the car, and we drove down Beverly Hills Boulevard and he said to me, 'You know, Patrick, anybody driving behind us would think Los Angeles has been invaded by an alien race!' "

Although he treasured the time he spent "hanging out" with Kingsley, Frakes, and his other male friends, Stewart, a self-described "passionate" man, longed for female companionship. Unfortunately, the long-distance relationship with his wife would eventually take its toll.

"More Sex and Shooting"

The second half of the third season produced some of the best episodes in *The Next Generation*'s seven-year TV life span. In *Yesterday's Enterprise,* cited by fans and critics alike as one of the series's most popular and powerful, the starship is unknowingly trapped in an alternate universe in which the Federation is still engaged in a bloody war with the Klingon Empire.

"A classic episode," remarked Stewart, obviously happy for a change. "Because our crew was in another . . . time line, the characters were allowed to change dramatically and they were permitted to engage in violent verbal opposition to one another. It was a lot of fun to finally bite Riker's head off and put him in his place. And, my God, Picard sends 500 people back to their death on the word of Guinan, really nothing more than a bartender."

Stewart also appreciated the minor touches that were used to subtly point out the differences between the real and alternate universes: the substitution of "military log" for captain's log, "combat date" for stardate, and the absence of a counselor and a Klingon. On the bridge, steps replaced the side bridge ramps, the captain's chair was more thronelike (some people on the set felt that Stewart finally got a chair that fit his personality), and sidearms were the norm.

Stewart's favorite scene was the climax in which Picard jumps over the railing (and several dead crew members) on the bridge of the *Enterprise*-D and fires on three attacking Klingon ships just long enough to allow the *Enterprise*-C to enter the temporal rift so that history could return to its normal course.

The next episode, *The Offspring*, was co-star Jonathan Frakes' directorial debut. This tale of Data's efforts to build a daughter, is well-loved by fans. "As a piece," Stewart said, "it represents the very best of what *Star Trek: The Next Generation* is. But the following show, *Sins of the Father* was pure Shakespeare. Klingon dynastic struggles with conspiracy and kinfolk at each other's throats. I loved it!" This landmark show gave the *Trek* audience its first-ever look at the Klingon homeworld and won art direction Emmys for production designer Richard James and set decorator Jim Mees.

"I really like the fact Worf took it on the chin in that episode," said episode writer, Ron Moore. "It said he was willing to stand up and do the right thing for his people, even if they weren't going to do the right thing by him."

In *Allegiance,* Picard is abducted by aliens as part of a futuristic lab experiment, and replaced by a duplicate who acts in an atypical manner: wooing and then dropping a stunned Dr. Crusher and leading the gang in Ten-Forward in a drinking song. Meanwhile, the real Picard along with three other captured aliens attempt to escape from their containment, discovering that one of them is actually the lab-keeper.

This episode represented director Winrich Kolbe's favorite of the numerous he helmed during *The Next Generation's* seven-year stint. "I like it because we did something stylistically interesting in the lit room where the four people were incarcerated. It was Patrick's show and I always know when it's going to be Patrick's show it's going to be a good one because he's so damn good in everything that he does."

Captain's Holiday, the directorial debut of assistant director Chip Chalmers, came about out of Stewart's desire for more "sex and shooting" for the captain. "It's one of my favorites because it was the first," admitted Chalmers. "This episode was also terrific because Patrick is such a wonderful actor. The other thing for me is that I got a wonderful actress, Jennifer Hetrick, and we had such a good time working on the show. . . . I can look back and smile for a lot of reasons, but certainly the happiest result is that we proved Patrick Stewart is extremely funny."

"I really don't watch much television at all," said Hetrick, the former model and commercial actress who portrayed Vash in the episode and would return in the fourth season's *Q-pid*. "I had watched the original *Star Trek* when I was kid on and off. I was never a Trekkie and was not really familiar with this show, but have since taken to it. I thought this episode was quite funny. It seemed like a *Romancing the Stone/Raiders of the Lost Ark*-type story."

At the close of *Captain's Holiday*, Picard and the brash, striking Vash muse on whether they'll see each other again. In a classic example of life imitating art, the married Stewart asked Hetrick if they, too, would see each other again. After exchanging telephone numbers and addresses, the couple attended a Hollywood party together and began openly dating only days after filming for the episode was completed, setting the stage for a *very* public scandal in the coming year.

King Bee

In *Sarek*, Spock's father is escorted aboard the *Enterprise* to a diplomatic conference, where it is discovered that the aged Vulcan's mind is gradually deteriorating with lapses into senility and illogic. When the tirade of emotions proves too much to keep suppressed, Picard volunteers to mind-meld with Sarek to give him the time to successfully complete negotiations.

Mark Lenard reprised the role he first played in 1967's *Journey to Babel* on the original series. His appearance in the character-driven episode was the first major uniting event tying together the *Star Trek* generations since Dr. McCoy's cameo in the *Encounter at*

Farpoint pilot. Lenard's work was complemented in the episode by the mind-meld scene in which Stewart *was* Sarek with a brilliant portrayal of pent-up emotional anguish.

"Trying to come up with a way to conceptualize and shoot that scene became a frustrating point," director Les Landau recalled. "I think, ultimately, when the two actors got to the set and showed me what they wanted to do, it just melded together and became a wonderful moment within the show. You always come to the set with a prepared framework for a particular scene, but you use that only as a schematic. When actors get to a set, all your planning can go out the window, and such was the case when Sarek finally says to Picard, 'Illogical, illogical,' to shed some kind of emotion. The dynamics between Picard and Sarek reach a level that I think is classic in *Star Trek* history."

The third season cliffhanger, *The Best of Both Worlds,* was the first true two-parter in the series and with its spectacular movie-quality offering is considered by most fans as one of the best episodes of *The Next Generation.* Michael Piller, who said he didn't know how the saga would end when he first sat down to write it, began with the need for a cliffhanger and came up with the Borg plot to kidnap Picard.

"We felt there had not been a worthy successor to the Klingons as adversaries in the new generation, and that was a very serious problem that a show like this has to wrestle with," Piller explained. "In the third season we spent a great deal of time developing the Romulans, and to a lesser degree the Ferengi, to be a continuing threat and a worthy adversary. But we also had always known that the Borg were there and that there had been a good response from the audience about them with the *Q Who?* episode from the second season. But when the Borg came up, most of the people here felt they were boring because there was no personality you could put your teeth into. The fact is because they were all one and there was no spokesman or star role, every time we talked about doing the cliffhanger and the Borg, we said, 'Why don't we create a 'queen bee' that can be the spokesman for this group, and make her a character instead of just cold steel?' "

But instead of a queen bee, Piller came up with the idea of a king bee: namely Jean-Luc Picard—or Locutus, as he came to be known for a while. The challenger however, was what would happen on the *Enterprise* once Picard was abducted. Even with the extra money for space battles and sets, Piller was determined not to have the episode turn into *Battlestar: Galactica,* but rather maintain the human drama which would serve as a backdrop to the epic drama he was weaving.

"The Best of Both Worlds was definitely a get down and dirty show," recalled then assistant director Chip Chalmers. "I also remember the moment when Patrick, first walks up to the viewscreen and says, 'I am Locustus of Borg.' He came on to the set—everybody was wowed with what they had done to Patrick—and we got everyone settled down and did one rehearsal. All he had to do was walk up to the camera. He did so and towered over everyone. It was just so creepy and spooky, and he said, 'I am Locutus of Borg. Have you considered buying a Pontiac?' And everyone was on the floor!"

Stewart relished portraying the newly transformed Borg Locutus but disliked the role's physical demands. Playing a Borg "was very uncomfortable. It was a four-hour makeup job. And of course, once it was all on, movement was very difficult—*sitting* down or *lying* down or *standing up*. But I enjoyed being the Borg.

"The character of Picard was not so much turned into a Borg but his personality underwent some adjustment. Essentially, Picard was always there. The interesting situation for me was how to create this murderous, autonomous figure while retaining, behind all that, the shadow of Jean-Luc. I was pleased with the final result. The Borg experience is one that lives with Picard forever."

After production wrapped, the Borg lay idle on stage 16, collecting dust while cast and crew enjoyed their hiatus and fans pondered possible outcomes of the saga, wondering what would happen after Riker ordered the *Enterprise* to fire on Locutus and the Borg ship. Over that summer of 1990, fan debates raged, computer bulletin board lines hummed, and fanzine letter-writers argued, fueled by rumors that Stewart's contract talks with Paramount had stalled: Would Picard die heroically? Would Riker be promoted to captain?

But the stories of Stewart's difficulties with the parent studio were just wildfire rumors, fanned by Paramount itself to create a *Who Shot JR.?* circus-type guessing game during the summer hiatus. Surprisingly, Stewart was no longer wrestling with the decision as whether to remain on the show or move on. The scripts during the second half of the third season had allowed his character to expand and develop and, more importantly, so dramatic was the impact of *The Best of Both Worlds,* that the actor had to concede that *The Next Generation* had finally arrived.

"The Borg was a great embodiment of evil," Stewart told an interviewer. "Mechanical evil, absence of soul. Hence the power of the episode where Picard, the very soul of the *Enterprise,* became a Borg: Anybody, even the best man, can lose his soul. This is a genuinely scary idea, a mature concept."

Stewart didn't lose *his* soul when he signed the new multi-year contract for *The Next Generation* after the third season Borg cliffhanger, but he did make one concession to luxury and bought a British-racing-green Jaguar XJS. "When I was a child, a 1937 or 1938 SS Jaguar—one of the most beautiful cars ever made—often came down the street. Whenever it went by, it was like looking into a window on another world that was desirable but utterly unattainable."

It was a wise decision on Stewart's part, however, that he elected to sign a new contract and remain on *The Next Generation*. Unbeknownst to the actor, Paramount had already given Michael Piller the green light to pen a script for which the Borgified Picard would be killed and the *Enterprise*-D would be destroyed while saving Earth, but a new *Enterprise*-E and the familiar crew would be commanded by the recently promoted Captain William Riker.

Stewart admitted a few years later, "[If I'd left] I think they would have replaced me without a backward glance. None of us are that exceptional that we can't be replaced, even though we'd like to think we are."

Only one question remained during the 1990 hiatus: could anybody write an ending to the seemingly impossible-to-solve cliffhanger?

Seven

All the World's a Stage

All the world's a stage, and all the men and women merely players. They have their exits and their entrances, and one man in his time plays many parts.

—Shakespeare, *As You Like It*, 2.7

If the fans were in a frenzy, the summer of 1990 was the calmest hiatus yet for *The Next Generation* cast and crew, thanks to Stewart's newly signed contract and the return of most of the staff, led again by Michael Piller, now settling into his second year as the creative force behind the series, and Rick Berman, who had definitely sidelined Roddenberry as the "top dog" in charge of the day-to-day operations. Ronald D. Moore returned and added "executive" to his story editor title and first season veterans David Livingston and Wendy Neuss were promoted to producer and associate producer, respectively.

Jeri Taylor, who joined the series as a supervising producer after Lee Sheldon left the show over the familiar "creative differences," also had her own ideas regarding what she wanted to see happen during the fourth year of the *Enterprise*'s continuing voyages. During the summer break, she met quite often with Stewart and discussed script ideas for the coming season. Fortunately, they discovered they were very much in sync about the way they wanted his Picard character to evolve and, more importantly, Stewart finally found a "soul mate" who saw a need to break into the "boy's club mentality" of the series and reward the women cast members with roles they could relish playing.

"If there's anything I wanted to do more of, it was developing the characters of Crusher and Troi," Taylor said, "because I thought they were underused and would like to flesh them out and make them more rounded and interesting people. I'm not saying that this was a staff of men and I had to come in and show them the way, but maybe it was something a little more in the foreground with me than some of the others."

Taylor's and Stewart's perceptions of the role of women on *Star Trek* were shared by Marina Sirtis, who, at Stewart's urging had been complaining repeatedly to Berman and Piller about her character's "underutilization, underdevelopment and lack of dimension."

"I don't think we've addressed feminism," she said. "The women on the show were very non-threatening and I don't think it's realistic, I don't think it's realistic in the 20th century so it's definitely not realistic in the 24th century. Ever since Denise [Crosby] left the show the two women that are left are both doctors in the caring professions so we don't see women in power positions. We do see female admirals but I have to say the fans don't really care about our guest stars, they care about the regulars and what they want to see are the regular women having more power."

Michael Piller acknowledged that servicing the lesser-used members of the *Next Generation* ensemble was a major consideration going into the new season. "One of our goals from the beginning of the fourth season was to find stories for each character, Troi among them."

Rick Berman, who had piloted the series through stormy waters during its early shakedown period, outlined his goals for the new season: "We knew which characters we wanted to focus on and what kind of stories we wanted to do in very broad strokes. Of course, we knew we had to start off with a show that finished up the Borg experience. Our ultimate goal was to do a lot of 'family' shows and really get to know the bridge crew inside and out."

David Carren, a fourth season story editor agreed. "There's one basic thing that never really changed and part of that evolution was the new *Star Trek* finding its way to being a family. The old show worked because it basically was a family. It was more like Kirk was a big brother than a father figure and everyone else was kind of his siblings and Spock was the wise uncle. There were all kinds of interesting dynamics to their relationships. The family didn't really jell per se on *The Next Generation* until deep into the second season or even third where it really came together. You saw there's Picard and he's the father and here's the rest of the members of his family."

To Stewart's immense satisfaction, nine of the season's first eleven shows concerned family. "Not only did we see the *Enterprise* crew evolving closer as a tight family unit, we got a glimpse of their *real* families," the actor explained. "Worf's mate K'Ehleyr, son Alexander and his foster parents all made appearances; Tasha Yar's manipulating sister, Ishara and Tasha's mystery daughter, Sela, came calling; Data was revisited by his 'father' Dr. Noonien Soong and his evil brother, Lore; and Picard himself journeyed back to his home in France to recuperate from the Borg attack with his brother, sister-in-law and nephew. The fourth season was sterling television and the quality of the writing and the storylines had improved so much over the previous seasons, climaxing in what was delivered to the audience that year."

Marina Sirtis observed, "The fans tend to say that the writing and the storylines have gotten much better over the last four years, but I think that's possibly to do with the fact that now we have more or less a fixed writing staff. In the first couple of seasons the turnover was so immense that I don't think they could ever get a hook, they were here for ten minutes and then they were gone which really wasn't long enough to establish any kind of continuity or character development in their scripts."

Michael Piller concurred, "I don't think there was one clinker in the whole group. Certainly in the third season we had some. Arguably you could say there were better shows during the third season, but week after week we maintained a much higher consistency of quality than we had or most shows ever achieve."

"The show has gotten better and better each year," agreed Rick Berman. "We all take it extremely seriously and that's the only way you can do it because it's such hard work and the second you start getting sloppy the audience sees it instantly. The fact that we have kept up the quality and integrity of the show and simultaneously the audience has gotten bigger is a wonderful achievement."

Stewart offered his own opinion on why the overall quality of *The Next Generation* had improved by the fourth season. "Lack of interference by Gene Roddenberry. Plain and simple."

Family Affair

In September 1990, Paramount's publicity department ran its first-ever promotional campaign for a single *Next Generation* episode since the *Encounter at Farpoint* two-hour pilot. In addition, ads and radio spots were specially prepared for the much-heralded fourth season premiere, *The Best of Both Worlds, Part II.*

"I thought Part One was much better than Part Two," recalled writer and executive producer Michael Piller. "The reason was that Part Two had to deliver the goods promised by Part One, but they were not as interesting. If you look at it as a two hour movie, it's really quite effective. As an episode by itself, I don't think Part Two really has a lot of character stuff. It has to have the battles and all the stuff I don't like writing. The one thing I will say about Part Two, about which I was extremely pleased, was how I figured out to defeat the Borg, because, frankly, when I was writing it I had no idea. I honestly believe that you let the characters take you and just listen to what the voices are saying in the script. Ultimately you'll find wonderful things."

Piller said he waited until he returned to the Paramount lot in late July to sit down to wrap up the story and the idea of using the Borg's interdependency as a weakness hit him just two days before filming was to start. "I basically discovered the solution at the same time the characters did," he admitted. "It just occurred to me that their strength was their interdependency, [so] why not make their weakness that same interdependency?"

Meanwhile, amid all the swashbuckling and space battles, supervising producer Jeri Taylor's newfound influence on the show greatly enhanced the female roles. Hand it to the women of the *Enterprise* crew for saving humanity: it is Beverly who discovers the Borg's fatal flaw of interdependency, and it's Troi who realizes that Picard is fighting through his programming.

"I had hopes that Picard would go *on* being the Borg a bit longer," Stewart said in an interview with a science-fiction magazine. "I thought it would be a lot of fun for Picard to be marauding around the galaxy for several episodes, destroying everything and beating up the universe. . . . The Borg experience changed Picard in some ways. I've tried to acknowledge that in certain episodes when they've come up. I think, for me, the Borg episodes were not as dramatic as they were for our audience. I can think of other episodes in which I felt that the character was expanding, developing and learning much more than in that one. It principally for me was a way of trying to find out technically how to make the Borg character work."

One of the points of contention which the creative team wrestled with early on in the season was the follow-up to Piller's two-part Borg epic. Upon the second part's conclusion, a clearly shaken Picard trembles upon reflection on his seizure by the Borg.

"It was my intention to wrap the two-parter with the feeling that although everything is solved," Piller said, "life isn't so smooth and a man does not walk away from something like that and go back to work without having a little extra flashback nightmare. It's just that little uncertainty, the moment of discomfort that I wanted to leave the audience with and Patrick did a stellar job of conveying that feeling on screen as the camera pulled back to see him gazing out a window of the *Enterprise*. He was clearly a shaken, disturbed man."

Some of the staff were equally uncomfortable with the notion of Piller and Stewart wanting to continue the story of Picard's abduction by the Borg into an unplanned third part. "The biggest decision of the summer hiatus was to extend the storyline of Picard's kidnapping into the third episode," Piller acknowledged. "That was very controversial and there were a lot of people who were very hesitant about doing a threesome and going down to earth. People felt it was not *Star Trek*."

Stewart successfully argued that it would not be fair to wrap up everything neat and tidy at the end of Part Two. He lobbied for an epilogue that would at least let Picard heal his emotional wounds on-camera after his virtual psychological and physical rape by the Borg. Stewart thought there was an opportunity to do something *Star Trek* had never done before—go home and do an episode about the captain finding himself again.

"The normal objections were that we were not serialized," Piller recalled. "We try to tell stories that can be told in one hour and that's what we do very well. When I got to the end of Part Two, we made the decision not to extend it and I called up Rick [Berman] and said, 'Hey, listen. Next week Picard can be fine, but for a show that prides itself on its realistic approach to storytelling, how can you have a guy who's basically been raped be fine next week? Patrick and I both believe there's a story in a man like Picard who's lost control. Delving into the psychological crisis that a man like that has to face, and what does he have to do?' Finally, I was persuasive enough to talk Rick into taking the chance, and I think everybody is glad we did."

At first Berman agreed to let Picard go to Earth to recuperate but insisted that a science subplot be used to round out the show. After weeks of trying various story lines that just didn't work, including a child stow-away, and a paranoid's nightmare of disappearing crew members, Berman relented and allowed the other family-theme subplots with Worf and the Crushers to fill out the hour.

Writer Ron Moore remembered: "We decided as long as we were there at Earth, let's make it a show about people's families and do some other characters on the ship and explore their backgrounds. It became a very off-concept show [looking] at the characters and how they got to be who and what they are."

Said Stewart himself, "I think the *Family* episode was one of my best and one of the best episodes of *Star Trek* ever. It was the perfect follow-up to the Borg shows and the conclusion of that story line. Picard was in a dilemma, what to do and what better place to do it than in the environs of one's 'home.' After all, his home is the universe, but his specific home is La Barre, France. That opening moment where Picard walks into the vineyard and sees his brother, who he hasn't spoken to in twenty years, on his hands and knees picking grapes and his brother doesn't even acknowledge him, is one of my favorite acting scenes."

Director Les Landau concurred. "I think it was certainly one of my best episodes of *Star Trek* and one of the best *Next Generation* episodes ever. I'm not talking about my work, but the story, the acting, the production values. Everything about that show worked."

Unfortunately, *Family* was the lowest-rated episode of the season, even though it presented what Stewart called, "a deeper insight into more of Picard's and the other show's characters than virtually any other episode."

"I have friends who are fans of the show who called and said I hope you never do that again," commented Michael Piller. "But I've got to tell you, for my money,

Family was one of the best pieces of film we did fourth season and it was also consistently the lowest rated in both the original and reruns. Maybe my friends were right—if you're not out in space, you're not hitting the audience where they want to be hit."

The family theme continued with *Suddenly Human* in which a human teenager, Jono, is found aboard a damaged Talarian ship and brought back to the *Enterprise* along with his comrades. Jono, who also shows signs of having been abused, is responsive only to Picard's command authority. The captain tries to reacclimate him to human culture when it is learned that his human grandmother, a Starfleet admiral, requests that the boy be brought back home. But Jono's adopted father and commander of the Talarian fleet, Endar, demands his return or war will be declared against the Federation.

Suddenly Human stirred rumors throughout *Trek* fandom that the episode would address the issue of child abuse. Instead, it dealt with the emotions and decisions faced by broken families and by cultures in collision. The subplot involving Jono's injuries and the ambiguous manner in which they were attained, stirred some controversy on the show and generated some heated comments from viewers who perceived the episode as condoning child abuse.

"We got some pretty angry letters on that show," recalled Michael Piller. "They said, 'How can you let an abused child go back to the people who are abusing him?' We really brought the child abuse issue up because it was the right and natural thing to bring up in the context of the story. There are real parallels to stories that go on in today's world about parents who fight over custody and one says there's been abuse. Who do you believe?"

Added Rick Berman, "We wanted to make the point that the interpretation of broken bones was nothing more than normal childhood broken bones, and that these people were sort of prejudiced in this direction. It was in no way intended to be an episode that had anything to do with child abuse."

Stewart, who worked closely with the episode's writer, Jeri Taylor, in developing the script, added some special "character enhancing moments" between Jono and Picard, who once again must confront his discomfort with children. Under Counselor Troi's gentle probing, the captain wonders if the feeling stems from his lack of friends as a duty-driven child who early on wanted to be in Starfleet.

"In three episodes within the first month of the new season, I was permitted to explore more of Picard's character than throughout the past three years," Stewart later said. "As an actor, I found this newfound ability most satisfying."

The Curse of Popularity

Stewart, always the lobbyist for stronger roles for the women on the show and an ardent supporter of hard-hitting political topics, was also invited by the producers to have some input into the scripts for *Remember Me*, which showcased Gates McFaddens' acting talents during about forty percent of the episode, and *Legacy*, which was an allegory on gang warfare.

The latter episode, however, was celebrated as the eightieth episode—the one that broke the record of the seventy-nine-episode run of the original *Star Trek*. To help mark the milestone, the cast and staff wrapped the filming with a party, reported by *Entertainment To-*

night, and a cake adorned by the art staff's special congratulatory logo.

Although the occasion was supposed to be festive, Stewart and Berman voiced their grievances to the *ET* crew about the Emmy Awards' old prejudices against science fiction in general and *The Next Generation* in particular. Berman, especially, was incensed that the series once again won only two Emmys from among its many technical nominations and none on the so-called creative side despite such excellent actors as Stewart and Brent Spiner, who portrays the android Commander Data.

"Because our show doesn't air on one of the traditional networks, we continually face the frustration of being an anomaly," Berman openly complained. "We can only hope that our show will be acknowledged by the industry, which an increasing number of viewers have obviously been enjoying for four seasons regardless of where they watch it."

When Stewart was told that some people in the entertainment business dismissed *Star Trek* as escapist entertainment, the actor went ballistic. "It's only dismissed by people who don't watch it. Even though it's full of fun, high adventure, dazzling technology, and all kinds of bizarre creatures, it's a very serious show, and that's the way serious things should be presented," Stewart said, struggling to retain his composure on an obviously "touchy subject."

"Shakespeare wrote entertainment, but clearly his plays could be very serious, too. We're conscious that some people think of us as 'that syndicated kids' show,' and as far as a large part of the TV industry is concerned, we are," he continued. "Otherwise, how can you explain the total absence of Emmy nominations, for directing, writing, and acting? Oh, I was angry for a while. I wondered: Are we so bad? Are we getting it wrong? Are our numbers somehow totally misleading as to the quality of the work? I watch the show and I think it's very good. In fact, it's as good as anything I've ever been around in my life as an actor. So how do we explain this? I think it's somehow a curse to be too popular."

Familiarity Breeds Contempt

Though thoroughly at ease as Picard, Stewart insisted on separating his high-profile character from his personal life as *The Next Generation* grew enormously popular around the world. "From the beginning I have absolutely refused to wear polyester costumes out in public," he has stated flatly in many interviews. "I have refused to use any jargon from *Star Trek* on any kind of commercials or voice-overs—and you wouldn't believe how many times the phrases 'Make it so' or 'Engage' have appeared in commercial scripts that I've read. My work on *Star Trek* is a self-contained thing. Beyond that, I have no responsibility to it whatsoever. A fan caught me at a particularly bad moment recently when he said, 'You're Jean-Luc Picard, aren't you?' My immediate retort was 'No!' "

Oddly, for an actor obsessed about being typecast forever as the character he played, Stewart had begun attending at least six *Star Trek* conventions a year. Whereas some of the show's actors would rather fight Klingons with water pistols than attend the conclaves (which were infamous for their unalloyed adulation), Stewart embraced the close encounters with *Trek* fandom with relish.

"I enjoy them," Stewart admitted. "It gets me back on the stage. It's like doing stand-up in front of the most adoring audience one could ever wish for. I get to be Sting and Bob Hope and Billy Connolly all rolled into one just for an hour, and it's a great workout. I consider myself extremely fortunate because there are very few television shows where actors can have direct contact with those people who love it and watch it regularly. You also can't afford to forget the names of episodes at these conventions. I can get away with it—that's what goes with being the captain. But these people are liable to rip your throat out. And I get slightly unnerved by certain people who dress and look like me, down to having their heads shaved. It's a compliment in a way, but going that far seems a little foolish to me."

Stewart also took enormous pride in *The Next Generation*'s broad appeal as it hooked viewers ranging from bellboys to female astronauts. "There are Trekkies that are mad for it and there are a lot of people who would not classify themselves as Trekkies who are mad for it, too. It is one of the delightful curiosities of the show that it does span all ages, all races, all educational backgrounds or social backgrounds, and it's a compliment to the show. Our fans range from vice-chancellors of universities to five and six year olds in school to Colin Powell, chairman of the Joint Chiefs of Staff, a big fan of the show who asked my permission to sit in the captain's chair when he once visited the set. It is because these people watch what we do that the show gets better."

Stewart was once asked in an interview what was it that kept the Trekkies so wildly enthusiastic—even obsessive—about *The Next Generation,* to which he replied: "People have written academic theses on this subject, and you want a short answer. There is a mystery at the heart of *Star Trek* that touches people. It's composed of elements like hope, optimism, companionship, comradeship and courtesy, legitimacy and boldness. It lies in the assurance, which can only be a theoretical assurance, that we're going to survive— that some of us will make it."

As *The Next Generation* became increasingly more popular, so did the merchandising attached to the series. Stewart, a man who cherished his privacy, was extremely uncomfortable with seeing his face plastered on lunch boxes, coffee mugs, calendars, mouse pads, T-shirts, and on the covers of *TV Guide* and *Entertainment Weekly.*

The days of anonymity were over for Stewart. With an easily recognizable and well-known face, he found it next to impossible to go anywhere without someone identifying him. "Leaving the studio very late one night, I went to a nearby bank to get some cash from an automated teller," Stewart said, relating the story of his most memorable encounter with a fan. "It's always risky doing that late at night, so I take precautions. While I was standing at the machine, a car cruised into the parking lot and stopped, and so I kept one eye on it while I was punching in my numbers. And the guy looked out of his window and watched me. I got my money and began to walk briskly toward my car, and the door of his car opened in the path between my car and his car. He stood up and he said, 'You're Patrick Stewart,' and I said, 'That's right.' And he said, 'Jean-Luc Picard,' and I said, 'Yes,' and he lifted up his arms and shouted, 'I love L.A.!' "

Sometimes, though, Stewart, an international star in his own right, faced the oddity of being confused with other well-known bald actors. "I have a collection of hats and caps I keep everywhere because I always feel this is the part that I have to conceal," Stewart said, pointing to his head, "but even then, they seem to know who I am. Ben Kingsley, one of my best friends, and I look alike. I was at one of those Hollywood events, black tie, and when I arrived, a very, very well-known elderly movie star saw me come in, and opened his arms. And I looked around to see who he was looking to embrace, because I knew he didn't know me. But I knew who he was. I was impressed. And he said out loud, 'My God, I love this man. Oh, you're fantastic . . . where's the photographer? Get him over here.' I was just dizzy with delight. And I called out, 'Hi. Hey, hi.' And so we had our photographs taken with his wife, and then he turned to me and said, 'Mr. Kingsley, this has been a great honor.' 'Well,' I said, 'it's been a great honor for me, too.' "

One woman accosted Stewart at a party and racked her brains, struggling to place the face with a name. "You fly the Endeavour," she told him triumphantly, when her memory finally clicked, "and you play William Shatner!"

The Other Woman

Stewart, when asked by a reporter how his life had been affected by his long-term role as Captain Picard, he answered, "It's been my lot to play most of the tortured, twisted, miserable wretches of classical tragedy. Some of those parts shook me to my foundation, and still go on shaking me. To my surprise, Captain Picard was identified as a classically romantic hero."

Stewart, a well-known method actor, evidently decided that the role of television heartthrob was a part he wanted to rehearse for in his private life as well. On the morning of February 2, 1991, he awoke as usual at 5 A.M. and listened to classical music for an hour on the radio while he read a book and drank a "proper cup of tea." After showering and shaving, he slipped on a purple robe belonging to the woman whose apartment he had spent the night and stepped outside at 6:50 A.M. for the morning paper.

Unfortunately, a reporter for the tabloid *National Enquirer,* who had been stalking Stewart for several weeks, was spying on the actor from across the street. A few days later, the reporter called Stewart's wife, choreographer Sheila Falconer, at their London home, and asked her what she thought of her husband openly romancing another woman in Hollywood. "You're being silly," she replied. "I don't believe it!"

In the February 26, 1991, edition of the *National Enquirer,* an entire page was devoted to Stewart's adulterous relationship under the headlines: "L.A. LAW" BEAUTY'S LOVE AFFAIR WITH "STAR TREK" CAPTAIN WRECKS HIS 25-YEAR MARRIAGE. The article identified the "other woman" as thirty-two-year-old Jennifer Hetrick, former Oil of Olay model, *L.A. Law* costar (she played Arnie Becker's wife Corrine) and, ironically, Captain Picard's love interest in the third season *Next Generation* episode *Captain's Holiday.*

Stewart and Hetrick had been romantically involved for over a year and had also been surprisingly open about their relationship in front of the cast and crew of the show. Hetrick, who was a regular visitor to the set, would spend time with Stewart in his trailer between the filming of scenes. On the set, they were always holding hands, kissing and whispering to each other. On Friday nights after filming was completed, the couple would go with other cast members and crew to the hilltop restaurant Yamashiro's and have dinner with everyone. They routinely left early and they almost always arrived at the Paramount Studios together on Saturday morning, where he taught an acting class.

"Jennifer and I have a wonderful time," Stewart admitted to a friend. "There are no pressures, we're in the same line of work and we enjoy spending romantic evenings together. It's the perfect relationship for me. I want to start life fresh with Jennifer. I'm in love with her and want to be with her all the time."

Three days after the news of Stewart's passionate romance with Hetrick went public with headlines that scandalously proclaimed, HE FELL SO HARD FOR HER HE FORGOT ALL ABOUT HIS WIFE IN ENGLAND the actor and his wife announced their separation, citing the familiar "irreconcilable differences." And after a year of "relentless and brutal" tabloid press coverage in both the United States and in England, Stewart and his wife of twenty-five years divorced in 1992. In almost all of the press accounts, the actor was described as a "womanizer who abandoned his faithful and loving wife for a much younger woman after becoming an international star."

Stewart was furious and took the opportunity to vent his anger when he made an appearance on Joan Rivers' show. "They [the press] wrote a lot of lies and they quoted friends inappropriately, and they hurt my children. They made them unhappy and they made their friends unhappy. It was a miserable experience."

Stewart refused to discuss the details of his divorce in public. Although the British press labeled the proceedings "ugly," Stewart and his wife announced that his relationship with Hetrick was not the reason that they had chosen to dissolve their marriage. They both stated publicly that they had simply "drifted apart over the years with different goals and plans in life."

Although the couple considered their divorce an amicable severance, the press continued to paint Sheila as a vengeful, scorned lover and Stewart as an unfaithful, philandering husband who didn't want to give his wife a fair settlement during the proceedings. Finally, a stressed-out Stewart suffered a heart attack scare when he collapsed on the set of *The Next Generation* and was rushed to L.A.'s Cedars-Sinai Medical Center by ambulance. But doctors in a press conference announced that the actor was simply exhausted and released him after five hours of tests and observation.

From that moment on, Stewart, citing the "numerous miserable experiences and pain" surrounding his divorce and the coverage by newspapers "in the business of smearing reputations," retreated into a private shell and refused to discuss his personal life in public for the next several years.

Eight

New Directions

People have written and said you are the crew of the Enterprise, *and we believe in that crew. They refer to a vivid contrast between the previous captain and myself.*

—Patrick Stewart's response to
the Kirk versus Picard debate

Stewart, wounded from the public disgrace and humiliation of the Hetrick affair, immersed himself in his profession and in the process invested Picard's character with a new level of dramatic intensity and complexity during the fourth season's second half.

The Wounded, a dark, fatalistic episode for *The Next Generation,* concerned a renegade starship captain who launches a one-man war against the Cardassians, an alien race with which the Federation has recently negotiated a peace treaty. "This episode aired during the Gulf War and was about Picard doing everything he could to prevent a war, happening during a time when the United States of America was doing everything it could to *start* a war," explained director Chip Chalmers. "That was one of the best written episodes that I've ever seen in a while and Stewart's on-screen philosophical conflict with the rogue captain where two strong and able people tee off against each other was some of his finest acting."

"It was sort of *Heart of Darkness,*" said producer/writer Jeri Taylor. "It started with the idea that if you had been at war with a country and now you are not at war with them anymore, you can't just immediately become friends. While in the 24th century people have a much more expansive view of the galaxy and are able to do it a little better, we planted the idea that some people had just a little more residual problem with that sort of thing, and harbored some resentment."

Stewart had his own opinions on the episode. "I would like to see aspects of the political world of the Federation in the 24th century addressed from a much less utopian point of view. Political life is ambivalent and filled with gray areas. I always felt the show could be more radical politically. My ambition is really a modest one. I just want to change the world."

Stewart also received critical acclaim for the following show, *Devil's Due,* which drew the series' highest-ever Nielsen rating of 14.4, breaking the record of 14.0 set in November 1987 during season one. Reworked from an original premise for the aborted *Star Trek* 1970s television revival, *Devil's Due* plays like a cross between *The Devil and Daniel Webster* and an original *Trek* series plot in which Picard must argue in court that a woman, Ardra, claiming to be the planet's devil, is really just another intergalactic con artist. The captain challenges the validity of her claim in a contest of wills which could cost Picard his soul . . . or something equally valuable, his pride and self-esteem.

In a humorous attempt to alleviate Stewart's recent dark mood, Michael Piller rewrote the final draft of the script, changing the male devil into a female. "Patrick was short-tempered and manic after the Hetrick thing was plastered all over the papers and then the divorce from his wife *really* had him pissed-off," Piller later recalled. "He was going around the set with his fists clenched and letting loose on the production people with that booming voice of his. I figured with all the women trouble lately, he could appreciate the humor of the devil being a female. Sure, we were poking fun at him, but we wanted him to lighten up and take it in strides."

Ironically, Jennifer Hetrick's character, Vash, was reunited with Stewart's Picard in the fourth season episode *Q-Pid*, in which the superbeing Q returns as a matchmaker who puts the two lovebirds and the crew of the *Enterprise* in a recreation of Robin Hood to teach Picard a lesson about love.

The writing staff had toyed with the idea of a shipboard marriage for some time and Piller, prior to the public scandal involving Stewart and Hetrick, even quietly inquired about marrying Picard and Vash to provide some new story dynamics. After a meeting with Vash creator Ira Steven Behr, the idea of a love triangle between Q, Picard and Vash was suggested as the premise for the *Q-Pid* episode.

"We decided to throw these characters into one of the classic love stories," Piller said. "King Arthur was discussed with Guenivere, and then Robin Hood with Maid Marian, which was in vogue with the soon-to-be-released Kevin Costner movie. It just seemed to be that Robin Hood and his band of merry men was a very nice group to put our guys into, and then we just played it for fun. That was what was so great about the fourth season. Each week you were never quite sure what was going to come on."

In the final scenes of the episode, Vash announces she plans to travel through the galaxy with Q. An uneasy Picard admits the two do have much in common—just before he kisses Vash goodbye and they promise to meet again. However, because of the adverse publicity surrounding the affair between Hetrick and Stewart in real life, Paramount reportedly sent word to *The Next Generation* writing staff to close the books on the Vash/Picard romantic relationship.

In a continued attempt to counteract the bad press of his much-publicized divorce, Stewart put everything he had into his performances and received both industry and fan kudos for his portrayal of the beleaguered Picard under siege in *The Drumhead,* which was praised as one of series's most provocative and chilling episodes. The show echoes the groundless investigation of Picard from season one's *Coming of Age* and weaves in references to his abduction by the Borg in *The Best of Both World,* the alien parasitic invaders *Conspiracy,* the T'Pel-Selok spy scandal in *Data's Day* and the developing Klingon-Romulan intrigue.

Jeri Taylor's script, the one she is most proud of, was inspired by a Ron Moore idea called *It Can't Happen Here.* "It's basically a witch-hunt with the idea it's taking the McCarthy era and the Salem witch hunts that can happen even in our enlightened 24th century, and how these individual personal liberties can be stepped on," Taylor explained. "It's a very provocative story and one which is a little darker than some of the others. It's nothing but talk and it was a real challenge as a writer to make that work."

"The risk is that shows like this are too chatty and people like a little action," said Jonathan Frakes, in his second directorial outing. "But if you like dialogue and acting, this is certainly the episode. It's the McCarthy trials, a real guilty until proven innocent approach that

Admiral Satie takes and she [Jean Simmons] was brilliant. She's an enormous Trekkie and watches the show every week, and then gets on the phone with her friends and they talk about the episode. The people who are fans of this show never cease to amaze me."

Stewart especially enjoyed working on *The Drumhead* with Ms. Simmons, a veteran classical actress. "She's one of my heroines," he admitted. "Her performance was marvelous, and she was such a warm, hard-working and dedicated person on the set. Of course, we've had many marvelous guest performances, but it was especially exciting for me to have Jean, and to be going on a kind of 'head-on' with her."

From the Captain's Chair to the Director's Chair

Following up on Jonathan Frakes' lead, Stewart became the second cast member to direct an episode. The story chosen for his directorial debut was *In Theory*, a no-fail Data show by Ron Moore and Joe Menosky that confronted the questions about the android commander and love.

"I was a virgin on that episode and those seven days [shooting it] were the most exciting of my career," Stewart would later say. "I was given an extraordinary lead by the example and standard that was set by Jonathan Frakes, whose work has been outstanding, and I was lucky to have Brent [Spiner] as my leading man and a fabulous guest star performance from Michelle Scarabelli. And finally, I was lucky that *In Theory* had no big set scenes, no Klingon halls and no shoot-outs. I was left simply to concentrate on structure and camera movements and more than anything else, to work with the actors."

When Stewart was asked what inspired his interest to direct, he replied, "It had become increasingly apparent to me that at some point I was going to direct. But I had always imagined it would be theater. I knew that I would do it, and that I could do it. I never expected my first formal directing job would be a television series. I wasn't sure that I was qualified to direct an episode of *Star Trek*. I was nervous and unsure but I was given plenty of time for preparation. But I found being in creative control of an episode of *Star Trek* very exciting.

"One director gave me a tip just before my show," Stewart continued. "He said, 'You know, no matter what has happened in pre-production, and no matter what will happen in post-production, never ever forget that the best times for a director are on the set with the camera and the actors. Don't let anyone take any of that away from you. Use it and enjoy it to the fullest.' And that's what I tried to do. I was very stimulated in every way to be able to tell a story in the way I wanted. Directing has been very fulfilling to me."

Ironically, it was the captain who turned to his first officer for advice when he took the helm of an episode for the first time.

"We had a couple of conversations," admitted Jonathan Frakes of Stewart's directorial debut. "He was fabulous and took to it beautifully. He's a very sensitive man and he did a great job. He was also lucky that he got a Data show as his first. Brent really is an incredible actor with an unbelievable range and technique, and certainly the most popular character, so it's a real plus to get that combination."

The Great Debate

The Next Generation ended its fourth season with an epic cliff-hanger in which Worf resigns his Starfleet commission to fight in the Klingon civil war and Picard returns to the role of Arbiter of Succession to oversee Gowron's installation as ruler of the High Council.

The series was now one hundred episodes strong, a success rate rarely equaled and even more rarely surpassed, especially by the original series which barely lasted though seventy-nine installments. *The Next Generation* had become the *Star Trek* standard bearer. Four years of adventures had given the characters of Picard, Riker, Data and the other *Enterprise*-D characters a history and a depth. What seemed like a long shot in the first season had become the new tradition. The original series had become old *Star Trek* while *The Next Generation* had become the new future of the *Enterprise* and its crew.

The torch may have clearly been passed between the original *Star Trek* crew to *The Next Generation,* but the inevitable comparisons between Captains Picard and Kirk continued with no end in sight. After returning from a scuba diving trip with the Whale Conservation Institute's research vessel *Odyssey* in the waters around Fiji during the summer hiatus of 1991, Stewart was confronted with a *TV Guide* cover story that spawned the debate with the questions: Who's the better commander of the USS *Enterprise?* Who would you rather have defend the Earth—James T. Kirk or Jean-Luc Picard?

In the article experts and fans debated who was truly the best. The late, famed science fiction author Isaac Asimov described William Shatner's portrayal of Kirk as "boyishly eager, open and vigorous . . . more the classic hero—young, strong, passionate, risk-taking." By contrast Patrick Stewart's Picard is "reminiscent of Spock"—more mature, more intellectual, an intensely complex man, seemingly in constant control of his emotions and apparently more open to taking advice and counsel from his executive officers. But there was no mistaking his commanding presence and intention behind his frequent instruction, "Make it so," which Stewart once interpreted as meaning, "Just do it, and talk about it later. It's sometimes not until you do something that you know whether you can possibly understand it or whether it's something you like."

Ron Moore, who wrote some of the best episodes of *The Next Generation,* compared the two commanders: "[Picard] and Kirk went through life quite differently. Kirk at the Academy was a bookworm, straight-laced, straight arrow and very uptight. You would call him a stack of books with legs—and then he became this wild man. He went out in the fleet and got comfortable and started doing all this crazy stuff. Picard went the other way. He was a wild man in his youth and then sort of became a little more mature and collected as he became an adult."

Mary Henderson, curator of a *Star Trek* exhibit at the Air and Space Museum in Washington, D.C., remembered watching the original series when she was a teenager and thinking Kirk was "really great." Several years later, however, he seemed too "brash." Her preference now was the more "paternal" Picard. "Kirk is a man of the '60s. Picard is a man of the '90s."

But who would NASA choose as the commander of its next shuttle mission if the space agency had to choose between the roguish space cowboy Kirk and the cool, authoritative Picard? "Picard deals with moral and ethical issues," said Dr. Robert Jastrow, founder of NASA's Goddard Institute. "He's less hardware-oriented." But Apollo 11 astronaut Buzz Aldrin thought both men had the "right stuff." On Picard: "More like an ambassador to the stars," and Kirk, "the explorer, shooting from the hip."

"Picard's command style is very different than Captain Kirk's," Stewart has said. "At the center of *The*

Next Generation is Picard, who is presented as a positive, polished individual, bold enough to make independent decisions even if they fly against the input he had invited from his crew. Yet, despite these kinds of decisions, Picard never loses the trust, respect and loyalty of his crew.

"When civilian airline pilots have to go for their refresher course, which they do I think every year, two years, they watch sequences from our show that are edited together in order to illustrate the 'On the Bridge/On the Flight Deck' command style of Picard as it's being an illustration of command at its best. It's a very different command style to that of Captain Kirk."

Dave McDonnell, editor of the science-fiction magazine *Starlog*, insisted that Picard talked too much. "Kirk's first thought is to break out the phasers." But what if the two captains were pitted against each other in a do-or-die battle to see who was the better commander? "Kirk would win," said McDonnell, "because Picard would stop and say, 'Now wait a minute. We should talk this over . . .' And, of course, Kirk would kill him."

Entertainment Weekly listed "Kirk versus Picard" as the single most discussed issue on the information highway. Ask even *casual* viewers of the original series or its spin-off and they're likely to have a strong opinion. And Trekkers can spend hours on the Internet comparing the two captains. With no hope of resolution, the discussions quickly break into two camps. Kirk lovers find Picard too cerebral, Picard partisans think Kirk lacks diplomatic skills. Is Picard too slow moving or Kirk too prone to insubordination? Kirk too emotional, Picard too reserved? Is this a generational battle? Is it a class thing? Or is it simply a matter of style—Kirk's dashing spontaneity versus Picard's almost professional bearing?

Since *The Next Generation* debuted in 1987, countless chat groups debating the relative merits of the two captains have made the rounds online: "Picard has had 80-plus years to learn from Kirk's mistakes and build on the things he did right." Or "If it's negotiation, I'll take Picard, but in a battle, give me Kirk any day." "Kirk has sex more than once a season." Rejoinder: "Sex with Picard is worth waiting for a whole season." "Kirk never once stood up and had to straighten his shirt." Rejoinder: "Picard never once stood up and had to suck in his gut." "'Kirk never asks his bartender for advice." Rejoinder: "Picard never asks his Chief Medical Officer to be bartender."

The Top 20 Reasons Why Picard is a Better Captain Than Kirk
Note: The following list in various manifestations is often posted on Internet message boards as the debate continues.

20. When Picard gets captured by Romulans, he fights his way out. When Kirk gets captured by Romulans, he pretends that he's dead until they go away.
19. Picard has the balls to stand among hundreds of Klingons and argue with them.
18. When Picard's senior officers get killed, they *stay dead.*
17. Picard's doctor looks better than Kirk's and never said, "Dammit, Jean-Luc, I'm a doctor not a bricklayer."
16. Picard's first officer doesn't play some wimpy harp—he jams with his trombone.
15. Picard speaks fluent Klingonese.
14. Picard didn't have to cheat at the *Kobayashi Maru* scenario while at Starfleet Academy as a cadet.

13. Picard never had to destroy the *Enterprise.*

12. Picard refused to take a command until he had enough experience. Kirk took a command as soon as he could and was captured and held prisoner on every third mission.

11. Picard was assigned to protect the Klingon Empire from invasion by Romulans. Kirk was assigned to protect bins of wheat from invasion of little fuzzballs known as Tribbles.

10. Picard's *Enterprise* has windows.

9. Do women swoon when they hear, "Beam me up, Scotty"? No? How about "Make it so"? See the difference?

8. If Kirk had met the Borg, they wouldn't have assimilated him because they only assimilate intelligent life. They would have discarded him as space debris.

7. Picard can tell the difference between a real woman and a mirage.

6. Picard admits he's made mistakes. It takes a real man to admit his errors.

5. If Kirk had been killed in the first episode, the show would have been reduced to thirty minutes of good acting.

4. Picard doesn't need to hop in the sack to prove his masculinity.

3. When Kirk was Picard's age, they made him retire.

2. Kirk has not aged well. Picard has aged beautifully.

1. Two words: No toupee!

William Shatner was especially concerned over discussions about which captain was the better commander of the starship *Enterprise.* Since *The Next Generation's* debut in 1987, he refused to acknowledge Stewart, making negative remarks like, "Stewart is not the captain, he's just a wonderful actor." Shatner offered his own opinion why Kirk was superior in a televised interview in December 1991.

"Kirk was the better captain," said Shatner, "because he was more three dimensional. He was a wonderful leader—not only an intelligent [man] but an emotional man. He was a passionate man, and he felt for his troops—and they knew it!"

In another interview, Shatner further inflamed the Kirk versus Picard debate: "Given a dire situation, Captain Kirk says 'Drop that gun. I'll count to three. One, two, three,' and he fires. But Captain Picard says, 'Drop that gun. I'll count to three. One, two, three. I'm not kidding.'" Stewart countered that Picard "would never have got himself into a situation where one, two, three was a consideration in the first place. . . . Picard's approach to most situations is diplomacy. He always strives to see someone else's point of view and not to act aggressively or impulsively."

Shatner truly believed that he had said good-bye to Captain Kirk once and for all in *Star Trek VI: The Undiscovered Country* when the movie was released during the 1991 holiday season. The last entry in the ship's log made it clear that Kirk had seen his last voyage and *The Next Generation* was waiting to have the *Star Trek* franchise handed to them:

Captain's log, stardate 9529.1.
This is the final cruise of the starship *Enterprise* under my command. This ship and her history will shortly become the care of a new generation. To them and their posterity will we commit our future. They will continue the voyages we have begun and journey to all the undiscovered countries, boldly going where no man, where no *one*, has gone before.

—James T. Kirk

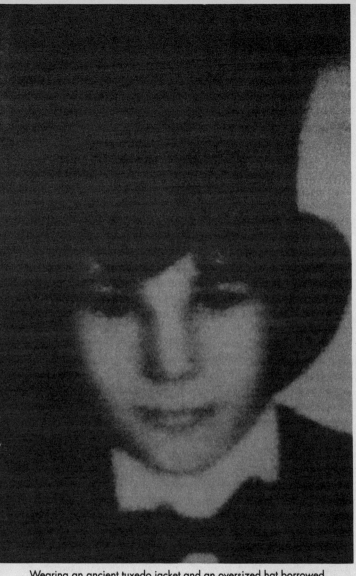

Wearing an ancient tuxedo jacket and an oversized hat borrowed from a local undertaker, Stewart began his acting career with "The Great Mesmo" mind-reading act when he was just a young boy. *(Courtesy of T.L. Adams/England)*

Stewart (far right) in a theatre club performance of *Hiss the Villain*. The victim of paternal child abuse, he quit school when he was fifteen years old and embarked on an acting career to "escape from the real world." *(Courtesy of T.L. Adams/England)*

Seventeen-year-old Stewart (front left) in the title role of *Harlequin's Dumbstruck*. *(Courtesy of T.L. Adams/England)*

One British theatre critic in 1976 questioned the director's decision of turning Stewart's Oberon in *A Midsummer Night's Dream* "into a Red Indian, clad only in a loincloth and going berserk from time to time," but he concluded nonetheless that "despite the handicap of his get-up, [Stewart] is virile and ethereal at the same time."
(*Courtesy of the Sue Harke Collection*)

Stewart and fellow RSC member Ben Kingsley rehearse *A Shakespeare Anthology* in the late 1970s. Looking more like brothers as they got older and balder, the two actors have remained close friends over the years, and are often seen partying together in L.A. when Kingsley is in America filming a movie.
(*Courtesy of Star Shots/Lori Yerger*)

Stewart's performance as the "monstrously unhappy" Leontes in the 1981 production of *The Winter's Tale*, only a few months after his abusive father's death. "For the first time I was prepared to directly draw on my own experiences and feelings and instincts in a role," he later admitted. *(Courtesy of T.L. Adams/England)*

Stewart participated in an ACTER-sponsored benefit performance at the University of California at Santa Barbara in 1988. From left to right: Stewart, John Ireland, UCSB Chancellor Barbara Uehling, Michael Douglas, and Mary Steenburgen.
(Courtesy of Star Shots/Lori Yerger)

Stewart's film roles in the 1980s were largely minor and forgettable.
He took up the sword and the shining armor of a knight in
Excalibur, a grim and bloody version of the Camelot legend. "I found
the director, John Boorman, a little remote, very, very preoccupied
with images and the look of the film," Stewart said. "But those were
the early days of filming for me and I was probably a little timid."
(Courtesy of Star Shots/Lori Yerger)

During *The Next Generation*'s first year on the air, a distant and aloof Stewart spent his time alone on the set preoccupied with memorizing his lines and finding ways to improve the scripts. "I was a pain in the ass when I first came to America," Stewart acknowledged. "I was pompous and altogether too full of myself." *(Courtesy of Mary Draganis)*

Stewart makes a point about the lack of development of the Captain Picard role during *The Next Generation*'s first season in 1987 with producer Rick Berman, who would later replace Gene Roddenberry as the creative force behind the *Star Trek* franchise. "Rick was more broadminded about what I was permitted to explore as a character," Stewart later acknowledged. *(Courtesy of Star Shots/Lori Yerger)*

Stewart and his *Next Generation* costar, Jonathan Frakes, sign autographs and meet with fans at a *Trek* convention. When they were not working 17 to 18 hours a day on the set of the series, Stewart spent much of his off-hours with Frakes, whose devil-may-care, live-life-to-the-fullest attitude Stewart particularly relished. *(Courtesy of Star Shots/Lori Yerger)*

Stewart and costar Marina Sirtis (Counselor Troi) discuss a scene on the bridge of the *Enterprise*. The actor challenged *Next Generation* writers to break away from Gene Roddenberry's male chauvinistic views of women on the series. "They were continually featured as sexual objects, as softer, weaker, and therefore—it always seemed to me—second-class individuals," Stewart complained. *(Courtesy of Star Shots/Lori Yerger)*

From 1991: Stewart with Jennifer Hetrick, the "other woman" who allegedly wrecked his 25-year marriage. Hetrick, a former Oil of Olay model and *L.A. Law* regular, played the part of Captain Picard's love interest during third and fourth season *Next Generation* episodes. (*Courtesy of* The National Enquirer)

During the early years of *The Next Generation*, Stewart attended at least six *Star Trek* fan conventions a year. "I enjoy them," he admitted. "It gets me back on stage. It's like doing stand-up in front of the most adoring audience one could ever wish for." (*Courtesy of the Sue Harke Collection*)

Stewart was all smiles at the dedication of the new Gene Roddenberry building on the Paramount Lot to celebrate *Star Trek*'s 25th anniversary in 1991. Behind the scenes, though, Stewart maintained a
stormy, tumultuous relationship with the creator of *The Next Generation* and allied himself with Rick Berman in Paramount's power struggle to oust Roddenberry. From left to right: Stewart, George Takei,
William Shatner, Rick Berman, and Roddenberry.
(Courtesy of Star Shots/Lori Yerger)

Stewart and Whoopi
Goldberg entertained questions from the audience at
a 1990 ACTER perfor-
mance at a California university. The two *Next Generation* costars began frequently rewriting some of
the third season episodes
to make them "go much
more on the nose" with political issues. *(Courtesy of
Star Shots/Lori Yerger)*

By 1991, during *The Next Generation*'s fifth season, Stewart's television stardom had given him the financial and artistic independence to create his own Broadway show, a one-man staging of Charles Dickens's *A Christmas Carol*, a work he adapted, revised, directed, and in which he portrayed some 35 characters.
(Courtesy of
Star Shots/Lori Yerger)

From 1993: Stewart and his one-time fiancée, Hollywood screenwriter Meredith Baer. Within a year, the engagement was cancelled and the two ended their relationship on a bitter note. Stewart went so far as to say in several interviews that he missed Baer's cat more than he missed her. *(Courtesy of The National Enquirer)*

On the set of *Star Trek Generations*: Stewart takes direction from David Carson, a fellow Brit and close friend of the actor. When Stewart threatened to quit *The Next Generation* at the beginning of the sixth season, however, Carson commented, "I believe the show is not about a star and not about a Captain Kirk or Jean-Luc Picard." *(Courtesy of Star Shots/Lori Yerger)*

From 1995: A relaxed and gregarious Stewart sips tea (Tetley's, not Earl Grey) and fields questions from members of one of his fan clubs while in New York for the Broadway production of the critically acclaimed *The Tempest*. *(Courtesy of Star Shots/Lori Yerger)*

Only weeks after the broken engagement to Meredith Baer, Stewart realized that the woman of his dreams was right under his nose: Wendy Neuss, the attractive co-producer of *The Next Generation*. "She's making me tremendously happy, and I'm feeling better about everything . . . my career, my relationships with my kids, better than I ever did before." *(Courtesy of The National Enquirer)*

Stewart and William Shatner, *Star Trek*'s two legendary captains courageous, take center stage at a New York convention. Prior to the crossover movie *Generations* in 1994, Shatner had angrily denounced his successor and asked *Trek* fans to boycott *The Next Generation*. But once filming began on the new movie, Shatner described Stewart as "an utterly delightful, sensitive and gentle man." *(Courtesy of Star Shots/Lori Yerger)*

Stewart (driving) and his brother, Trevor, were mobbed by British fans when the world-famous actor returned home to his native England.   (*Copyright © 1996 by Anita Van-Gelder*)

Stewart at the *Star Trek* 30th Anniversary "Grand Slam" convention in 1996, his first appearance at a *Trek* conclave in almost two years. After *The Next Generation*'s final episode in 1994, the actor distanced himself from the franchise with roles "that would dynamite the Captain Picard image." *(Courtesy of the Sue Harke Collection)*

By borrowing sets from *The Next Generation,* the original crew's final voyage in *Star Trek VI* kept within its $26 million budget and became one of the twenty-five top-grossing films of 1991. With box office receipts of nearly $150 million, *Star Trek* remained a reliably profitable movie-making franchise, but the perception began to circulate around Paramount Studios that clearly the glory days of Captain Kirk and the *Enterprise's* original crew were behind them.

"That notion, combined with the inescapable realities of an ever-more-expensive and ever-more-wrinkled crew, soon served to remove most of the remaining sheen from the formerly high-gloss hull of the *Enterprise,*" Shatner related in his second autobiography, *Star Trek Movie Memories.* "Despite *Star Trek VI's* success, the standard rumors in regard to yet another sequel were nonexistent, replaced by rumors that a *Next Generation* movie would soon become a realty."

"I felt strongly that this sixth movie was 'it'—the ending," Leonard Nimoy later recalled. "Why? I felt like life was going to imitate art again: At the end of *Star Trek VI,* the crew has been called home to retire, and pass the torch on to a 'new generation.' Word on the Paramount lot was that there was plenty of momentum for a *Next Generation* movie.'"

"By the end of our fourth season," Rick Berman explained, "we had already initiated a plan to take *Star Trek: The Next Generation* off the air just after our seventh season. Reason number one was that the series was about to get a lot more expensive to produce as television shows always do when they get into their sixth, seventh and eighth seasons. The directors, the producers, the actors, all of these people start asking for a lot more money. Two, the feeling was, 'You can't begin a movie franchise when people can still see these same actors in first-run television episodes for free.' There'd be no incentive there for anyone to plunk down their $7.50."

As Paramount pressed forward on a *Next Generation* movie, it was Stewart who originally proposed a transitional film involving members of both the original *Trek* and *Next Generation* casts. At first, the studio was dead set against a cross-pollination movie, but eventually Stewart convinced Paramount executives that the resulting hybrid between the two crews would most definitely attain must-see status among Trekkers everywhere, while serving to establish *The Next Generation* as a viable cinematic franchise all its own.

"From the moment our elevation to film status was being discussed, I'd argued—and I think I was a lone voice that it must be a transitional movie—that it should include as many members of the original cast as possible," Stewart later said. "Given that Bill [Shatner] and his colleagues had already made six movies, just to cut them off and start up with us would've been missing a golden opportunity to do something quite intense and dramatic. Critical to all of this was to have Bill. Having the two captains share screen space was something I thought people would enjoy seeing. There is something worth noting about the passing of the baton from one hand to the other. In a sense Bill validates me, that is, Captain Picard, but also *The Next Generation*."

Nine

The Fullest Living

The fullest living is a constant dying of the past, enjoying the present fully, but holding it lightly.

—Patrick Stewart, eulogizing Gene Roddenberry

The Next Generation enjoyed some of its highest ratings to date during its fifth season, while also sharing in the hoopla of *Star Trek*'s year-long twenty-fifth anniversary celebration. From TV specials and videos (which paired *Enterprise* crews from both series) to the original cast's last movie voyage, *The Undiscovered Country* (which featured Worf's Michael Dorn playing one of his Klingon ancestors), it appeared that the two fractious *Trek* franchises were finally striving to live peacefully together in the same galaxy.

Although there were two camps in *Trek* fandom, the die-hard loyalists, and those who embraced the new series, and who may or may not have felt a bit of unease about their "defection," one thing is certain: buoyed by the two-part Spock episode *Unification* and the anniversary commemorations during the November 1991 sweeps period, *The Next Generation*'s Nielsen ratings hit an all-time *Trek* high. In the key demographic group of men age eighteen to forty-nine the show received a rating of 14.6 against prime-time competition, with the composite for both sexes not far behind. Astonishingly, that rating left other major TV series in the dust. *The Next Generation* beat *60 Minutes* (10.7), *Coach* (11.6), *Roseanne* (12.7), *Cheers* (12.8), and even *Monday Night Football* (13.9). Paramount executives publicly boasted to the media that if the *Trek* series were a network show it would have been in Nielsens' Top Ten consistently every week.

Stewart strongly believed that one of the major reasons for the series' continuing success was stability in the ranks. "For the first time, *The Next Generation*'s upper echelon stayed relatively unchanged all season long," he said at the time. "That steadiness, security and firmness of purpose showed in the scripts, the character development, the production values and, hopefully, in the performances of the show's actors. I, for one, am certain that our fifth year was one of our finest seasons."

Rick Berman, Michael Piller, Jeri Taylor, Peter Lauritson, David Livingston, and Wendy Neuss retained their titles while Ronald Moore and Joe Menosky were promoted to co-producers. For a time they were joined by Herbert J. Wright, a veteran of *The Next Generation*'s chaotic first season who was coaxed back to the series by Berman to juice up the science-fiction content.

When Wright returned to the show in 1991, he discovered things had dramatically changed, both on screen and off. "Fifth season was no comparison," he later said. "People were so much happier and calmer and quieter and really helping each other. It was a kinder, gentler place to be."

Wright recalled meetings during the first season in which Roddenberry's longtime friend and attorney, Leonard Maizlish, would be involved in story conferences. His assistance was not appreciated by the members of the Writer's Guild,* who made a complaint to their union. Maizlish, who argued that he was only attempting to conserve Roddenberry's time and energy, was told to quit "helping out" with the script and asked to vacate the lot.

"It was so bizarre," Wright remembered. "Gene was bringing his attorney to staff meetings and he was giving us notes and secretly rewriting at night and taking people's names off and putting other people's names on. He would call up writers at home, free-lancers, ask them what was going on, how they were doing. It was horrible, one of the principle reasons I left."

"The first year was very chaotic," agreed Stewart. "But the second year Roddenberry stepped away and Rick Berman and Maurice Hurley took the reins and there was additional shakedown but things smoothed out a little and in the third year Michael Piller came and it was shaky at first and then started to stabilize and it was very stable on all fronts ever since. It was a well-oiled machine and it got better and more consistent and the key is that everybody continues to be as demanding upon themselves and take it as seriously as they have taken it."

* The Writers Guild of America had previously been involved with Roddenberry over another dispute regarding the series. Longtime *Star Trek* writer David Gerrold wrote most of *The Next Generation* 'bible,' devising the show's setup. Roddenberry then shamelessly claimed credit—and the glory and the money. But the controversy eventually was settled in Gerrold's favor by the Writer's Guild.

Roddenberry's Final Frontier

A booze-addled, pill-popping Gene Roddenberry suffered two strokes in 1991 and was confined to a wheelchair. A mere forty-eight hours before his death, he previewed *Star Trek VI: The Undiscovered Country* at a private screening. As usual, he fought for a more utopian vision of the future and vehemently denounced the militaristic thinking displayed by Federation and Starfleet officers in the film. Although Paramount executives were diplomatic it was obvious from the tone of the meeting that they had no intention of honoring his recommendations.

Roddenberry went back to his office, phoned his attorney, and angrily demanded that at least fifteen minutes of the movie be removed. Despite the fact that the original *Star Trek* crew's last picture was dedicated to his memory, his last wishes were ignored and it was released as screened.

"I always felt that Gene understood the kind of man that I was, the kind of actor that I was," Stewart said, reflecting a year later on Roddenberry's death. "Gene had, of course, a very firm view of what *Star Trek* was and was intolerant of interference. In fact, Gene died during the time that I was directing my second episode. Rick Berman came to my trailer, just after noon break, while they were setting up a scene, and told me. I knew, of course, that Gene had been very ill. Rick asked me if I wanted to suspend production for the day and, if I wished that, he would support my wish and would communicate it to the cast and crew. It didn't take long to decide to go on with the work. There actually was some unhappiness about that— some people felt that, in respect, we should have taken the day off."

Even though the announcement had erroneously been made that Roddenberry's memorial service on November 1, 1991, at the Hall of Liberty at Forest Lawn was private, over 1,200 people showed up and hundreds of fans, many in Starfleet uniforms, lined the winding road. It was truly a memorial befitting the creator of the greatest science-fiction show in the history of entertainment.

Nichelle Nichols, who had at one time been Roddenberry's mistress and played Lieutenant Uhura on the original *Star Trek*, sang two songs. Renowned science-fiction writer Ray Bradbury eloquently and movingly saluted his friend and Whoopi Goldberg recalled how she literally begged Roddenberry for the role of Guinan on *The Next Generation*. Following the Academy Award-winning actress were several writer-producers who delivered short, heartfelt tributes. Finally, Stewart, his posture impeccable and his distinctly resonant voice echoing throughout the building, spoke the last public testament of respect for a man he had desperately sought to have ousted as creative force behind *The Next Generation*. (Less than a week later, a transcript of Stewart's remarks had appeared online and at *Trek* conventions around the country.)

"The first impression of Gene Roddenberry was size. Bulk, stature, bigness. Gene dominated by the space that he filled and when Gene opened his arms, not only were the dimensions involved impressive, but he suggested dimensions that went on, beyond his fingertips. The next, unexpected, impression, when he spoke, was of gentleness. A surprisingly light, tenor voice with a rising inflection that gave a lilt, an airness, an almost whimsical tone to his statements. And only in the past few days, when reading the obituaries, the appreciations, the editorials, did I discover that, had he lived there longer, I might have heard the sound of Southwest Texas, because Gene was born in El Paso.

"I wish I had known that, because for a short time I lived in a neighboring city across the Rio Grande: Juarez. And I stood under those skies and felt the heat, and looked at those hard, bare mountains. Considering the impact that Gene Roddenberry was to have on our culture and the culture of the world, what a perfect location El Paso was for him to draw his first breath. Straddling the old world and the new. A meeting point of people and cultures: Aztec, Olmec, Tigua, European, Oriental, African. On the banks of a great continental river, this place of diversity, a mixing, a flow of challenge and space. How appropriate!

"There are many people here who are much more qualified than I to speak of the life of Gene Roddenberry that followed his first appearance in 1921," Stewart continued. "I have known Gene for only five years, and though we were always promising each other lunch or dinner, times of quiet away from the set, when we can exchange thoughts and experiences and ideas, we only in fact found them twice. Two lunches. Of course, had we really wanted to, we would have found those times more often. But I never called and Gene never called and the seasons went by.

"It seems to me that I sensed why. Gene had launched *The Next Generation* and now he expected us to get on with it. He had other pressing matters to absorb his attention: living for one thing. And dying.

"Dying. Gene certainly thought about that, and he wrote about it. It has become a standing joke on our sets that whenever the good captain begins to philosophize, the crew and cast will burst into universal groans. Eventually somebody will cry out, 'Give us the death speech, Captain!' Well, Jonathan, Marina, you're going to get it. LeVar, Gates, Brent, Michael, here it comes: that speech that we've so often laughed about.

"It occurred very early, in the start of the second season. It was written by Gene in an episode, I believe, mostly written by another writer, and once again, the good *Enterprise* was in peril and all of us were convinced that we were going to die. The android, Data, paid an unexpected visit to the captain's quarters and asked him, 'Captain, what is death?'

"Picard replied, 'Well, Data, some explain it as our changing into an indestructible form, forever unchanging. They argue that the purpose of the entire universe is to then maintain us in an earthlike garden which will give us pleasure through all eternity. At the other extreme are those who prefer the idea of our blinking into nothingness, with all our experiences, our hopes, our dreams, only a delusion.'

"And Data asked, 'And which do you believe sir?' 'Well,' says Picard, 'considering the marvelous complexity of our universe, its clockwork perfection, its balances of this against that, matter, energy, gravitation, time, dimension, pattern, I believe that our existence must mean more than either of those choices. I prefer to believe that what we are goes beyond Euclidean and other practical measuring systems and that, in ways we cannot yet fathom, our existence is part of a reality beyond what we understand now as reality.'

"I wonder how many popular television series would have the guts to place a speech like that in the middle of a prime time broadcast? The Old Testament, atheism, Euclid! And a few weeks ago, a fifth season episode described the legend of Gilgamesh and spoke of the Homeric hymns, and in a letter to Rick Berman, a fan, thrilled and amazed by these references, reflected that in one week of that show's transmission, more people were probably made curious about that literature than at any times since their creation!

"Even at its most frivolous, which sometimes *The Next Generation* is, it is concerning itself with ideas, with issues. . . . That is Gene's gift to us, which we actors and producers and crew and technicians and staff strive to sustain.

"Gene's gift to me was this job, and that endowment will last a lifetime—sometimes as a curse, but more as an unexpected, life-transforming, life-bestowing blessing. Five years ago, first in his home, then twice in his office, he looked at and listened to a middle-aged, bald, opinionated, working-class British Shakespearean actor and he said, 'He will be captain.' Inexplicable!

"Gene at the beginning was challenged on all these counts. Our American icon played by this, this . . . ! How to describe him? Even my hairline was subject to heated questioning. When a journalist remarked that 'Surely, in the 24th century there would be a cure for male pattern baldness,' Gene responded, 'But, why? In the 24th century nobody will care!' With that remark, millions of men stood taller. Even without hair.

"That is what Gene did. He readjusted our view. He corrected our vision, our vision of where we were going and what our values were. What our values will become. And the view wasn't always consistent, especially where it concerned women. Infuriatingly, *Star Trek* remains simultaneously liberated and sexist. Maybe even in that, Gene remains, sadly, a visionary. We discussed this particularly contentious issue, Gene and I, and he reminded me that before we began shooting the pilot he had said to me, 'Patrick, if you have something important to say about this show, say it to me.'

"Gene always made it easy to be honest and frank with him. He never intimidated, though he could impress. I was reminded of that this week when A.C. Lyles spoke of an incident when President Reagan visited the set in the spring. He and Gene stood side by side, and somehow Gene's stick got knocked to the ground and at once, the president bent on one knee to pick it up. When this was referred to later, Mr. Reagan said, 'You know, in that moment, I felt I was about to be knighted.' In one way or another, Gene graced all of us while he was alive and he will go on doing so.

"Almost a year ago I was here, taking my farewell of another friend who died too soon. I'm going to repeat some words of a British doctor on the subject of dying:

" 'To walk we have to lean forward, lose our balance, and begin to fall. We let go, constantly, of the previous stability, falling, all the time, trusting that we will find a succession of new stabilities with each step. The fullest living is a constant dying of the past, enjoying the present fully, but holding it lightly; letting it go without clinging and moving freely into new experiences. Our experience of the past and of those dear to us is not lost at all, but remains richly within us.' "

In conclusion, Stewart straightened his posture and held his head high, as if looking toward the heavens. "Gene, I have something important to say about the show. Thank you!"

As the lights dimmed and the memorial came to a close, outside in the distance, four Air Force fighter jets approached from the east, flying in a slight V-formation. As the aircraft approached the San Fernando Valley, the plane second from the right peeled off in the famous "Missing Man" maneuver, aviation's honor to a fallen flyer. Roddenberry, who volunteered as a pilot for the U.S. Army Air Corps in 1941 (before it was changed to the Air Force), took part in eighty-nine wartime missions and was decorated with the Distinguished Flying Cross and the Air Medal.

Roddenberry's first *Enterprise* captain, William Shatner (who was conspicuously absent from the memorial), summed up the essence of his former employer's life during an online eulogy: "Very few people have the ability to fire up our imaginations and make us think about the human condition. Gene Roddenberry, the creator of *Star Trek,* was one of those people. He took us where no man has gone before—and beyond. He created a starship, its crew, an entire universe—and brought them to life for millions of people. Without Gene, there would have been no *Star Trek."*

In October 1992, a year after his death, the space shuttle *Columbia* blasted off into space—the final frontier—carrying the cremated remains of Roddenberry in a stainless-steel canister.

It wasn't the *Enterprise,* but the creator of *Star Trek* was finally home.

Bridging the Generations Gap

Although it was well known that Roddenberry considered both *Star Trek* series his "children," the whole idea of a new generation of *Trek* actors originally did not sit too well with Shatner's former co-star, Leonard Nimoy. He wasn't pleased by the attention paid to Stewart, Brent Spiner (who played the android Data, *The Next Generation's* version of Spock), and the other cast members at the apparent expense of the original series and, like his former captain, Nimoy believed that the name *Star Trek* should apply only to the first show and the first *Enterprise* crew.

After Nimoy agreed to reprise the role of Spock during the fifth season of the new series, he was reminded of a 1986 comment in which, in regard to *The Next Generation*'s premiere, he wondered if Gene Roddenberry could once again "catch lightning in a bottle."

Years later, Nimoy admitted in his autobiography: "Part of me was *really* saying, 'How can you ever hope to do it without *us?*' *The Next Generation* was a well-done, logical extension of the premise that the original *Star Trek* laid down. The characters and the stories were consistently good, and it lasted longer than our show did, which has to tell you something."

Ironically, Paramount executives called Nimoy to a meeting in 1986 at which they discussed a new television series based on *Star Trek*, with new actors, set at a time even further in the future than the original show's twenty-third century. After Nimoy was asked to be the new *Trek* series's executive producer, he thanked them, wished them well on the project, and explained it simply couldn't work.

"I felt the original *Star Trek*'s success was due to many factors," Nimoy said. "The themes, the characters, the chemistry between the actors, the timing. . . . There was simply no way that anyone could duplicate all those things and be successful with a second *Star Trek* show. And so I opted out."

If any doubts remained that *The Next Generation* had become a worthy successor to its namesake after five highly rated seasons, even the most skeptical loyalist had to confess that Nimoy's presence in 1991 as the legendary Spock silenced them. There had always been rumors that more of the original cast would turn up following De Forest Kelly's brief appearance as the 137-year-old Admiral McCoy in the pilot, and scripts had actually floated around to that effect. A second-season opener, called *Return to Forever*, had been penned, bringing the movie-era Spock together with the Spock of the twenty-fourth century through the

Guardian of Forever time portal from the 1966 episode *City on the Edge of Forever.* But during the Writer's Guild strike that summer, negotiations with Nimoy collapsed just as the outline was being completed, and the project never again got off the launchpad.

"Things happen when they're supposed to," Nimoy later commented. "You let things unfold as they should. It seemed like the right time and all the right reasons to do the two-part adventure *Unification.* . . . Returning to television was comfortable for me. I know the character so well, even though I was working with a different cast. But, Spock is Spock, and bringing this character back to TV was coming full circle for me."

Who was ultimately responsible for bringing Spock into *The Next Generation*'s twenty-fourth century? Stewart, who was adamant about bridging the original series and its spin-off, to tie the two *Treks* together, to somehow unite them with a common story thread during the franchise's silver anniversary. As *Star Trek VI: The Undiscovered Country* went into planning, the formidable Stewart lobbied Berman, who, in turn, proposed the idea to Paramount president Frank Mancuso.

Nimoy later recalled: "During the making of *VI,* he [Mancuso] called me up one day, and said, 'Leonard, I've got an interesting proposition for you. How would you feel about appearing as Spock in an episode of *The Next Generation*? Maybe you could make some elements of *VI* that reflect on *The Next Generation,* and work with Berman to make *Next Generation* reflect *VI* to have some backpacking.'"

The idea intrigued Nimoy, so he met with Berman and Michael Piller. *Star Trek VI* director Nick Meyer was brought in to discover ways to bridge references between the generations in his movie script and in

Unification, since the motion picture filmed long before the episode did. "Nimoy loved the idea of making slight references in the future to the Kirk era," Berman recalled. "[But] I don't have any great belief in paying homage to the original show."

Nimoy gave his blessing to the script and agreed to a very modest salary (union salary minimum) even though his commercial success as the director of *Star Trek III* and *IV* and *Three Men and a Baby* had positioned him to command a salary that by itself would have soaked up one *Next Generation* episode's budget.

"When the time came, I reported for work," Nimoy said. "[However] I'd met all the cast before, at a party at my home when we kicked off production for *Star Trek VI,* so I knew them, liked them, and felt comfortable around them. I enjoyed the sense of camaraderie on the set, although I have to admit, there was a little bit of an 'Uh-oh! Big Daddy's here! We'd better behave!' feeling among the crew, which amused me at the same time that it made me a little self-conscious."

Nimoy was particularly impressed with Stewart, who he later described as "extremely likable" and "an exceptional actor whom I sincerely admire." He found the final scene in which Picard (who had mind-melded with Spock's father in the episode *Sarek*) graciously consents to let Spock contact the part of Sarek's mind that still remained with the captain, "an extremely moving, dramatic moment." He went on to say that Stewart's acting is "clean, clear, intelligent, and witty. . . . Patrick is in some ways rather like his character, Picard—absolutely charming, yet authoritative in speech and manner."

"I was delighted that Leonard came to do two episodes of our show," Stewart said in response, "although I know the fans felt a little cheated by the brevity of his appearance in the first half. I have always hoped that the actors from the original series would work with us at some time and I've always been enthusiastic about that. But it was grand to have an opportunity to get to know Leonard, who is a truly delightful individual. He is a charming man, relaxed and amusing and it was a delight to have him with us."

Piller, who co-wrote the episode's second part with Berman, used the unification of Germany as his basic thematic metaphor but was disappointed that his script couldn't provide more chemistry in the Picard-Spock scenes. "We got some good moments, and Leonard was splendid, but I thought a lot of it was flat, talky and dull. I thought it was an historic opportunity and I don't think we delivered what the potential of it was.

"I wanted to tell a story about the maturity of one of drama's great characters. What happens to Spock in the 85 years between then and now? How has logic and emotion played a part in his life? What is the growth of the man beyond logic? What was the conflict between he and his father and the death and passing of generations? I thought they were meaningful pieces of business to explore the man. I did not want a lot of plot to get in the way of the examination of the man and I felt the show would be carried by the conflict between Spock and Picard, with Picard ironically representing the father through the mind-meld. In fact, it was Picard who represented the original philosophy of *Star Trek* and Spock who was moving onto the future, so when the two came together it was sort of a reversal. It was all great stuff and it sounded wonderful in my mind and on paper, but the bottom line for me was that the relationship between Picard and Spock didn't have the chemistry. I don't think it was in the script and I don't think it came out on screen."

With Spock deciding to remain on Romulus and work with the underground for real peace at the end of the two-part episode, obviously the door was left open for Nimoy's return on *The Next Generation* as the legendary Vulcan. "I felt we were finished at the [original series's] second season's end, but then, there was that big outcry and we were renewed for a third season. After the third season, I thought, 'Now we're really done.' In '79, we made the first movie and I thought, 'OK, now we've made the movie and now we're done.' In the second film I died and was resurrected in the third. With *VI*, I felt a sense of closure—a sense that the sixth film would indeed be the Vulcan's final appearance on the large screen. But I wound up reprising the role of Spock much sooner than I ever dreamed I would. None of us could have predicted that we *might* never be done with *Star Trek*."

Even though Stewart repeatedly lobbied Berman for Spock's return in the series' last two seasons, one of *Star Trek*'s most memorable characters never made another appearance. Yet, Nimoy's role in the two-part *Unification* accomplished exactly what Stewart so desperately sought and its title proclaimed: Spock (which means "Uniter" in the Vulcan language) had bridged the gap between the two worlds of *Star Trek*. Clearly, the torch had been passed.

A Lifetime of Memories

Another phenomenally popular episode of *The Next Generation* during its fifth season was the Hugo award-winning *The Inner Light* in which Picard lived an entirely different life in some twenty-two minutes as Kamin, iron weaver of the planet Kataan. The captain experienced all the things Starfleet could never give him: a wife and children, stability and a home.

"It was a fascinating script, and it gave me the opportunity to explore a different kind of Picard," Stewart said. "That episode, probably more than any other, gave me more acting opportunities because we had to take the same Picard character and put that man into a completely different environment. I then had to create a man who would have obviously developed very differently, grown old very differently, because of the society he was living in. He was away from Starfleet, away from the *Enterprise* and his crew and friends. It was an interesting situation and an interesting problem for me to try to discover what would have become of Picard if he had just been an ordinary family man living a quiet life in a small community on some small obscure planet. How would this man have developed and changed? It was a very important experience to investigate the potential domestic side of Picard which, of course, we know simply does not exist on the *Enterprise.*

"I found aspects of that show very moving to play," Stewart continued, "and quite emotionally involving. There were moments in it where I felt my emotions deeply connected with the character, particularly at the very last scene when he realizes that his whole existence on this planet had been predetermined for him by the probe. That moment, when his wife and friends come back to say goodbye to him, was a very powerful scene."

"This episode allows us to bring Picard and a wonderful group of guest actors together and create a world," Rick Berman told the press at the time. "We see Picard at half a dozen different ages involving wonderful prosthetics and a man's lifetime in the course of an hour. It's quite dramatic."

Michael Piller added: "It's a great premise about a man who lives forty-five years of his life in twenty-five minutes. Patrick gives a remarkable performance. He gets to be six or seven different ages and it works. As we were breaking the story with the writers, I remember putting all the lines on the board and with each one creating the blocks to have connections and relationships grow in this other life for Picard, so that by the end of the show when they die or they are lost, there is an emotional impact that the audience should absolutely be heartbroken that he's lost three other people he loved and spent his life with. I actually had tears in my eyes when we were breaking this story."

Executive script consultant Peter Fields, who wrote the episode's final draft recalled, "It was an opportunity to give Captain Picard an entire lifetime which is the antithesis of the kind of life he had always lived aboard the *Enterprise*. I understand Patrick enjoyed playing it very much, and it was a delight to be able to write it. Picard doesn't change, even though he's not the captain his personality doesn't change. But now he has a life he's never had; he has love, a home, marriage, a family and things that are not burdens; things he never thought he needed before. He not only has them but he loves them and is used to them and loses them."

As *The Inner Light* demonstrated, Stewart had become a much more active participant in the show's fourth and fifth seasons than he had been in the first three. "They addressed the romantic, the *real* romantic side of Picard," the actor said. "Perhaps, if there's one area which I would personally enjoy because it gives me a lot of pleasure and they haven't had much of it in the past, is the humorous, ironic, wittier side of our good captain. Two or three seasons ago I might have been complaining about being too much of a desk captain, a briefcase captain. My body count has risen dramatically in the last few episodes."

Although Stewart often cited *The Inner Light* as one of his favorite episodes of *The Next Generation*, the "powerfully dramatic script" was not the major reason for his obvious passion for the show. In a classic case of art imitating life, Stewart's real-life son Daniel played Batai, Picard's son on Kataan, after several auditions for the show.

"The work Daniel did in that was his *own* work," said Stewart with fatherly pride. However, both Stewarts "ran the lines together and talked about the scenes, because the Captain Picard I was being was not the Captain Picard that would be on the ship, but a man who has lived forty years in another environment. That's what Daniel and I talked about: What kind of father would Picard be if his life had changed so radically, and therefore what kind of son he would have."

Stewart found the experience of working with his son "was *very* satisfying and exciting for me. If you're going to have a child who becomes a performer like you, to be sharing a professional situation together is *deeply* rewarding. I thought he did an excellent job. One of the things that a number of people said which has particularly pleased me is that they think Daniel was very much the son of that relationship."

Stewart didn't encourage either one of his children to take up the acting profession "because ninety-odd percent of all actors simply don't work," he said with a deep sigh. "I know a lot of bitter, unhappy and frustrated actors for that very reason and I didn't want that kind of life and outlook for my children. My daughter [Sophie] received her theater training in England and I was unable to see her grow, but Daniel went to school in California. It was a momentous day in my life when Daniel graduated from CalArts in 1992. There he stood, Bachelor of Fine Arts, the first member of my family to receive a degree. It was as significant for me as it would, under other circumstances, had he been the first member of the family to read or write. I was tremendously proud and somewhat in awe of it."

After Stewart was awarded the role of Captain Picard in 1987, Daniel literally begged his father to allow him to come to America and attend college. Sophie, however, elected to remain in England with her mother, where she now operates Soul 555, a boutique owned by Stewart in London. Friends and relatives of Daniel and Sophie have said that after the much-publicized divorce of their parents, each of the children seemed to gravitate to one parent in particular.

Although Daniel eventually returned to England, he and his father spent a great deal of time together while he lived and attended college in the United States. On one occasion, Stewart had to borrow his son's pickup truck and drive it to the *Dennis Miller Show,* when his car didn't start. "He [Daniel] drove it out to me because I'm too cheap to get a taxi," Stewart told Miller and the audience when he appeared on the comedian's short-lived talk show. He went on to reveal that he had driven all the way to Hollywood with the hand brake of his son's pickup still engaged.

After *The Next Generation*'s successful seven-year run on TV ended, an interviewer asked Stewart if he had any regrets about being involved in *Star Trek.* "One," he quickly replied. "It separated me from my daughter for long periods of time, and I'll never get that back. I've been focused so entirely on my work for so many decades, I haven't paid attention as a father and I am now trying to pay attention."

Ten

From First Love to Sex Symbol

All the good things happening in his career still surprise him. You would never look at him and think, "Oh, that's an actor." He's a real person.

—Actress Leslie Caron on Patrick Stewart

As much as Stewart enjoyed playing Captain Picard, he longed to return to his first love—the stage. "I just couldn't be cut off from live theater," he explained to Glenn Collins of the *New York Times*. "Working in front of a camera is a very sterile experience." By 1991, during *The Next Generation*'s fifth season, Stewart's television stardom had given him the financial and artistic independence to create his own Broadway show, a one-man staging of Charles Dickens' *A Christmas Carol*, a work he adapted, revised, directed—in which he portrayed some thirty-five characters, including a dead-as-a-doornail Jacob Marley, Bob Cratchit, those dancing

Fezziwigs, frail and gentle Tiny Tim, and Ebenezer Scrooge himself.

Looking for something to occupy his time off the set of the 1985 film *Lady Jane,* Stewart came across Dickens' 1843 novel and began to read. "And I was suddenly aware that, although I *knew* the *Christmas Carol*—I had never actually *read* it," Stewart admitted. "I have a feeling that probably applies to the majority of people. So, I read it, and before I had finished, I knew that all of my impressions about *A Christmas Carol* had been substantially adjusted.

"I had thought of it as being a rather sentimental and somewhat melodramatic, whimsical, Victorian Christmas story," Stewart continued. "What I saw in the book was a very powerful piece about the power of redemption, as well as being a very tough, uncompromising picture of the harsh social conditions in Victorian London. Most particularly, I was moved by the almost-Shakespearean major theme, that of a man leading a bad life who's given a vision of his future and invited to change. Not *changed,* but to change himself and acquire redemption."

A short time later, Stewart read portions of the novel at a fund-raiser and then fashioned a one-man Broadway show from the book during the holiday season in 1991. "I think in many respects my performance in *A Christmas Carol* might prove to be the most significant theater experience for me for a good many years," Stewart later said, "because it was a piece of work that I had adapted myself, directed myself and is a solo show. There are no other actors in the show so the responsibility for me was much greater than it had been for anything else that I ever attempted. It almost seemed the very first thing I was going to do on a Broadway stage was vomit!"

A Christmas Carol "is difficult for an audience, too. They have to sit for two hours and watch *one* actor, without costume, with no set or props and minimal furniture, not just *telling* a story, but inviting them to use their imaginations in quite a demanding way," Stewart explained. "The show won't work unless an audience is prepared to come a long way to meet me in the performance. And listening to Dickens is *hard*. But the big production numbers of my show lie in the language—in the breathtaking, heart-stopping, dazzling kaleidoscope of words that pour out. And I feel their effect on an audience. You can hear them gasp at hearing language."

In his adaptation of Dickens' fantastic tale of redemption, Stewart communicated three primary themes ensconced in large doses of creativity and humor: "You cannot do good in the world until you first do good yourself. You have to correct the imbalances in yourself before you can begin to look outwards. *A Christmas Carol* also tells us not to despair. That's a powerful message."

Stewart found miserly Ebenezer Scrooge the most challenging to portray "because he's the character who undergoes the most change. And in the same way that a major dramatic character in a fine play will have an arc of development and change, that applies to Scrooge. If Scrooge doesn't work, the show doesn't work. The other character that gives me a lot of difficulty is the Ghost of Christmas Yet To Come. He barely exists. He's a pointing hand and little else."

Stewart must shoulder alone what he considers to be a trio of responsibilities each time he takes the stage. The first, he said simply, was "telling the story. The next thing is to keep them interested, not to bore them. It's the worst thing an actor can do. And, after that, it's necessary that the audiences are *changed*. I see it as my responsibility to send an audience out of a theater with a different perception of the world than the one they had when the came in."

The experiences of working large ensembles with the Royal Shakespeare Company, however, did not prepare Stewart for the challenge of presenting a one-man version of *A Christmas Carol*. "It presents a whole different set of problems. One of the reasons I became an actor was that I was permitted, in an approved context, to indulge my fantasies, to enter into a world of make-believe—and whatever world I entered was a damn sight more pleasant than the world I was living. In *A Christmas Carol*, I found a format where my imagination could be indulged to the ultimate. There are no boundaries to this make-believe world. When I say, 'And in that moment all vanished, the ruddy glow, the fire, the night, and Scrooge found himself on an open country lane on Christmas morning with clean white snow all around'—*boom!* It's like a cut in a movie. What pleased me about *A Christmas Carol* was finding that this imaginative world that Dickens created can have the same impact on twelve hundred people in a New York theater."

Stewart's virtuoso enactment of the holiday classic also had a thrilling impact on the critics, including an initially skeptical Clive Barnes of the *New York Post,* who wrote, "Stewart, with his stunningly effective and deviously imaginative portrayal of Scrooge and Company in his multivoiced, many-faceted *A Christmas Carol* . . . , won over every single one of my doubts and gift-wrapped them up as a Christmas bouquet."

Mel Gussow of the *New York Times* commented that Stewart made the "audience believe it has entered a magical world dense with character, atmosphere, and action. . . . His supple look and voice enable him to portray the widest range of Dickens characters without altering his costume or makeup. . . . The Cratchit Christmas dinner, in which the actor portrays the entire family, Scrooge, and the Ghost of Christmas Present and is also on the verge of impersonating the goose on the table and the Christmas pudding with holly stuck into the top, is a tour de force. It reminds us not only of what an inventive actor he is, but also of Dickens' own great theatricality."

"It was a thrilling time in New York doing *A Christmas Carol,*" Stewart remembered. "It had been twenty years since I had been on Broadway. To find myself back on the Broadway stage in something like that was both very frightening and very exciting. But the show was, fortunately, very successful, critically and at the box office. It broke all box office records for a solo performer on Broadway. I'm not unaware of the fact that a large number of people that came to see me were people who came because they had seen me on *The Next Generation.* I have quite an audience through that series and a wonderful audience, I might add. They've given me fantastic support when I have done other projects and the series has given me independence in a way that, frankly, I never really would have expected. And that independence, of course, is what makes all these other things possible."

Stewart's presentation of *A Christmas Carol* won a Drama Desk Award for best solo performance of the 1991-92 theater year, and in 1993 he received a Grammy nomination for his album version of the show. In 1994, Stewart won the Laurence Olivier Award for Best Entertainment, when he performed the acclaimed holiday classic at his beloved Old Vic in England.

Stewart had come a long way since his first stage review at the age of twelve, when the local newspaper wrote, "Patrick Stewart had nice movement, but not enough variety."

A Bad Morning, America

After stage performances of *A Christmas Carol*, Stewart would meet his fans at the stage door to sign autographs and occasionally talk to one or two, even though the crowds that gathered could be rather unruly. The production crew and others that worked backstage also described him as gracious and often funny, lending credence to his reputation as a "gentleman's gentleman."

Karen Droms of the Patrick Stewart Estrogen Brigade, an international fan club comprised of women who come together through the technology of the Internet, related the story of waiting for Stewart to emerge from a New York performance of *A Christmas Carol:* "I managed to get a spot right next to his limo. There must have been 200 fans lined up on the sidewalk and across the street (climbing up onto things to get a better view). Patrick's bodyguard asked us to please step back and keep a clear path to the limo. That was easier said than done, though, as I was continually shoved forward. Finally Patrick appeared, and as the crowd surged I was pushed into the side of the limo and into a police officer's holstered gun. It was all very disconcerting and disappointing to see Patrick's fans behaving so immature and self-centered. Patrick himself called for calm, saying, 'Let's not have anyone hurt!'

"The next day, we went back and talked to the stage-door manager," continued Karen, "who had many nice things to say about Patrick (and if the backstage people say nice things about an actor, you can pretty much bet they're true). He pointed to police barricades that were lying on the ground next to the door, and said that after the crowd the night before, the theater wanted to erect barriers to keep everyone back. But the stagedoor manager told us that Patrick had said, 'No, that would be like putting his fans in cages.' "

The Patrick Stewart on the set of *The Next Generation*, however, was light years away from the image of the proper Englishman. As a matter of fact, there were several Stewarts working on the series. Sometimes he was solemn, and other times he displayed a wicked sense of humor. He would be enchanting and warm one minute and short-tempered and explosive the next. There was a presence about him that commanded respect, yet those associated with *Star Trek* called him an insecure actor with a supercharged ego and prima donna attitude. Given to extreme mood swings, there was no single event that epitomized his manic behavior more than the time he stormed off the set of *Good Morning America*.

On February 12, 1992, midway through *The Next Generation*'s fifth season and during the all-important sweeps month, the production crew of ABC's popular morning news and entertainment show *Good Morning America* originated its broadcast that day from Paramount Studios and the actual sets of *The Next Generation*.

The show opened with co-host Charlie Gibson cheerfully stating, "Good morning, America, from the USS *Enterprise,* home to the cast of *Star Trek: The Next Generation.*" Gibson and his co-host, Joan Lunden, introduced themselves and announced that this was the fourth day of their Great Hollywood Wake-up Tour.

"It is 1992. But we really come to you from the 24th century," Gibson said solemnly as the red-alert warnings clamored in the background. He looked around as if wondering if a stage hand had somehow tripped an alarm. "They know we're here. I think they spotted us. But we are going to be on the sets, really, of *Star Trek: The Next Generation* through the day."

Holding up a model of the *Enterprise*, Gibson continued. "Theoretically the ship is half a mile long, and theoretically we are right here in the top. That's where the bridge is located. But in reality the USS *Enterprise* is really about a dozen sets, scattered around three sound stages here on the Paramount lot.

"For instance, the Ten-Forward lounge, that's supposed to be ten decks down and in the front of the ship—in truth it's about twenty-five feet over here," he said, gesturing to one side of the sound stage. "But the detail on this set, on the bridge, is really amazing. For instance, back here where the crew sits, the control seats, they all swivel, and there's some very authentic looking things here, built into the arms. I love the way these control panels swivel around, and you can use them just about any which way."

Gibson then pointed out the dedication plaque on the wall, rarely seen in the episodes themselves, which dedicated when and where the *Enterprise* was built. "It says here it was launched Stardate 40759.5, which I'm told translates to year 2363. That's when the ship was launched: made in the Utopia Planetia Fleet Yards in Mars. Where else would it be built?"

Then Gibson explained that they would be moving around the dozen sets, and Joan Lunden pointed out that they'd also be talking to the *entire* cast in the "intergalactic lounge," and to stay tuned, but first the news and weather . . .

After spotlighting 1992's catastrophic winter rainstorm which was pelting Los Angeles, even directly affecting the broadcast itself, former astronaut Alan Shephard wished the country "good morning" and said, "As America's first man in space, let me express my very best wishes to the crew of the USS *Enterprise* as they explore new galaxies and unknown worlds!" The theme music from *The Next Generation* played in the background of his greeting.

"So many of the astronauts, apparently, are big fans of *Star Trek,*" Gibson said, "and it is interesting that many of the cast were inspired by the astronauts. One of the cast members, that I'm going to be talking to in this half hour, Michael Dorn who plays one of the Klingons, Lieutenant Werf [sic], I believe, wanted to be an astronaut when he was a kid. It didn't happen, but he got the next best thing which is to be in this cast."

Backstage, Dorn groaned over the mispronunciation of his character's name. "You think he's ever seen an episode of *The Next Generation?*" he asked an already red-faced Stewart backstage. The *Enterprise* captain had been doing a slow-burn all morning while the two "hokey and mawkish" hosts, he felt, were irreverently treating the series' set like it was "some sort of kids' Saturday morning show." Stewart was highly defensive of *The Next Generation,* often calling it a "quality show that I consider an honor to be associated with." The actor was on the verge of getting up and walking off the set, but Paramount had promised the producers of *Good Morning America* that the entire cast would participate. Walking off a set meant that somebody broke their word, and in television walking off a set often costs somebody money.

"These are the guest accommodations on the USS *Enterprise,*" Gibson continued as they entered the set for one of the crew quarters, a set which was redressed and rearranged depending upon whose quarters it was meant to represent in a particular episode being filmed. "We're going to be talking about where we are.

It is interesting that on these very sound stages on the Paramount lot, the original *Star Trek* was made here. And they use it still for *Star Trek: The Next Generation*. But there is so much history on the Paramount lot," he explained. "It's interesting that these studios that grew up in the movie age now devote so many of their resources to television. I guess that's sort of a sign of the times."

After another news segment, *Good Morning America's* weatherman, Spencer Christian returned wearing a Starfleet uniform and sitting at the bar in Ten-Forward. He was being served by an actor in full Romulan makeup, apparently from the episode that was scheduled to be filmed that day. Making a joke when the Romulan served him, the weatherman said, "Hmmm, that doesn't look like coffee. What is this?"

"Gorgon stomach extract," the Romulan soberly replied.

"I see. Regular or decaffeinated?"

"Both," the pointy-eared Romulan answered.

"Great way to start the morning, with Gorgon stomach extract. Here's looking at you," Christian said as he picked up the cup to drink.

It was at that point in the program that Stewart, who was about to be introduced, decided that the hosts of *Good Morning America* had poked enough fun at his series and the actor walked off the set in a huff. The show continued, lurching from one subject to the next, from one set to the next and from one vacuous and superficial interview to the next. Lunden talked to Jonathan Frakes, Marina Sirtis, and Brent Spiner and Gibson questioned the other cast members from *The Next Generation,* although Stewart wasn't in the group, a fact never discussed the entire morning. Ordinarily, when the cast—minus one—appears on a talk show, they say something about the absent member of their ensemble even if it's nothing more than a lame joke. But no one said anything about Stewart.

A few weeks later an item appeared in the April 1992 issue of *Spy* magazine: "Just how does a celebrity draw the line between infotainment, good sportsmanship and unseemly shtick? One morning recently on *Good Morning America,* Patrick Stewart, who plays Captain Picard on the syndicated show *Star Trek: The Next Generation,* was about to be interviewed. As Stewart awaited his moment, he noticed that Spencer Christian, *GMA's* weatherman, was dressed up in a *Star Trek* getup. Stewart, perhaps all too keenly aware that he risks the camp fate of William Shatner, stalked out of the studio, enraged. As it happened, the botched segment was on the same morning as an on-air discussion among the four men who control TV programming in America—Bob Iger from ABC, Warren Littlefield from NBC, Jeff Sagansky from CBS and Peter Chernin from Fox—and they evidently witnessed Stewart's mad scene. 'So,' one of the network presidents said with a smile to a fellow network president, 'we're agreed—nobody will give Patrick Stewart any more work?' "

Whether the remark was said in jest or not, having the entertainment chiefs of America's four television networks see an actor throw a temper tantrum over something that could be viewed as trivial could not have enhanced Stewart's professional reputation. The actor himself confirmed the incident himself in the July 31, 1992, issue of *TV Guide,* just five months after it occurred. We'll never really know exactly how much trouble he created for himself with Paramount, but he was more than willing to express a public apology, when David Rensin asked about walking off the set of *Good Morning America.*

"They were broadcasting from *The Next Generation* set, and the weatherman was dressed in a Starfleet uniform," Stewart said, becoming slightly angry as he recalled the incident. "I thought that it was disrespectful. They were doing shtick in our costumes, and I thought it was demeaning to the show. I know I sound pompous, and I don't give a damn. Nevertheless, I should not have done what I did. I regret it."

It would not be the first or the last time Stewart would display a fit of bad temper and then have to issue a public apology afterward. In fact, presumably as a time-saver, he recycled his remorse—when he apologized two years later for screaming at an *Entertainment Tonight* crew on the set of the series' finale, he expressed the same regret, almost word for word!

Picard Bonds with the Perfect Mate

Stewart was once asked by an interviewer, "If Picard and Kirk walked into a singles' bar, who'd nab a date first?"

"I think they'd pool their resources and round up the whole place together," the actor jokingly replied. "And then they'd beam the beauties en masse to a nearby Hyatt. The captains are so used to being in command, I think they could handle all of them. As for me, I'd settle for just one."

Actually, Captain Kirk's intergalactic amorous pursuits were legendary and his love interests ranged through a dozen alien species and several anatomically correct android women. Nearly every episode of the original series had scenes of Kirk flirting with or bedding down some alien female. *Entertainment Weekly* writer Bob Cannon in a special *Star Trek* edition called James T. Kirk "the swingingest bachelor of the 23rd century."

"Kirk's success with women was uncanny," Shatner told one reporter. "It was miraculous how well he did with women across the universe, especially alien women and the various techniques they require. It's not like he spent his off-hours reading how-to books on alien women."

Captain Picard, on the other hand, never seemed to be with a woman. "Well, there have been episodes of romance. For the first couple of years, there were several," Stewart said, defensively. "Most of the romancing in the series was based upon the sudden appearance in Picard's life of someone from his past, with a pastel-colored, wistful sense of what might have been if things had been different. It's boring, very boring.

"It's pathetic that I have to count on my fingers how many times he got laid," Stewart continued, actually counting. "Well, I imagine he [and his occasional love interest] Vash probably did it more than once. There are those who would say that it probably should have happened more often, but it was never quite that explicit. But yes, indeed, he did get laid, and you know what? It was good for him. It generally is."

In the fifth season episode *The Perfect Mate,* a Kriosian ambassador arrives aboard the *Enterprise* with Kamala, a sexually empathic "mesomorph," as the peace offering from his people to the ruler of Valt Minor, intending to end years of war between the two worlds. The beautifully exotic humanoid female is a genetic rarity among her people with such a creature born only once every seven generations. Educated to fulfill her role as peacemaker, she has been prepared from birth to bond with Valt's leader, but when Picard is forced to turn to her for help in performing his ambassadorial duties he soon finds his legendary resistance weakening as he succumbs to her sexual attraction. Kamala is drawn to him as well, telling the captain that he is the first man who has suggested she has value in and of herself.

"On a positive note, I think, like the Borg show, it showed that Picard has a flaw, you can cut into his character," explained episode director Cliff Bole. "When I say that's positive, that means you can continue to make the character work. I think this is a real case for Picard, because he normally wouldn't have allowed himself to be vulnerable."

"We have Beverly argue the point that Kamala's mission amounts to prostitution," Michael Piller said. "She [Kamala] is an empathic metamorph and has the ability to be whatever a man wants her to be. This is the adolescent male fantasy of all time. I think the challenge of the show is if Picard is confronted with his perfect mate, could he resist her? This show does not work if the audience, at least the men, do not fall in love with this woman, too. She must be fully rounded, bright, engaging, with a great personality and the audience should say, 'I see the problem for Picard.' If there's no magnetic electricity between the two of them and it doesn't happen for me as a man watching her, then the audience will not accept for one second that Picard would even give her a second thought."

"I'm very pleased with it," enthused Rick Berman. "The actress [Famke Janssen, who later played the thigh-crushing villainess in the 1995 Bond film *Goldeneye*] is about as beautiful as any woman any of us have ever seen and gave a delightful performance. We shot two different endings and there were two more we didn't shoot. None of us will ever know which of the four would have been best."

A disappointed Piller, who co-authored the script, explained: "The trick ending which no one liked but me and Patrick, may have been the product of a writer who was trying too hard, but I was overruled. . . . I wanted to do an ending where he stopped the ceremony and said, 'No, she's staying with me.' [Then] he interrupts and says, 'I'm sorry, I can't allow this to continue,' and so while they're walking down the aisle and it seems each time it's the end of the show, we in fact cut back to them walking down the aisle so it's continuing and we understand these are things happening in Picard's mind. Finally he gets to the end, and the third ending is she interrupts and tells both of them she isn't staying for either of them. She says through Picard's influence she's been enlightened and is going off in search of adventure, leaving both men standing there. I was overruled. Those who overruled me would say that her leaving was not justified by anything else in the script, but I would argue with that."

What could have easily been just another Picard romance became a much more significant story. Stewart found *The Perfect Mate* moving "to see Picard, against his judgment and wishes, finding himself becoming attracted to a woman he could never have, with whom he could never be. The pressure that put him under made for a very interesting episode."

Bald, Beautiful, and Bodacious

During the summer hiatus of *The Next Generation* in 1992, Stewart was "confused and a little distressed, but extremely flattered and charmed" when the July 18th issue of *TV Guide* revealed that in a poll of readers, he was voted "the most bodacious man on TV" with 54% of the votes, beating out perennial sex symbols such as Burt Reynolds and Luke Perry.

"I was astonished that I should even be a contender and stunned that I won by such a significant margin,"

Stewart later said. "It pleased me enormously. It's good to get pats on the back, especially from a lot of people. It was a great compliment that was paid to me, I believe. To be in such delightful and gorgeous company was an honor as well. Of course, many people said nice things about it and you will understand that I also had to withstand a great deal of teasing from my fellow actors here on the show."

For several weeks Stewart was in total denial of the magazine's award, falling back on the persona of a deeply embarrassed Englishman. But as time went by, he began to confess, first to himself and then to others, that the honor of being the sexiest man on television gave him nothing but pleasure.

With the newfound role of TV sex symbol, Stewart also received an increase in the number of indecent proposals, which forced him to put "huge numbers of locks" on his door. "While that edition [of *TV Guide*] was on the newsstand, I kept a very low profile. I particularly didn't go into my market to do any grocery shopping! [A few weeks later] when I was speaking at a convention in Phoenix, this young man stood up, and he said, 'Mr. Stewart, please, will you marry my mother?' An attractive-looking woman sitting beside him bent forward and put her head into her hands."

While on *The Arsenio Hall Show* only days after the *TV Guide* cover story went public, Stewart was asked by the comedian and talk show host how it felt to be the most bodacious man on TV. "It feels better than being the man with the worst halitosis in the world," he answered. "It feels better than being the man with the flattest feet in the world. And very surprising. But I wish I had been voted it when I was sixteen or seventeen. I was a very unconfident teenager . . . I remember my first crush. But it never developed into a girlfriend. I could never make that step into asking somebody out. I was talking to a friend the other day about sitting in the back row of the movies waiting for the right moment, not quite knowing when it would be, and sometimes getting through the whole movie and never, ever taking that risk. I was very, very shy, and very insecure around girls."

With elegance, grace, and an overwhelming modesty, Stewart always took the opportunity on talk shows and in print interviews to thank the readers of *TV Guide* who voted for him, sincerely believing that it was his self-confidence that they found attractive. "I think attractiveness or whatever this thing is has very little to do with looks in a conventional sense or sex appeal. Self-confidence is attractive. Not arrogance but self-confidence. I think a lot of young people need to understand that it is very necessary to like yourself and I think I spent a large amount of my life not liking myself very much."

Ever since he lost all his hair when he was nineteen, Stewart was so traumatized that he felt women found him "ugly and would never look twice" at him. After skyrocketing to international fame in his role as Captain Picard on *The Next Generation,* Stewart had grown weary dealing with the inevitable questions concerning his baldness. In an interview in the November 1992 edition of *Playboy* magazine, Stewart went ballistic: "This is the last time that I will ever discuss my hair—ever, at any time, with any journalist," Stewart angrily told interviewer Neil Tesser. "I can never understand it. What if I were to say to you, 'You have an extraordinarily hooked and pointed nose that looks as though somebody got hold of the end of it and dragged it downward; what are your feelings about that?' You see, I was brought up to believe you do not make personal comments about someone's appearance. It's bad manners. And yet, with baldness it's open season—always. If I had a huge wart, you wouldn't refer to it. You might keep looking at it, but you wouldn't refer to it."

Stewart, finally realized that in the grand tradition of Yul Brynner and Telly Savalas, he seemed to have made hairlessness sexy for a new generation. "I've come to the point where I wouldn't replace my hair if I could. I now have actually been cutting my hair closer and closer. And I think that is the product of beginning to feel now, in my fifties, that it's all right—that I don't have to duck my head. I'm finally at peace with how I look. My lack of hair has turned out to be an identifiable trait. And the ladies seem to like it."

Besides *TV Guide*'s Most Bodacious Man on TV award in 1992, the 15,000 members of Man Watchers, Inc., picked Stewart, along with Sean Connery, Harrison Ford, and Paul Newman among the fan club's Top 10 World's Sexiest Men Over 50 in 1993: "As Captain Jean-Luc Picard on *Star Trek: The Next Generation,* this dashing 53-year-old has become the latest bald sex symbol. Women are bowled over by his strength and vulnerability." And in 1995, Stewart was named one of the 10 Sexiest Men by *Playgirl* and one of the 50 Most Beautiful People in the World by *People* magazine.

"Please, do not think for a moment," Stewart said in response to his newfound sex symbol image, "that I am not enjoying it to the fullest now!"

Eleven

Action and Romance

It is not possible that there are five better male actors in this town than Patrick Stewart!

—Jeri Taylor, co-executive producer of
The Next Generation

In the summer of 1987 Paramount believed that the odds were astronomical against Gene Roddenberry pulling off a *Star Trek* phenomenon a second time, so the studio executives hedged their bets on the new *Next Generation* series. The regular cast members had three contracts: one for the pilot, one for the first thirteen episodes, and one for multiple years. The studio could bail out if it became necessary, with no long-term financial obligation to the series's actors.

With the original contract options ending at the beginning of *The Next Generation*'s sixth season in the fall of 1992, rumors amid fans and the industry press surrounded the cast—especially Stewart—about their plans for a seventh season.

"There was concern, but I think we all felt that Paramount was going to do features and that was a big carrot to get him to commit to another year," Michael Piller later explained. "When we were doing *Chain of Command*, that's when the first inkling that Patrick might not be coming back was heard. Bringing in a new captain in Part One, you could see how that could give the show a really fresh start if you could find somebody good. Frankly, we were more concerned that Brent [Spiner] wasn't going to come back, because Brent is irreplaceable. You don't just bring on another android or cart out a Vulcan or something to fill his role. You have to have a captain and there was, in fact, some enthusiasm about the possibility of getting someone new. We were talking about bringing a woman in."

While shooting the pilot for *Deep Space Nine*, veteran *Star Trek* director David Carson considered the departure of Stewart, a long-time friend and fellow Englishman, a strong possibility. "I believe the show is not about a star and not about a Captain Kirk or Jean-Luc Picard," he said at the time. "I think there will inevitably be some sort of shake-up, as there always is when a captain leaves a ship, and there will be a feeling of the ground. But you may find that you get a different, richer *Next Generation* out of it and you're not simply retreading the same waters with the same people. The regrouping of the cast and the realignment of the actors towards either new people or redistribution of their own strengths, will inevitably make *Next Generation* different."

During the intense contract negotiations, Stewart let it be known that he wanted to end his association with *Star Trek*, with the exception of an occasional theatrical movie, and took his case public in several interviews he granted at the time. "I want it [*The Next Generation*] to continue but it has to be in something of a more modified form—possibly feature films. . . . There is something I would like to say and it is most genuine and significantly felt and that is the indebtedness that I personally owe to the fans of the show. They were behind Captain Picard and my work very early on and, although I, myself, was suspicious of the fan world of *Star Trek*, I very quickly learned that I had very little to fear. I am, weekly, delighted with the responses I get and the support and affection from the fans of the show. Again, whatever happens in the future, the memory of my experience with the *Star Trek* fans will always be a very, very warm one."

"There were for thirty minutes or so some real concerns that Patrick wouldn't be back," recalled Jeri Taylor, who had been promoted from supervising producer to co-executive producer. "Most of the people felt in all probability he *would* be back. The negotiations were difficult and had he not come back then the door would have been wide open." Reportedly, Stewart and his agent convinced Paramount and *The Next Generation*'s producers that he was ready to walk if he didn't receive a significant pay increase commensurate with his position and stature on the show, even more freedom to pursue other acting interests without the roles conflicting with the series' film schedule, and a contractual obligation by the producers that allowed him more input into the development of the Picard character. In addition, Stewart was vocal in expressing his desire to see the seventh season be the final year of his contract, whether or not the series was renewed for an eighth year.

Stewart agreed to return to the weekly grind of episodic television for one final year, with the promise that after *The Next Generation*'s seventh season the series would be canceled and the cast would make the leap to the silver screen. Although Paramount wouldn't make the announcement for several more months, *The Next Generation* theatrical feature was planned for release by Christmas 1994, to be shot after a brief respite following a moved-up seventh and final TV season.

Sergio Stewart

With a new contract structured to his liking, Stewart took an even more activist role in making *The Next Generation*'s sixth season more daring and provocative, often breaking its traditional format and dealing with more controversial issues.

"It was conscious," emphasized Michael Piller. "From the beginning of the sixth season we said let's take more chances. One of the problems in the fifth season was we said, 'Okay, it's not a great story but we need another story for this week so let's keep going,' and I think we said let's wake up and see how far out we can go the sixth year. We had some episodes that are as far out as any you've ever seen on this show."

In many ways, however, *The Next Generation*'s sixth season seemed like two completely different seasons. The year began with Part Two of *Time's Arrow,* in which Picard and his senior officers travel back to 1890s San Francisco to prevent Data's destruction by energy-consuming aliens. It was followed by several heavy high-concept science-fiction episodes, including *Realm of Fear,* in which nervous engineer Reginald Barclay encounters creatures in the transporter; *Man of the People,* where Counselor Troi becomes a receptacle for the negative emotions of an ambassador; and *A Fistful of Datas,* a Stewart-directed episode in which the holodeck malfunctions and results in a deadly Data gunfighter facing off against Worf in the center of a computer-generated town.

"I'm not a Western fan," said episode writer Brannon Braga. "I never really saw Westerns and Patrick Stewart, a British guy who's not familiar with the Western genre—and here we are doing our big Western show! But, I think, we brought a fresh sensibility to it."

"Patrick approached this with such zealousness—he went out and rented two classic Westerns every night," co-executive producer Jeri Taylor remembered. "The next morning he'd come in and tell us what great ideas he'd had, and we could always tell what he'd watched!"

The opening big boots/little boots scene was right from the Sergio Leone spaghetti Westerns—whose Clint Eastwood vehicle *A Fistful of Dollars* inspired the title—while the *Enterprise* flying off into the sunset at the episode's end was just the right touch. Even the music had a familiar feel: harmonica virtuoso Tommy Morgan, veteran of all those distinctive Western soundtracks of the past, was brought in with his packet of hand-filed instruments to record the soundtrack.

"This was a hoot! It was never meant to be anything more than old *Star Trek,*" said Michael Piller, who noted that the script met two of his pre-season goals: be more lighthearted and give Brent Spiner something more interesting to do. "The tricky part was not to make it broad parody but make it believable Western storytelling and still have fun just from seeing the characters in those situations."

"I had the chance to play five or six characters in a show and Patrick directed," enthused Spiner, "which made it additionally fun. It's certainly the most fun episode I've ever had to do and I would have liked to have done a show called *For a Few Datas More.*"

Stewart himself recalled the episode fondly. "There is nothing I have done in my career anywhere that could match the amazing thrill of directing a Western. There had been rumors around the production offices for some months that there was a Western episode coming up, and, of course, every director was eager to get a hold of it because everyone feels they have at least one Western in them. I was actually supposed to direct another episode when things were switched and the Western landed in my lap. I think there was a lot of gnashing teeth from some of my colleagues and the other directors, but it provided me with a fabulous opportunity to have an enormous amount of fun entering into the western.

"If I were to isolate the five or six best days of my thirty-year career to date, I think the one day, working from long before sunrise until after the sun had set, was at the Warner Brothers western town in the Valley," continued Stewart. "That was one of the most exciting days of my life. I had three cameras rolling almost all the time there, including an action slow-motion camera. I had the biggest crane that you could get in Hollywood. I had some wonderful toys to play with and it was an absolutely fantastic day. It was also one of the hottest days of the year, too, so it was truly a sunbaked Western scene. I shall never forget it."

Snubbed Again

The Next Generation's numbers for the first half of the season were so strong that its success led to a November 6 *Los Angeles Times* feature examining why the series had suffered so little from the death of Gene Roddenberry a year earlier, with the show's own average rating now at 13.5, or over twelve and a half million households—a 22 percent jump over even the prior year's new highs.

Intent on getting away from what Stewart termed "the soap opera" plots of the past year, *The Next Generation* writing staff's new focus on "high-concept science-fiction"—or—"weird shit," as Michael Piller phrased it— lasted through the first third of the season. With *Chain of Command*, a dark and conflict-ridden two-part episode, the season appeared to make a dramatic departure in tone and substance.

Originally scheduled to be a single episode, Michael Piller made the suggestion that the show be split into two parts to save money. "We were in budget trouble," said Jeri Taylor, "and Michael said, 'You know, I think what we could do is make this a two-parter. Have Picard captured and then make it an episode about his relationship with his torturer that takes place in one room. It's a fascinating two-person play and we'll get another episode out of it that way and we'll save a lot of money that will bring us even with the budget."

"The fundamental pitch the gang came in with was you have Picard on a mission and a new captain comes in and how does the crew react to the new captain," recalled Piller. "They wanted to put Picard in a real rugged adventure story where he gets caught by the Cardassians and we rescue him and that's about it. I knew if we divided it into two parts and made the first part the mission and then Picard gets caught, instead of resolving that in an hour, you put Patrick Stewart in a room with another great actor and you do the torture show. You call up Amnesty International and you get their cooperation, which is very important to Patrick, and you build a relationship between two men; one who is trying to beat the other and the other who is trying to survive."

Stewart, who is a member of Amnesty International and very good friends with the secretary-general of American Amnesty, was excited about the chance to delve into such a thorny subject and read numerous books and watched videotapes on the psychology of torturers, their survivors and everything else the organization could supply him with. Stewart also worked with a group that are surviving torture victims and he talked with a psychiatrist who specializes in treating torture victims.

"Patrick called me after reading the first draft," Jeri Taylor later remarked, "to say he was delighted to know that we were doing this and told me of his involvement with Amnesty International. I said, 'Great. I have to tell you that it's going to be rather substantially rewritten.' Patrick got very concerned because he assumed that meant we were going to back off from the very strong nature of it. He said, 'I don't want that to happen. I think that this hits it head on. I want to do that. I don't want this to become another talky episode where we simply talk about and around something and don't really tell it the way it is.'"

Stewart's concerns, however were shared by Taylor, who just didn't feel the script was working yet. "I said, 'Patrick, please trust me. We won't do that, but I think that we can get more out of the script.' And he was very uncertain and disconcerted. He said, 'Well, I'll wait until I see the rewrite, but . . .' and then he got the rewrite and called back. He was thrilled because we didn't back off an inch. It was very strong stuff."

Pleased that the episode's intensity had not been diluted, Stewart turned in a tour de force performance, in what many believed to be his most profound and focused acting on the series to date, if not in his career. In Part Two, Picard finds himself unable to prevent being mentally and physically assaulted and stripped and cuffed to a rack. A method actor, Stewart was, at his insistence, nude during the interrogation part of the episode but performed the scene on a set closed to almost everyone but absolutely essential crewmembers.

"It's a very gutsy and nude performance," said Brannon Braga of Stewart's acting, which provoked some protest among viewers. Added Jeri Taylor, "They didn't want to see Patrick Stewart or anybody else writhing in pain. They felt that it was too excessive, that it went too far and that it was disturbing to children. I can't disagree. It's certainly very intense for children. I wish there had been a disclaimer."

"Ultimately, the victory for Picard is just surviving," explained Michael Piller. "We made the decision early on that we couldn't say that Captain Picard was such a great man that he would not break under torture, because that would be doing a great disservice to everybody in the human rights struggle who has broken. Nobody can resist torture. Anybody who wants to get you to speak will get you to talk if they're willing to do the hideous things necessary. There had to be a different kind of victory. I can't imagine a better show than *Chain of Command, Part II* and it had no tricks or whiz bang stuff. David Warner [as the Cardassian torturer] was sensational and Patrick Stewart was even better. I don't think there's been a better show in the history of this series, and certainly there was not a better hour of television that year."

Piller took out a full-page ad in *Variety* to back an unsuccessful Emmy nomination for the actor. "There's just nothing better than putting Patrick Stewart alone in a room with one other good actor and really letting him go for an hour."

"It is not possible that there are five better male actors in this town than Patrick Stewart!" Taylor agreed. "It's probably his finest performance—he literally threw himself, physically and mentally, into that."

As usual, The Next Generation was snubbed in the so-called creative categories of TV's Emmy Awards, such as acting, writing, and direction—a division Rick Berman outright rejected. "Why somebody decides writing a screenplay is 'creative' and somebody scoring a soundtrack isn't is just ego," he said after Stewart's Emmy-worthy performance in Chain of Command was ignored.

"I'd like to think the Academy [of Television Arts and Sciences, awarders of the Emmy] is coming around, but we're a 'science-fiction' show, a 'sequel,' and syndicated," he noted—the three strikes against the series in a system dominated by traditional network-oriented voters.

Picard versus Sisko

In January 1993, midway through The Next Generation's sixth season, Stewart guest-starred in the two-hour pilot for Star Trek: Deep Space Nine, which drew a syndication high 18.8 for the season. By grounding the space station's Commander Sisko in the battle of Wolf 359 with the Borg (The Best of Both Worlds, Part I and Part II), it allowed appearances in both past and present by Stewart's Locutus and Picard, helping christen the new show as a guest star to lend the needed continuity.

"DS9's Commander Sisko is somebody who's lived a life of tragedy," explained Michael Piller, co-creator and an executive producer of the new spin-off series. "When Picard was with the Borg and led the Borg on their attack, he was a commander on one of the ships destroyed. Sisko lost his wife and now he's raising his son by himself and he hasn't really been able to go on with his life since he lost her. One of the arcs of the first story is some conflicts with Picard and how he gets by some of those things."

Just as Stewart had been compared to his illustrious predecessor, Avery Brooks, who plays Commander Sisko, immediately began hearing complaints from ardent *Next Generation* fans that he was certainly not a leader along the lines of the *Enterprise's* strong and admirable captain. Fans repeatedly voiced their objections that Sisko was too somber and stuffy, that he was no Jean-Luc Picard, for that matter, Benjamin Sisko was no James T. Kirk, either.

Offered Michael Piller: "The Picards and the Kirks were the explorers who made the first contacts. But after spending an hour on somebody's planet, it was 'Hey, whatever happens to ya, good luck!' Then there are the builders, the architects, the ones hanging around and making lasting contributions—and that's Sisko."

Fans also found *The Next Generation* spin-off's fundamental elements to be less attractive than its progenitor because the show was grounded in a space station. "*Next Generation* was already out there on the *Enterprise* and these two shows were supposed to run concurrently," Rick Berman explained in numerous interviews, "so there was no question that we needed to come up with something different—which we did. This show is definitely a little darker and there's a lot more conflict. . . . We also had to deal with the problem of doing a *Star Trek* show without a starship—trying to do a show based on a stationary location . . . and one of the things that Michael [Piller] and I did was take an entire season of *Star Trek* episodes and check to see how many of them could have easily been renovated to work on *DS9*. We found that all of them could have been, so there wasn't a big problem there."

Piller drew an interesting analogy between *Deep Space Nine* and its predecessor by comparing them to two popular comic book superheroes. "*Next Generation* is like Superman and *Deep Space Nine* is like Batman. Clearly, the complications and the psychological underpinnings and the quality of the storytelling and the angst is greater in Batman, but they both exist in the same DC comic universe and they occasionally meet. The point is, if you think of all the pale imitations of Superman, they have all gone right out the window but Batman has endured because it touches people in a certain, specific way. It is a more adult comic book and somehow we have managed to do that with *Deep Space Nine*. Batman was never as popular as Superman was, but it has its own special audience. I think we've got that on *Deep Space Nine*—at least I hope so."

Stewart had ambivalent feelings toward the new *Star Trek* series. "I feel a little protective of *The Next Generation*," he said. "It may be that I feel a little that *The Next Generation* might become less significant to people than it has been, and that there will be a newer, younger, hotter group of people working on *Star Trek*. Yet, as I know the kind of new series that it is going to be, I find myself very excited about its potential. It's going to be very different from *The Next Generation*. I think, in many respects, a much grittier show—a much rougher, tougher show. I think in the same way that *The Next Generation* has helped to intensify the enormous affection, love and enthusiasm for the original series, *Deep Space Nine* will probably do the same for us.

"When you look back over the last five years to the deep suspicion that many people had about *The Next Generation*," Stewart continued, "and how it was going to trash the original series and be a shallow, money-making rip-off and, now, it has become such a respected show with totally its own identity, its own characteristics, its own jargon, its own idols and icons, it really is amazing. I think *Deep Space Nine* could help us."

Piller believed that the arrival of *DS9* was the sole reason that *The Next Generation*'s revitalized sixth year is considered one of the series's most successful seasons both in terms of increasing viewership and quality. "*DS9* suddenly stoked the creative fires in a very constructive way. I concentrated on communicating that there was not an 'us-against-them' situation; that these were all people working on *Star Trek*, all in the same building, and we should help each other and contribute to the other's show and learn about each other's show and help the universe grow. What did come, however, was an attitude that we have to be on our toes because there is a parallel development going on, and whatever they're doing on that show over there, I have to be doing just as well over here. So it became a very healthy situation as far as I'm concerned and we began to see a restart of serious creativity in *The Next Generation*."

Stewart Gets Physical

After donning the "very uncomfortable" Borg makeup again for *DS9*'s two-hour premiere, Stewart returned to *The Next Generation* for *Tapestry*, one of his favorite episodes in which Picard finds himself in heaven with Q after being gravely wounded by terrorists during a diplomatic mission.

"I'm very proud of *Tapestry*," reflected writer Ron Moore. "I liked it a lot. I immediately fastened onto the idea of Picard going into the white light and having a near death experience and there's Q." Moore's first draft departed from the final script in many respects. Entitled *A Q Carol*, Q led Picard through pivotal scenes in his life much the way the ghosts of *A Christmas Carol* took Scrooge to the past, present, and future. The irony was not lost on Moore who was of course cognizant of Stewart's recent star-turn on Broadway as all the characters in the Dickens holiday classic.

"Q took Picard back to several points in his life," recalled Moore. "The *Samaritan Snare* story was one where he is attacked and needs to get an artificial heart. There was a scene in France with him as a kid with his parents and I even considered doing the *Stargazer* and having Jack Crusher there."

The premise for the episode, however, was not only too expensive but failed to excite Michael Piller. "He thought it was pointless," Moore said. "Here are some scenes from your life basically. It didn't have the right resonance so I went back and tried to focus in on one incident to make it a little more meaningful."

In the final draft of *Tapestry*, Picard tells Q that he cannot deny the regrets he feels about his rambunctious youth and wishes that he could change them. Q instantly wisks him back to the eve of one of his life's biggest turning points: the fight where, as a fresh-faced ensign just before shipping out, he is almost killed in a fight with three large Nausicaans. Determined to change history, Picard avoids the conflict which caused the brawl and Q returns him to the present where Picard finds himself in the midst of disintegrating friendships, a failed love affair and, ultimately, an unfulfilling career in Starfleet when he is returned to the *Enterprise* as a junior grade lieutenant assigned to astrophysics.

"It was an interesting little story about him," noted Moore. "That story, to me, said a lot about Picard's character—that he was a different guy in those days. Then he changed. Why did he change? What would be the difference in the young, womanizing, hard-drinking, hard-fighting Jean-Luc Picard and the guy that we know today?"

Even though Stewart thought it was an "excellent script which made a lot of people think about their lives and how they should accept themselves rather than wishing they had done something else," *Tapestry* was received less warmly by many fans who felt that the episode glorified violence.

"Some people were of the opinion that the episode basically says Picard tries to go back and not do the violent thing and solve things by reason and it makes him bland and not captain material," explained Stewart. "We got stacks of letters from fans complaining that the episode went against everything *Star Trek* stood for. I think they lost sight of the message."

Trekkers also protested the violent action/adventure concept of *Starship Mine,* the episode in which intergalactic thieves raid the *Enterprise* and Picard grapples with women in Ten-Forward, shoots another man with a crossbow, and pulls the plug on a container that destroys an entire ship.

This take on the movie *Die Hard* was so far off *The Next Generation* norm that Jeri Taylor predicted it probably wouldn't have been done in the years past. "It was very violent," Piller agreed, "but it's good to have one of these kind in the mix [of stories]. It didn't feel like *Star Trek* to me. I liked the show and thought it was very effective and well directed by Cliff Bole, but I was worried that it was very violent, which troubled me. Picard slugging it out with the two women wasn't silly, and Patrick did his usual fine job, but it was derivative."

"This was a classic example of a bravura role for Picard," countered Rick Berman. "It had a real tone and style to the look of the show and I think Cliff Bole did a nice job directing it. I enjoyed seeing Patrick as an actor being able to get physical."

Stewart enjoyed the break from the "sitting and talking" norm and did several of his own stunts, as he had in *Tapestry.* "I enjoyed the episode enormously," the actor said with a smile. "It's now in my top half of a dozen episodes. It was wonderful to be out of uniform for an entire episode and to be on the ship without any of the other boring crew members."

In a complete contrast from *Starship Mine,* the following episode, *Lessons,* which Michael Piller dubbed *Brief Encounter on the Enterprise,* sparkles from the chemistry between Stewart and actress Wendy Hughes. In the episode, Picard becomes romantically involved with the new chief of the Stellar Sciences departments, who shares a mutual love of music.

"We started thinking about this back in the fifth season when we were brainstorming ideas," recalled Jeri Taylor, "and Michael [Piller] said maybe it would be interesting to do a love story in which Picard is attracted to someone who is serving under his command. It had honesty and simplicity to it that was very engaging. Wendy Hughes, who is a wonderful actress, made the whole relationship believable. You believed that Picard would be enchanted with this woman."

The captain is seen wearing a shirt in *Lessons* from the Picard/Vash episode *Captain's Holiday,* but unlike Vash, this time around Picard is given a real peer and equal in Nella Darren—a quality that Stewart felt gave the match-up "true substance and genuine warmth" the actors could play from.

"We cast a woman who's closer to Picard's age than the women we've see him with in the past, like Jennifer Hetrick and Michelle Phillips, and we're all very happy about it," said recently promoted senior staff writer René Echevarria, who polished the script's final draft. "We wanted somebody who had weight as opposed to it being just purely sexual."

Lessons in Love

After ending the torrid affair with Jennifer Hetrick, Stewart, who was fifty-one years old at the time, started dating a string of young beauties, all of them eager to be seen with the sexiest man on television. But like his alter ego, the actor quickly grew tired of romancing women only half his age and longed for a woman who was truly his peer.

One day early in 1992, Stewart told Whoopi Goldberg how he felt about his love life while the two were sitting in makeup on *The Next Generation* set. A few weeks later, Whoopi ran into her close friend, forty-six-year-old Hollywood screenwriter Meredith Baer, at the Disney Studios, where Whoopi was filming the theatrical movie *Sister Act*. While the two women were having frozen yogurt in the studio commissary, Baer said she'd practically given up on finding a decent man to date in Hollywood. "They're all losers," she told Whoopi.

A week later, Whoopi invited Baer to a *Star Trek* cast party at Paramount and introduced her to Stewart. According to several of those in attendance, the two "were drawn together like magnets." The couple began dating and in mid-January 1993, Stewart proposed to Baer during a romantic weekend at an inn in Santa Barbara.

Reportedly, Stewart said, "I love you and I want us to be together for the rest of my life." Baer accepted and the first person she called with the news of her engagement was Whoopi. Although the couple didn't set a firm wedding date, they had made up their minds to tie the knot by the end of 1993 and wanted Whoopi to be the matron of honor at their marriage ceremony.

Within a year, the engagement was canceled and Stewart and Baer ended their relationship on a bitter note. Stewart went so far as to say in several interviews that he missed her cat much more than he missed her. But he was obviously heartbroken by the break-up. A short time later, Stewart described himself in an another interview as "passionate, intense, and who very much enjoys being in love" and "very susceptible to being hurt."

Stewart didn't mope around the set of *The Next Generation* very long, though. Only weeks after the broken engagement to Baer, the actor realized that the woman of his dreams was right under his own nose: Wendy Neuss, the attractive co-producer of *The Next Generation*. Although it took him almost a year to work up the courage to finally ask her out, the couple fell madly in love and began talking about her moving into his Hollywood Hills home.

Friends of the couple said that Stewart found Wendy to be the "perfect lady at all times" and she was charmed by the British actor's "elegant manners and his wit."

"I love her dearly—we're the perfect match for one another," Stewart happily announced. "We've known each other for seven years. It's been curious. I've heard about this happening, but I've never understood how it worked—when people who are good friends find a deeper relationship. And now it's happened to me, and it's just delightful. . . . She's making me tremendously happy, and I'm feeling better about everything . . . my career, my relationships with my kids, better than I ever did before."

Wendy, however, thought her significant other was anything but a proper British gentleman when he appeared on *The Tonight Show* in October 1993 and behaved like a lovestruck teenage boy with country-and-western megastar Reba McEntire.

"I remember the very first time I saw her [McEntire]," Stewart later recalled. "In my first year living in America, I was switching channels and this event was happening, and my finger hovered over the button, but it just went on hovering, because I didn't understand what was going on, but there were these extraordinary-looking people. What I had tuned in to was the Country Music Awards. The camera was panning along people sitting in the front row, and it passed by this redhead. That's all it did. And I leaned forward in my chair, as if I could have made the camera pan back again. Literally, my heart skipped a beat when I saw this woman. . . . And anyone who can sing, 'I walked into the kitchen, silverware's gone, furniture's missing, guess he got it all . . .' that's my kind of woman. One night I was on Leno. It was only some fifteen minutes before we went on the air, and I said, 'By the way, who's doing the show?' And they said, 'Reba McEntire.' My knees turned to jelly. So I immediately found out where her dressing room was and knocked on the door and gushed."

After Stewart went on the show, he spent most of the time talking about McEntire, telling Leno that his heart was still "going pitter-patter." When it came time to finally introduce the "Queen of Country Music," Leno told the audience that he felt "like one of those afternoon shows where the stalkers meet their victims."

"In fact, she asked if I could come on all her appearances," Stewart later said. "She even kissed me on camera, which was just delightful." He closed his eyes and smiled.

A year later, Stewart returned to *The Tonight Show* and told Leno that Wendy had not appreciated the ungentlemanly way he had behaved with McEntire during his last appearance on the late-night talk show. Leno then showed a videotape of McEntire admitting rather melodramatically that she "drew inspiration" from Stewart and gushed about how she wanted to drop her cloaking device and beam him on to her bridge anytime.

An obviously embarrassed Stewart told Leno that he was "really in trouble now."

Twelve

The Final TV Voyage

The character found the man, and the man found and made the character.

—Rick Berman on Patrick Stewart and Captain Picard

In May 1993, as *The Next Generation's* sixth season drew to a close with another Borg cliffhanger, it became official: Picard and Company were taking the *Enterprise* to the silver screen. Ending Paramount's promotion reel of upcoming projects at Las Vegas's *ShoWest* film exhibitor's convention, the studio announced to great fanfare the scheduled December 1994 release of the seventh film in the successful *Star Trek* movie franchise. Although they didn't make the announcement until August of that year, the seventh season of *The Next Generation* would be its last TV voyage.

The idea that the series was ending amid high ratings and critical acclaim angered many fans and the question remained: How could such a phenomenally successful show leave the air waves at the height of its popularity? Publicly, Paramount stated that they had gone as far as they could with a movie series featuring the original crew. The time had come for *Star Trek* to boldly take *The Next Generation* to the big screen. The studio reasoned that removing the series from television while still so popular would guarantee box office success. In addition, reruns of *The Next Generation* would undoubtedly air for years and years and there were two spin-offs to fill the vacuum: *Deep Space Nine* and the recently announced *Voyager* on Paramount's new television network.

"Paramount was looking at a 'mature asset' that could only get costlier," Associated Press reporter Scott Williams wrote a week before the series' finale aired. "At the same time, its revenues would remain relatively flat. . . . Folding *The Next Generation* tent lets Paramount close its books on one set of syndication deals and open them, more profitably, on another."

Stewart, however, was pleased that the series was ending after seven years. It was widely reported that his resistance to doing season eight was one of the main reasons Paramount canceled *The Next Generation*. "I am flattered by those remarks, that people should think that I have that much power," Stewart said. "I felt their timing was perfect. I liked the idea that we would end the series when we were on top. . . . I started to fear that I as an actor might start repeating myself. Days were not as interesting and as exciting as they had been and I was looking for fresh fields and pastures new."

Like Stewart, Brent Spiner was reluctant to play the android Data for an eighth season, and probably would not have returned had the series continued. "We had done 178 hours," he explained. "One hundred and seventy-eight hours of anything is just about enough, I think, and it was a brutal sort of seven years of work. I was glad not to have to get up at five in the morning anymore. I think we were really almost all ready to stop doing it. Maybe a couple of people would have been interested in doing an eighth season, but not many of us really. I think we felt, 'Yeah, we have done this now for seven years and with luck, we will get to come back and do it every couple of years.' I'd like to do more movies for the reason that I get to come back together with my friends and have some fun again. It would be like going to summer camp every couple of years."

Terrorist Suspect

But it was certainly no fun-filled day at camp during the summer of 1993, when Stewart was apprehended in London as an Irish Republican Army (IRA) terrorist suspect while visiting his children in England before filming began on *The Next Generation's* final season.

"The harrowing experience really unnerved me," the normally stoic actor admitted. "Around 6:30 A.M. I left my hotel for my customary morning jog. I chose to run in Green Park, which is right next to Buckingham Palace and near the side entrance to Clarence House, the residence of the Queen Mother and Princess Margaret."

Stewart decided to run around the edge of the park three times, which is equal to a distance of three miles. Unfortunately, he was not aware that the outlawed IRA had London in a panic with a widespread bombing campaign. Camouflaged soldiers with assault rifles and bulletproof vests had replaced traditional guards at Buckingham Palace and Windsor Castle, where Queen Elizabeth was spending a long weekend with family members. Security also was increased at St. James Palace and around No. 22 Downing Street, the working residence of the prime minister. Princess Diana, accustomed to driving around London without a bodyguard, was accompanied by a police officer twenty-four hours a day and told to vary her routine. Similar security was arranged for the Princess of York, Sarah Ferguson.

Earlier that day, a British citizen passing Clarence House had spotted a suspicious-looking package placed in a trash can and the area around Green Park was cordoned off by Scotland Yard's antiterrorist squad. "As I ran, I saw no other joggers or pedestrians anywhere. That seemed odd, but it was very early in the morning," Stewart said. "But I did see something unnerving. The usual unarmed guards at Clarence House and Buckingham Palace had been replaced by fatigue-wearing soldiers carrying automatic weapons. On my second lap they watched me closely. It made me feel uncomfortable. Then, as I started my third lap, a police car suddenly drove off the road, roared across the grass and screeched to a stop right in front of me. An armed uniformed police officer jumped out of the car and said, 'Sir, hold it for a moment! I want to speak with you!'

"The tough-looking officer asked me my name and what I was doing there, and he demanded to see some identification," Stewart continued. "That's when I realized I had no ID. I was wearing only jogging shoes, a T-shirt and shorts. The officer said, 'A man fitting your exact description has been observed placing suspicious packages in a rubbish container close to Clarence House.' He patted me down for weapons. Then I heard his partner inside the car refer to me on the police radio as a suspect."

Stewart was sure at that point that he was going to be jailed as a terrorist, but was extricated when the police officer in the car suddenly recognized him. "Ah, I know who this is! It's Captain Picard of the *Enterprise!*" Fortunately for the actor, *The Next Generation* was as popular in England as it was in America.

After a stern lecture about the need to always carry identification, even when jogging, the Scotland Yard officers released him. "If it had been *Star Trek*, I would have asked them to beam me up!" a relieved Stewart admitted.

Close Encounters

The Next Generation's seventh and final year on TV presented the series's staff and cast with some of its greatest challenges. It also proved one of the most difficult seasons for its writers, who were charged with creating another twenty-six hours of thought-provoking and entertaining episodes while Rick Berman and Michael Piller continued to expand the *Star Trek* franchise into new frontiers.

The Thanksgiving 1994 release date of the new *Next Generation* movie pushed up the series's shooting schedule a month and cut short everyone's summer vacation. "I'm not sure how everything got done," said Jeri Taylor, who supervised the writing staff during the show's final season. "Rick Berman not only took on developing a new series, *Voyager,* but also continued the development of a feature film. I think we were all being kind of pushed to our limits."

Taylor admitted that each year it got harder and harder to come up with fresh story ideas. "I talked to Patrick and Brent at one point and asked if there was any facet of their characters that they thought we hadn't explored yet, and both of them turned to me and said, 'Nope.' They couldn't come up with anything."

But the writers believed that the long-simmering relationship between Picard and Dr. Crusher needed to be explored in the series's final season with the episode *Attached*, in which the two are kidnapped, and through a telepathic link discover their true feelings for each other.

"I believe the actors wanted it, the fans wanted it, the writing staff wanted it," explained the episode's writer, Nick Sagan, son of the well-known physicist Carl Sagan. "But it was just the very top guys who felt that everything should be done with looks and suggestions and let the audience assume what they wanted from that."

Writing producer Ron Moore offered in his own view of the long-hinted-at spark between Picard and Crusher. "There was a real hesitancy of whether we should say any of the stuff up front or whether it should be all subtext. I thought, let's just do it and stop toying around with this nonexistent relationship. I wanted to do something that explained how he [Picard] felt and why he never acted on it."

Jonathan Frakes, who directed the episode, added, "We finally saw Picard and Crusher together and I thought it was great. I particularly liked the long scene of them together by the campfire where they really explored their relationship and their attraction to each other." A shared kiss and a hint of possibly more by the couple around the fire was vetoed by Michael Piller at a story break conference with "Absolutely not!"

Taylor recalled the fan buzz about the episode and addressed the complaint about Picard and Crusher not drawing closer at the show's end. "It's the question of how far do you go? How much do you push this? What do you say? What do you not say? Where do you leave it? Where do you go from there? It starts to become a soap opera, and Picard would be sealed off from other stories. Also it seems perfectly legitimate to me, emotionally, that two people must have gone that long without ever coming together—there must be a reason for it. I think the fans universally liked this episode up until the last scene and then many, many of them felt very cheated. There's a very vocal group out there that wants this to be explored even more and have them get married. Patrick doesn't feel that Jean-Luc Picard would move in that direction. We didn't consciously want to wrap up arcs or bring things to neat conclusions because, of course, the feature film series will continue so we didn't want that sense that we had sewn things nicely into a box."*

Sagan noted that the final scene in which Beverly rebuffs Picard's romantic advances was one of the most important scenes of the show. "I wanted to make the ending as heartbreaking as possible. I heard criticism of the episode from fans who said what was the point of the episode if they didn't actually get together, and I think that's really missing the point. It's really about people who make choices that prevent them from getting together."

When Beverly informs Picard over a wine and candlelight dinner in his quarters that she prefers to remain just friends, the usually stoic captain is obviously devastated emotionally. "I think Picard was shocked and very dismayed," commented Stewart. "I think it took a long time for him to get to the point where

---

* In the series' final episode *All Good Things* . . . Picard and Crusher have married and divorced twenty-five years in the future. However, *The Next Generation* writing staff consider that particular episode an alternate time-line, evidenced by the fact that the *Enterprise*-D is still intact although it is clearly destroyed in the *Star Trek* theatrical movie *Generations*.

he could make that proposal, and I think with customary male vanity he was a little surprised."

"That was really terrific," recalled Gates McFadden, who portrays Beverly Crusher. "I think Jeri Taylor has always been in agreement that we should do something with Dr. Crusher and Picard and pick up that thread again, which all the fans who write Patrick and me want to see. We've got so many letters asking what happened to their relationship. I thought the episode was terrific because it doesn't close the door at all."

The Last Hurrah

The season boasted several standout episodes as the series's final year evolved into a sort of family reunion, with more of the regular cast's backgrounds finally being revealed through the dangling threads of real or imagined relatives: La Forge's parents in *Interface*, Troi's drowned older sister in *Dark Page*, Crusher's grandmother in *Sub Rosa*, Worf's foster brother in *Homeward*, Data's "mother" in *Inheritance*, and even Picard's "son" in *Bloodlines*.

The workload of the actors and the frantic production schedule, however, took its toll on the cast, as evidenced by the rash of bad press they received during the weeks preceding the airing of the final episode. "The poor cast was exhausted," said Jeri Taylor. "Patrick, who directed *Preemptive Strike* just before the finale . . . was really going on adrenaline. I think everybody was stretched thin, but nobody slacked off."

"I was at times, anxious as to whether or not I would get through the end of the season," admitted Stewart. "I'm not being melodramatic. The producers had, once again, been very generous in allowing me to go off and do my *Christmas Carol* one-man show. This time

I had done it in London, so my entire Christmas holiday, which is the one substantial break we get in ten months, I was on stage doing a solo show. I flew straight back and went right back into production. Of course, they had saved a lot of heavy episodes for me. I still had one show to direct and I wasn't sure that I was going to be able to stay upright long enough to direct it. They found one for me, which was *Preemptive Strike*, and it turned out to be a show that I was very [performance] heavy in, which had never happened before. This was immediately followed by the final show. . . . It was a difficult time for me."

With the exception of *M*A*S*H*'s series finale or perhaps when Dr. Kimble finally caught the one-armed man and proved his innocence in the last episode of the classic *Fugitive*, it would be difficult to find two hours of television that was more eagerly anticipated than the finale of *Star Trek: The Next Generation*.

All Good Things . . . drew a 15.4 rating and 26 share in the 36 metered Nielsen ratings markets to become the all-time first-run syndication and *Next Generation* leader. According to Paramount Research figures, 35 million viewers caught the series's two-hour finale. But the highest-rated and most complex *Next Generation* episode ever had anything but a smooth ride, as one might expect from its scope and epic qualities.

"We knew since the beginning of the season that that episode was coming at us and would have to be done, and it was intimidating," said Jeri Taylor. "Any final episode of a series is unique and important and for a series like *Star Trek*, which has cut such a niche in the American consciousness, the expectations are really very high. When we started breaking the story, we were really flying by the seat of our pants. It seems that some of our best work gets done under pressure, because the adrenaline starts running and we just started brainstorming."

Recalled writing producer Ron Moore, who co-wrote the finale with Brannon Braga: "Michael Piller had some ideas we talked about early on. I had originally mentioned that Q should be in the final episode in a different context and Michael liked that idea and hung onto it. He said, 'I think you should have Q and I think it should focus on Picard and I think it should have some time travel elements in it," and then it was just a matter of trying to bring those ideas together."

"We wanted to end with a sweeping story that embodies the themes that have made *Star Trek* important to us," said Rick Berman, elaborating. "We don't tie up every loose thread because, hopefully, there will be a series of movies. But there is a very strong sense of finality—we owe that to the audience. Riker will not wake up in the shower and say it's all been a dream."

Complicating production on *All Good Things . . .* was a major script rewrite mandated by executive producer Michael Piller at the last minute. "I got more involved in this than I have on any show on *The Next Generation* for two years," he admitted. "I actually went into the room with the guys and we rewrote the story because it wasn't working. This became controversial because for the first time in four years, Patrick Stewart called me up after seeing the first and later drafts and said, 'I'm terribly unhappy with the changes made in the script.' "

Brent Spiner was another of the actors disappointed by the rewrites on the finale. "The first draft that Ron and Brannon wrote was extraordinary. I think it would have easily been thought of as the greatest *Star Trek* episode of all time. Michael [Piller] came in and added a few thousand words of technobabble to it and took out some of the character scenes, which he is not keen on. There were moments when I read the first draft that my heart jumped into my throat because I was so excited. There were some wonderful moments between Picard, Geordi, and Data. Nonetheless, it's still a very good episode."

Added Jeri Taylor of the *Christmas Carol*-like awakening Picard undergoes in the episode, "We wanted to tell a story in which we realized that all the parts of a person's life contribute to making them what they are. Their past informs the present, the present informs the future and determines what they will be. That was the underlying kind of thematic material that we addressed in the context of an epic/adventure which was still laden with a rich character story that we thought would leave no one disappointed. It has scope, it has action, it has humor, it has mystery and it's all packed into two romping hours. It's the quintessential episode."

Director Winrich Kolbe acknowledged the widely reported tensions among the cast members on the finale. "Even though they might say they're glad it's over, I'm sure they all have an ambiguous feeling," Kolbe said. "That's what created the tension. Yes, we want it to end because we have done it and we're bored with it. On the other hand, it's safety, and we don't have to sell shoes. Unfortunately, the movie was there and everybody, especially Patrick, was involved in the movie making, the script conferences. There were all these problems and those problems took away from attention being given to this particular show. So the best laid plans of mice and men began to crumble rather early in the shooting and we had to struggle. There was a lot of tension."

"It's been crazy here these past few weeks," admitted Gates McFadden at the time. "Last Friday I was on the set for literally *twenty-three* hours. These have been *inhuman* hours. People are just exhausted."

Marina Sirtis sounded like her alter ego, the *Enterprise*'s empathic counselor, Deanna Troi: "Psychologically, I think everyone is trying to detach themselves from the show and each other. People are subconsciously being pissy on the set so that it won't hurt so much when the show is finally over. I'm really very sad. In my head I thought we had another season left in us. So I feel a little cut short. I'd love to have done a little more with Deanna and then wrapped it up. Although I'm really very excited about the film, which I'm sure will be great, I'd be lying if I didn't say I wish everything were one more year away."

"If there's any truth to the rumor that our show makes Paramount $80 million a year, why in God's name do they take off the cash cow?" demanded Jonathan Frakes. "But they don't ask us, do they? One wonders if they aren't going to the well one too many times. I hope not. But it's certainly got to be a fear the creators have."

Michael Dorn tried to have a conversation with one of *The Next Generation* producers about the series finale. "But," he said, "she was [more interested] in talking about going on to *Voyager*. She's on her way and I felt like an old shoe. It's sorta like [they are saying], 'Hey, we've got a new group showing up, it's been wonderful, see ya later, have a good finale.' "

Although the cast had been throwing what *TV Guide* reporter Michael Logan called "hissy fits" about the ceaseless bombardment of news crews on the set, it was Stewart who showed the least amount of patience and tolerance during filming of the series finale, especially when he screamed at an interviewer and cameramen from *Entertainment Tonight*. "Towards the end, I got so tired that things got a little rough and raw for me," he acknowledged. "I know that there were all kinds of rumors circulating—all of them, for the most part, exaggerated—about my bad behavior on the set. It was entirely due to the fact that I was in every scene and I was trying to do the best job that I could and, at the same time, there were a lot of people with other needs and demands. I found it all a bit distracting."

But as the time arrived to shoot the show's concluding moments in which Picard joins the senior staff at the poker table, Stewart and the others couldn't help but wax nostalgic over the completion of filming on the series.

"This is an extraordinary ensemble show," Stewart said. "The people I work with on this show are the best people I've ever known. Their commitment, dedication, generosity, humor and willingness to accept such an oddity as myself into the group has been among the most significant experiences of the past seven years for me. . . . My saddest moment will be in the breaking up of this group. They are an outstanding group of individuals."

"A slight little pang of despair runs through me every time I realize we're going to be on the Bridge or in Picard's quarters for the last time," said Rick Berman. "There's no real sense of closure."

Marina Sirtis, a British expatriate who was cast as Counselor Troi just six months after arriving in the United States, was actually crying as the last scenes were being filmed. "These people—and my husband—are the only family I have in this country."

"Emotionally, I really haven't come to grips with the end of the series yet," said Michael Dorn. "I'll miss the laughter. I kept telling everyone I'll miss the laughter and the fun we had more than anything else. I never had this much fun on any of the sets that I worked on. But it's not an ending, we'll still have the conventions and the films."

"I actually feel great about it," said LeVar Burton. "This has been a very fulfilling seven-year cycle in my life, but I feel in my very being that it's time to move on."

"This is all very bittersweet . . . very bittersweet," admitted Jonathan Frakes. "It's a very revealing time for us all. I've been very lucky with Riker—he's a good and honorable man. I've always begged for a little more irony, but irony's tough to write. All things being equal, it's been a good lick, as they say. . . . I think *The Next Generation* was one of the best shows on television. When it was good, it was a great show. When it was bad, it was still good."

"It was good television which is a rare animal in itself," said Brent Spiner. "I think we satisfied the entertainment angle and, to a large extent, we made allusions to the world we live in. I think we could have been more hard-hitting. I think we waffled on a few issues because there were so many rules that were attached to the world of *Star Trek* and it would have been nice to break some of those rules and stretch the envelope and go beyond what we did do with this wonderful format. . . . I've done a lot of jobs I didn't particularly enjoy. I've done episodes as Data that I've enjoyed and episodes I haven't enjoyed. The one constant on this show has been the relationship with the cast. We've developed some really rich friendships, and I expect those will go on forever."

"The day I went down to say goodbye to Patrick on the stage, I felt a loss," recalled Michael Piller, who visited Stage 16 during the final evening of shooting *All Good Things* . . . "It's the loss I felt from missing a character that I've really become attached to. I think Picard is a remarkable character and Patrick Stewart made him that way. I'm singling out Patrick because he is a special talent."

One of the reporters visiting *The Next Generation's* set during the series's final hours of filming asked Stewart if he and his character shared similar personalities. "The edges between Picard and myself have become somewhat blurred," Stewart answered. "I'm not sure where one leaves off and the other begins. I think we've grown closer over the years. A lot of what I believe and what interests me and gets me attention has gone into Jean-Luc Picard. And some of him, I hope, has rubbed off on me. Politically, I think he and I share the same point of view. The fact he makes no distinction between people of different races, cultures, colors, educational backgrounds, economic circumstances, that is something that I have always believed in very strongly—equality for everybody. His loyalty is something I share. I also believe we have a similar stamina. We are great stayers. And I would like to think we share the same sense of humor."

Over the past seven years, Stewart was often described as being a prankster on the set. Gates McFadden said in a *TV Guide* interview that, "Patrick has a fabulous sense of humor, and you don't always see that in his character." Many times over the years when the cast regularly worked ten- and twelve-hour days on *The Next Generation,* it was Stewart who kept things loose on the set.

"At the end of a scene that had gone particularly well, I'd say 'Grown-up men doing make-believe in silly costumes,' which is how it often seemed," recalled Stewart. "We came to write alternative versions of almost every scene that we did. My favorite one was that Captain Picard was an unequivocal, mouth-foaming, ass-paralyzing coward who at the slightest mention of any trouble would leap into Number One's arms and howl that he didn't want to die, please, he didn't want to die."

When a *Playboy* interviewer asked him whom would he fire from the *Enterprise* if he didn't have to go through proper Starfleet channels, Stewart displayed even more of his wicked sense of humor. "I would fire Commander Riker because he perpetually reminds Captain Picard of his mortality, certainly as far as sexual matters are concerned. I would fire Commander Data because he doesn't seem to understand the meaning of the word concise. I would fire Geordi La Forge because his technical terminology invariably goes right over the captain's head and, therefore, I have to take recourse in simply saying 'Make it so' when it's perfectly clear that the captain hasn't understood a word. I'd fire Lieutenant Worf simply for being Lieutenant Worf. I'd fire Dr. Crusher because she has a look that is capable of suggesting not just two things but a dozen things—most of which the captain feels inadequate to cope with. And I would certainly fire Counselor Troi because her costume reminds me of how unattractive I feel mine is."

Stewart, who was rather solemn, rather overserious, and admittedly pompous at times during the first few years on the series, eventually ejected the persona of the conceited Englishman with a Shakespearean background. "By my age, I'm not supposed to change very much, and yet all my colleagues are convinced that has happened. Apart from the fact they claim that I've become Americanized, I feel that only means that I've become nicer. . . . The American way is to be much more open, much more frank, much more free with your emotions, to confess how you feel to people more frankly than the British do. I think that has been the major change in my life since I came to live here. I feel much more relaxed now. . . . But perhaps more important it has given me more fun and laughter than in all the forty-five years that have gone before.

"It will seem it has also changed the way I sound," Stewart continued. "After a recent interview with the BBC, the journalist, with an unmistakable sneer in his voice, commented upon my 'American accent.' Sadly, sneers seem to be one of the commonest sounds emanating from the United Kingdom these days. Well, I certainly wasn't aware that my accent had changed, but if it has, that's just fine with me. If nothing else, it means that I am still open to change."

Not one to adhere to any single genre of entertainment, Stewart hosted *Saturday Night Live* on February 5, 1994. In the opening monologue, he admitted that the only reason he was asked to be on the late-night comedy series was because of his role on the hugely popular *Star Trek: The Next Generation,* to which the audience replied with thunderous applause.

"Well, thank you very much," he began, "but I have a confession to make. When I was first given the role of Captain Jean-Luc Picard, I pretended to take it all in my stride. I was so cool in interviews. I claimed never to have seen the original classic *Trek.* But it was all an act, because inside I was so ecstatic . . . I was delirious. . . . You see, not only am I probably the biggest *Star Trek* fan of all time, but well, as my friends can tell you, I am virtually an encyclopedia of *Star Trek* facts and trivia.

"Everyone knows that the part of Captain James M. Kirk was played by William Shiner," Stewart continued straight-faced. "Then, of course, later he was to become very famous as *The Six Million Dollar Man.* . . . But can you name to me the ship's other medical officer . . . because of course, there were two. You see, you're stumped. You're forgetting Dr. Spock. Now you remember, right? He was the pointy-eared creature, you know?

Half-human, half volcano, and was forever tormenting old Boney with his cold volcano logic, and uh . . . all right . . . here's another bit of trivia. Did you know that another *Star Trek* character, Captain Sulu, was the first black woman ever on television? Anyway, being the *Star Trek* maniac that I am, well, you can imagine my feelings when I first learned that I won the role of Captain Picard. I felt a kinship, you know, with all those unforgettable, legendary characters. . . ."

Stewart concluded the monologue with a totally un-Vulcan-like greeting, "Live long and be happy," while simultaneously flashing the Boy Scout hand sign.

Unlike Shatner, who in his appearance as *Saturday Night Live* host infuriated *Trek* fans when he told them to "get a life," Stewart had the live audience rolling in the aisles and the show garnered impressive enough ratings to place it among the top five *Saturday Night Live* episodes for the 1993-94 season, a further testament to Stewart's enormous span of appeal.

Best Buddies

Unlike Captain Picard, who was remote and distant with his crew, Stewart became "best buddies" with the other cast members over the course of *The Next Generation*'s seven years on TV. He entertained them at his house in the Hollywood Hills quite frequently, laid down backup vocals with several of the cast on one of the tunes from Brent Spiner's album *Old Yellow Eyes Is Back* ("one of the best nights of my life"), took scuba diving certification lessons with Spiner, and during the series's sixth season, he starred in and directed his fellow shipmates, Spiner, Jonathan Frakes, Gates McFadden, and Colm Meaney in a production of Tom Stoppard and Andre Previn's *Every Good Boy Deserves Favour* A complex musical drama backed by a sixty-piece orchestra, the play opened to sell-out crowds and rave critical reviews in a four-city tour. "It never occurred to me to cast anybody else," said Stewart. "I wanted to work with my pals, and I wanted to have a new experience with them."

When asked by an interviewer what he thought the future held for his former cast members after *The Next Generation* ended, Stewart responded: "I have no doubt that Jonathan Frakes will have a marvelous career as a director. Brent Spiner is so multitalented that, given a personal choice, I would love to see him get a leading role in a musical or some dramatic play. In fact, one day I wish to see Brent play Stan Laurel—his likeness to Stan in his middle years is extraordinary. Within five years Michael Dorn will be a leading member of either the Royal Shakespeare Company or the National Theatre of Great Britain. Marina Sirtis will have a movie career. LeVar Burton will be a significant movie producer or director. And Gates McFadden will do some of everything: acting, directing, choreographing, producing."

A few months after *All Good Things . . .* aired and *The Next Generation* had gone into perpetual orbit in reruns, Stewart was asked if he missed doing the series. "I don't miss the work," he admitted. "But I miss my colleagues acutely. I know this sounds like sentimental hogwash, and you've probably heard it one hundred times before, but I speak it from my heart. We had the grandest group of people I've ever worked with and I miss them every day. I miss walking into the makeup trailer and starting to laugh. I would never have believed that one would start laughing so hard so early in the morning, as I always did. I laughed my way through seven years. I miss that."

Thirteen

Generations Gap

He's got great inner dignity. He has had to make things happen for himself. He is talented. He has a good heart, great soul, great generosity. He's steadfast and loyal. All the things you want in a friend.

—William Shatner on Patrick Stewart

It was hailed as "the most spectacular intergalactic moment since Spock was resurrected from the dead in *Star Trek III.*" In February 1994, at ShoWest, the movie theater owners' convention, Stewart and William Shatner, *Star Trek's* two legendary captains courageous, announced the highly anticipated motion picture melding of their two generations.

"The morning after *The Next Generation* aired for the first time [in 1987]," began Stewart, "I was gassing my car when someone stopped me and said, 'I loved your show—are you guys making a movie?' But I knew that a [*Next Generation*] movie would have to have Bill Shatner." He then turned to his *Enterprise* predecessor and proudly said, "In three weeks we will be sharing the same set."

The *Star Trek* captains past and present held hands at center stage while telling the assembled film exhibitors what a momentous occasion it was going to be to have the two *Star Trek* captains co-starring in the same movie. Fifteen minutes later, amid several rounds of applause and hearty pats on the back, they were backstage and ready to make a quick exit from what Shatner unflatteringly called the "hype and schmoozing."

"It was just past 11:00 P.M. and because both of us had early morning appointments, neither Patrick nor I was particularly looking forward to spending the night in Las Vegas," Shatner related in his *Star Trek* movie memoirs. "We quickly formulated a plan by which we might take advantage of our combined clout to commandeer Paramount's company jet."

That they did, and after years of rumors about one or both "captains" disliking the other, Stewart and Shatner's first lengthy face-to-face meeting took place in the middle of the night, over a "nice supper and a bottle of wine," while the Gulf Stream jet roared over the starry skies of Southern California.

"It was a little awkward," Stewart revealed. "Bill has a reputation, you know. He has a reputation of being rough, tough and pretty uncompromising with colleagues. Also, there were stories that he had made certain negative comments about *The Next Generation* when the series was first airing, back in 1987 and 1988. And it must have struck me that one day I would slap him about some of those remarks."

Shatner had said in many interviews: "I've never liked the idea of the new television show. I think it's a dangerous thing to call something *Star Trek* which, when asked, 'What is *Star Trek*?' and you enumerate the various things that are *Star Trek,* none of the things you enumerate apply to that particular series. . . . Frankly, until the movie came up, I hadn't given the idea of meeting Patrick much thought. I hadn't even watched the show because it was on at hours when I was busy."

During the hour flight, the two men effectively "cleared the air" and discussed their feelings about each other and their respective *Star Trek* series. Shatner conceded that he had initially vowed with other original cast members to stay away from *The Next Generation* and was extremely agitated and disappointed when he heard that Leonard Nimoy and James Doohan were going to appear on the new series. Stewart, in turn, confessed that he had deeply resented Shatner urging *Trek* fans in interviews and at conventions to boycott *The Next Generation* when it first premiered and was especially angered by Shatner's public remarks that "Stewart is not the captain, he's just a wonderful actor."

The two men talked about their very similar Shakespearean backgrounds (although according to several sources Stewart considered Shatner's name to be synonymous with brazen overacting). Stewart particularly found interesting Shatner's story of his triumphant turn in *Henry V* at Stratford, Ontario, when he went on unprepared in place of an ill Christopher Plummer in the title role and developed the distinctive Shatner acting style while groping for half remembered-lines. The performance earned him a standing ovation and great reviews from critics.

Shatner also admitted that the problem with his acting was that he apparently had never made the transition in style from stage acting to television acting. He confessed that his overacting and wild motions worked fine on stage, just not as well on a TV set where the camera picked up every move much better. A sympathetic Stewart agreed that he had had the same problem during *The Next Generation's* first season.

Stewart told Shatner about an old farmhouse that he had recently bought in his native Yorkshire, which

the Air Force flew high-speed sorties directly over.
Shatner urged him to march into the commandant's
office and say, "I am an actor who has returned home.
I am Captain Picard. And I request that, with all due
speed, you change the sorties to two to three miles
down the road, not over my house." Stewart looked
at Shatner and asked, "Do you think I could do that?"
Shatner replied, "Absolutely, Patrick! You go get it!"

Complicating their relationship to *Star Trek* was the
unique relationship between the two men and the legions
of Trekkers. Like Shatner, Stewart had begun resisting the
countless lucrative offers to attend science-fiction and *Trek*
gatherings.*

---

* Stewart was noticeably absent from a black-tie thirtieth anniversary
extravaganza for *Star Trek* fans in Dallas in the fall of 1995, which
was scheduled to celebrate the first time the captains from all four
Trek series would have appeared together at a single event. Although
a bleary-eyed Shatner had been on connecting flights for twenty-six
hours from safari in Africa and Kate Mulgrew and Avery Brooks' plane
had to make an emergency landing in Arizona on their trip from Los
Angeles, Jonathan Frakes had to fill in for the missing Stewart, who
was "preparing for the Broadway run of Shakespeare's *The Tempest*".

In thirtieth anniversary print ads for "The Grand Slam Show," *Star
Trek's* biggest convention in Pasadena, California in April 1996, or-
ganizer Creation Entertainment invited fans to "celebrate 30 years of
Star Trek, starring Patrick Stewart in his first US convention in over
TWO YEARS!"

Although his appearance was questionable because of on-location
filming for *Star Trek: First Contact* in Arizona, Stewart showed up
practically at the last minute and spent a great deal of time defending
accusations by fans that he was distancing himself from *Star Trek*.
One slightly angry Trekker compared him to Marlon Brando who
badmouths his employers and "bites the hand that feeds him." A red-
faced Stewart admitted that he would take Captain Kirk's advice in
Generations and "never give up the big chair."

"I was filming the TV movie *Death Train* in Zagreb [in 1992] in the new country of Croatia, which used to be Yugoslavia, during the hiatus from the series," Stewart recalled. "My girlfriend [Wendy Neuss] and I went to a restaurant in the old part of Zagreb late one Sunday evening. It was a very obscure restaurant in an ancient converted monastery, a very charming place, quaint, and old-fashioned in every way. It was almost empty and, in fact, I think there was only one other table occupied when we arrived without a reservation. An extremely dignified Croation in a tailcoat took our order speaking moderately good English, which was a relief to us since we didn't speak their language. Without any reference to the fact that he might've known who I was, he served us a bottle of wine and then brought us the salad that we had ordered as first course. I looked down at my dish and then looked at my girlfriend's and my jaw dropped open and my eyes filled with tears because, sitting in the middle of each of our salads, was an *Enterprise* carved out of peppers, carrots and cucumber! It was an immediately identifiable replica of the *Enterprise*— not our *Enterprise* but the original series ship. And not a remark was made throughout the entire evening, but the chef in the kitchen had done this thing for us. I can think of no more extraordinary confirmation that *Star Trek* is indeed everywhere!"

Shatner, in turn, related to Stewart the story of the time when he was in a taxi cab and the driver told him he was a big fan of the original series. "I thought, 'Oh, great! Stuck with a Trekkie and no escape.' But then the guy told me he had been a POW in North Vietnam, locked up in a tiger cage. He told me that he and the other prisoners kept their sanity by reenacting episodes from *Star Trek*, with each prisoner playing a role. The cabbie said, 'I just wanted to thank you for saving my life.' "

Stewart confessed that he was glad the weekly grind of the television series had ended, enthusiastically explaining that he could now return home and spend an extended period of time in London, really for the first time in almost eight years. Additionally, free of the grueling workweeks he'd grown accustomed to during the seven-year run of *The Next Generation*, Stewart was going to refocus his creative energies toward mounting other projects. "I have no doubt Captain Picard is going to dominate people's impressions of what I do," he said, "but I'm working damn hard to be seen as other things too."

Shatner, on the other hand, found himself regretting his decision to let Kirk die in the new *Generations* film and had begun feeling the emotional effects of saying good-bye to *Star Trek*. He declared the five-year mission that stretched to more than a quarter-century a good ride. "Because of *Star Trek*," he told Stewart, "I've had life-changing, joyous experiences, the likes of which only a handful of people have had. Nothing could have happened to me as a result of *Star Trek* that would mitigate the joy that I've had."

Shatner recounted a story that he'd heard about an African tribe who lived in the desert with barely enough food to survive. Their culture prescribed that the elders, the aged ones, the ones who depended on the younger members of the tribe for their welfare, go out into the desert and die. "That's how *I* feel," he told Stewart, as his eyes widened. "It's like this elderly captain's been asked to dodder off into the desert, lay down, gasp his last few breaths and die."

Finally, the two men discussed their interpretation of the *Generations* script and how they planned to play off the differences between the two captains. They agreed that Picard's quiet, dignified strength and reserve would best be accented by allowing Kirk's humor, energy and the rest of the larger, broader aspects of his character to rise to the surface.

When the Paramount jet finally landed at L.A. International Airport a little after 3 A.M., the two *Enterprise* captains disembarked as friends instead of enemies, despite tabloid reports that suggested that the Gulf Stream wasn't big enough for the two actors' combined egos. "When we finally came face to face in a properly relaxed way, I found him to be an utterly delightful, sensitive and gentle man," Stewart said of his *Generations* co-star.

"In terms of time and space, I feel that we would be very good friends indeed," Shatner later said. "He's a wonderfully interesting, extremely warmhearted man, and I was very much taken with both the man and the professional."

"This isn't a buddy movie"

"So you're the captain of the Enterprise?" *asks James T. Kirk.*

"That's right," says Jean-Luc Picard.

"Close to retirement?"

"I hadn't planned on it."

"Well, let me tell you something," Kirk says, reining his horse closer "Don't. Don't let them transfer you. Don't let anything take you off the bridge of that ship, because while you're there . . . you can make a difference."

The Next Generation movie rumor mill had been working for years. But Berman recalled being formally approached by Paramount motion picture executive⁻

Sherry Lansing and John Goldwyn about the possibility of the film in late 1992, four months before it was publicly announced. Including the original series cast was not part of their initial plan, but Berman and the eventual story developers ultimately agreed with Stewart's adamant recommendation that *The Next Generation* movie be a transitional film including Captain Kirk and the rest of the classic *Trek* crew.

"It had been an argument of mine that the film should include as many of the original *Star Trek* members as we could get," Stewart recalled. "For the most part, I was alone in this feeling. Most of my colleagues didn't share this point-of-view and felt, since this would be a transitional movie, we should just cut the original cast off. I felt having members of the original cast would provide the opportunity to present something really intense and dramatic. I was thrilled and relieved when offers did go out to the original cast."

According to co-screenwriter Ron Moore, one of the earliest concerns was exactly how the two crews would be brought together, and to what extent. "For a while, we were intrigued with the 'poster' image that we wanted, which was the two *Enterprises* fighting each other. We thought that would be really cool: Kirk versus Picard! But we just couldn't come up with something where it was plausible that they would both be at such odds that they'd be fighting against each other, and the audience is still rooting for them both. It just had too many difficulties to set in place, so we abandoned it. And then it was Rick [Berman] who came up with the format of 'how about a mystery that starts at the time of the original series—fade out—and then pick up *The Next Generation.*' That is, a mystery that spans two generations. Once we had that in place, then we started looking for ideas—what story it was going to be in. How would the two crews meet? Would there be time travel? Do the *Next Generation* characters go back? Do the original series characters go forward?"

Initially when the first draft of the script was handed in, it featured an opening sequence that starred the entire original cast. For various reasons—including the displeasure of some actors with the size of their roles and/or salaries—only Shatner, James Doohan, and Walter Koenig signed on.

"It saddened me when only three of the original cast were in *Generations,*" Stewart said. "I was particularly saddened that Leonard [Nimoy] and De [DeForest Kelly] were not in it. I felt they would have made a marvelous contribution for the final send-off, no matter how small their speaking parts might have been."

Leonard Nimoy later recalled: "I was sent the script that Rick Berman wrote and was asked to direct as well as act in it. I had a number of concerns. For one thing, Spock's role was no more than a cameo, a walk-on; he served no function at all in the story. He was simply there for his marquee value. So when I went to meet with Berman, I relayed that concern, along with others. He told me he thought there wasn't enough time to address them, and we parted company. . . . Later, I spoke with my dear old friend De Kelly on the subject. De had also met with Berman, and his response was one that echoed my sentiments: 'I had a better exit in *Star Trek VI,*' De had said. 'Why should I muddy it up?' He also had told Rick, 'If Leonard isn't going to be involved, then I won't be, either.' "

"The other characters all had relatively minor roles," admitted Berman. "And in the case of Leonard and De Kelley, they both felt that they had made appropriate good-byes in *Star Trek VI* and there was no reason to bring their characters back—I wouldn't call them cameos, but they were only in the first fifteen minutes and that was it. In the case of Bill [Shatner], it was a whole different story. His part has a great deal more depth to it."

Although Stewart was disappointed that most of the original cast members declined to be in the movie, he believed that the only integral character from the first series was Kirk. "Critical to all this was to have Bill," admitted Stewart. "I was so anxious about whether or not he would want to do it. It would have been a bitter disappointment if he had pulled out. I felt that having the two captains share screen space was something audiences would enjoy seeing."

Generations director David Carson understood the implications of bringing together the two pop-culture legends. "I'm well aware that Kirk and his crew are American icons who have achieved a certain mythology in American folk art, if you like. They have a very specific place beyond simply being characters in a TV show. And I am aware of the responsibility of having Kirk and Picard together. It's very tantalizing to have them in the same place, interacting."

Similar problems arose from within, when several members of *The Next Generation* ensemble complained about the cameos relegated to series regulars. One cast member lodged enough protests that the role lacked meat that a fate worse than death was finally threatened—being written out of *Star Trek* altogether. Another, Gates McFadden, who played Dr. Crusher, said, "I was very disappointed in the size of my role. I was hoping to have something more substantial."

"The script changed so much and we were really cut out of the other part of the story," said a disenchanted Jonathan Frakes. "Worf and I have the 'B' story now and, originally, we were tied in a little bit to the Nexus story. Now we no longer are. It's like a big Picard episode."

Co-screenwriter Brannon Braga pointed out that through the course of a television season there were twenty-six hours to explore the various characters, where as *Generations* would have, at the most, two hours to tell its story. "The movie's about Picard and Data. To an extent, it's about Kirk. The other characters all have great moments, Dr. Crusher the least of which. But this is just the reality of our time situation. We just felt it had to be about Picard because he's our captain and our primary focus."

"Actually, I had some misgivings about doing the movie," Stewart confessed. "I felt we had done many excellent TV episodes, but once the writers gave the movie an 'epic adventure' quality rather than a 'television' feel, I was hooked. During the months prior to filming my attention shifted to the character of Picard and in creating a storyline for the captain which had something more than just the narrative sequences in it.

"One of the things I was happy with was that through meetings with the writers and producers," continued Stewart, "we developed a B story for Picard that is very private, personal, and a very intense emotional story that runs parallel to the main action story. I'm a little disappointed, though, because I had come up with a good name for the movie: *Star Trek: Rites of Passage,* and for a while it looked like they were going to use it. But then they went back to *Generations.*"

Originally, Picard's personal tragedy was limited to his brother, Robert, dying of a heart attack in his vineyard in France. But then Stewart suggested that a horrific fire killing both Robert and nephew Rene would add emotional impact. "I felt that those scenes deepened the emotional experience for Picard of what was going on elsewhere in the film. I found that what we did with Picard in the film was what we were trying to do in the series. I did not want us to ever lose any of that character substance, which is what made Picard so substantial over the years."

Stewart strongly believed that the biggest challenge in making the first *Next Generation* movie was to make the best film first and to make the best *Star Trek* movie second. "Although we know there is a massive worldwide audience out there that will go see the movie," he said, "I didn't want this to be something that would be so elitist that it could only appeal to fans or to those people who had been watching the series for the past seven years. I wanted it to be a movie that someone who had never heard of *Star Trek*—if such a person exists—could sit down and enjoy it and not feel excluded. In advance, I felt that would be the biggest challenge."

Some fans expected fireworks from the teaming of Stewart and Shatner—on screen and off. While the tabloids focused on a persistent feud between the two* (categorically denied by both actors), the greatest amount of attention was probably aimed at the reshooting of the film's climax. Several publications, most notably *Entertainment Weekly,* indicated that a test screening turned out to be a "major disappointment." Those surveyed reportedly complained that they'd expected more Kirk—specifically, more Kirk and Picard. "This isn't a buddy movie," said *Generations* screenwriter Brannon Braga. "People may be anticipating a Kirk-Picard *Lethal Weapon* experience. That's not what they're going to see."

---

* Interestingly, all the tabloid reports and industry rumors circulating in March, April, and early May 1994 about the two actors not getting along on the *Generations* set were absolutely untrue. Shatner and Stewart didn't even work together until May 24, when they filmed their first scene.

"The problem," Stewart explained, "occurs after we've brought the two captains together. It's the moment where Bill says, 'It sounds like fun,' and we go galloping off to save the universe. When we arrived down on the planet, basically I said, 'Okay, Captain, you go that way and I'll go this way,' and we split up. Whereas what the fans wanted to see was the two captains shoulder to shoulder. That was the whole point of bringing us together, and that's not what it was. So the reshoot was a very sensible action. I think there could have been even more of that 'buddy' quality about the last part."

Stewart detested returning to the 105 degree temperatures, hot winds, and fierce sand storms atop a rise in the remote Valley of Fire in the Nevada desert to refilm the climax, but nevertheless was pleased that the ending was being reshot in order to enhance the movie. "The new ending has much more interaction between Kirk and Picard. You see that they like each other, they're friends, and when Kirk does make a heroic gesture that ends in his death, it's that much more poignant that these two friends, having barely gotten to know and respect each other, have parted so soon."

Stewart admitted that he was extremely nervous when he sat down to watch the finished product at one of the studio's private movie theaters. "My biggest fear was that I would find that what we had made was just an extended version of the series. I don't think there is a scent of TV anywhere about this movie, and it was a great source of satisfaction for me. It looks like a super movie from the beginning to the very end. That I was most pleased about. I was very uncomfortable that we might be embarrassed by the end product, but it is a *substantial* feature film and I'm really proud of it."

Stewart's co-star Jonathan Frakes concurred with his captain. "I liked the movie very much. I liked the tone of it, I liked the look of it and I thought William Shatner was fabulous. He had his tongue so deeply embedded in his cheek—his character was so perfectly tuned that he was just on the edge. He had that twinkle in his eye. I thought he and Patrick worked brilliantly together. I was very impressed with the way we all made our transition to the big screen. I think the movie came off better than people anticipated. I think it's the best *Star Trek* movie ever made."

Generations opened in theaters across America on November 18, 1994, and boldly went where no previous *Star Trek* movie had gone before—grossing $23.2 million at the box office during its first weekend in release, which was the largest opening for any of the previous six *Trek* films.

But *The Next Generation's* first silver screen voyage was unmercifully savaged by the critics. *USA Today's* reviewer Susan Wloszczyna wrote, "Bottom line: The highly awaited time-travel teaming of Picard and Kirk . . . isn't quite the clash of the follicle-impaired titans that it's meant to be."

Michael Medved of *Sneak Previews* complained, "This bloated bomb turns *Star Trek* into *Star Drek*. It's the seventh motion picture in this profitable series and by far the worst—even less satisfying than *Star Trek V: The Final Frontier,* the previous runt of the litter. . . . Unfortunately, the lavish sets and dazzling explosions only provide distractions in the midst of the plodding plot, which culminates in an old-fashioned fist-fight involving three superannuated actors (Shatner, Stewart, and McDowell) whose stodgily choreographed fisticuffs resemble the bare-knuckle brawls in Grade-B westerns of sixty years ago."

The cruelest remarks came publicly from within the *Star Trek* family. Even Leonard Nimoy said he had a sense of deterioration about *Generations*. "I think it had more sales tools to work with than, say, *Star Trek V*—the two captains—and therefore it was a crossover movie that attracted a lot of press and fan attention. *Generations* was a media event—two captains meet at the Nexus. Okay. Something to sell. And they sold very hard on it. The campaign was a slogging campaign—get it out there, talk about it, sell it. But I didn't think the picture was very good. . . . My God, what are they doing? Why that scene? What's this scene about? Where are they going with this, and with that? That was the reason I wasn't involved in making it, though it was offered to me to direct."

Generations marked Rick Berman's first outing as a major film producer, but he was also dissatisfied with the final cut. "I think it did well by both captains. If I have one criticism of the movie, it's that we had too much plot. If I had to do it all over again, I'd simplify the story."

The general consensus among film critics was that *Generations* succeeded mostly due to Shatner's presence in the movie. Michael Logan of *TV Guide* commented that "William Shatner was an absolute delight. In fact, many feel he stole it right out from under Stewart." Another critic blasted the classically trained actor during his review of *Generations* on a syndicated radio show by saying, "Shatner, with his trademark hamminess, quite handily eclipsed the Shakespearean-trained Stewart, who in the past has always remained a master at suggesting the complex emotions that underlie Picard's stalwart exterior."

Mark Altman, writing for *Sci-Fi Universe,* wrote that "Shatner's charismatic Kirk blows the more subdued Stewart off the screen. The writers make the fatal mistake of making Stewart's Picard a passive hero who is constantly reacting to everything going on around him, practically begging Kirk to join him in fighting the nefarious Soran who is bent on destroying a sun to change the course of an interstellar Nexus in which time and place converge. Shatner's Kirk, true to form, is an active hero full of humor and bravado and a far more commanding presence than Picard, who is reduced to taking orders from Kirk."

"I think the film has some good points about it," Shatner later said. "But I thought it was a little disjointed, a little slow. It lacked an emotional cohesiveness."

The morning after the New York premier for *Generations,* a reporter asked Stewart how it felt for a Shakespeare veteran of his background and stature to be upstaged by Shatner's shtick. "I got top billing," he answered, "but Bill obviously got the big scene."

Fourteen

Finally Out of Uniform

I hope I have a lot of working life ahead of me and I don't want to become handicapped by Star Trek.

> —Patrick Stewart explaining why he made a conscientious effort to distance himself from the Captain Picard role

William Shatner played an aging Los Angeles police officer named *T.J. Hooker* Leonard Nimoy directed successful mainstream Hollywood films like *Three Men and a Baby.* And Patrick Stewart managed to avoid typecasting by accepting other acting offers while he was still employed as Captain Jean-Luc Picard.

"The Next Generation has opened up many exciting possibilities for me as an actor and has allowed me to focus on the role and not the paycheck," Stewart said at the time. "I'm in a position to initiate work myself which I have never been able to do before. I think, for any actor, arriving at that stage, it's got to be a very exciting time because it takes me out of the situation

of being simply a passive individual, waiting for the phone to ring and someone to offer you a job, to being in a situation where I can plan my future and plan my work and particularly do that which I most want to do."

During the last four years of *Star Trek*, Stewart's famous vocal chords were hired to portray Number One, the leader of a secret brotherhood on *The Simpsons*, and film audiences saw him in Steve Martin's *L.A. Story*, as King Richard in *Robin Hood: Men in Tights*, and in the made-for-TV movie *Death Train*, in which he played the senior member of the United Nations Anti-Crime Unit. "There are some aspects of Picard in that character and the fans of the show will probably see some similarities. Although he's much more British than Picard."

Blood and violence dominated his next movie, *Gunmen*, which co-starred Christopher Lambert and Mario Van Peebles. "I'm at the right age now to play the heavies. . . . [In the film] I'm an utterly despicable, vicious, cruel drug baron, who creates horrible deaths for people and he, himself, dies equally horribly at the end of the movie," Stewart said. "Although this man is the head of a huge, elite criminal organization, I suppose the leadership qualities are there. But that's where any of the similarities end with Picard. I'm sure it will be amusing for fans of the show to see me in a role of that kind."

Although Stewart was finally nominated in 1994 for an Emmy as well as for a Screen Actors Guild award for his portrayal of Picard, Stewart did not rest on such accolades and made a conscientious effort to distance himself from *Star Trek*. "All of this was very deliberately and carefully chosen because I did have genuine fears that the role might become an albatross around my neck," Stewart confessed. "I hope I have a lot of working life ahead of me and I don't want to become handicapped by *Star Trek*. So far, it seems that, on the contrary, it has opened up all kinds of interesting opportunities for me. It changed everything. Now I have entered somewhat uncharted territory where I now have the luxury of picking and choosing projects."

Picard made him a star, but Stewart wanted to work whenever he could. "I refuse to get sucked into this debilitating class structure of the 'Hollywood actors' world," he told an interviewer. "I get so angry at the thought of narrowing these parameters of work, just to stick to a supposed 'image' the world might have of you. Blow that image apart as often as possible, I say."

After completing *Generations* and licking his wounds from the universal criticism that he was upstaged by the showboating Shatner in the movie, Stewart moved swiftly from one project to the next. In the live action/animated feature *The Pagemaster*, he voiced a character along with other *Trek* veterans Leonard Nimoy and Whoopi Goldberg, though he never actually worked with them due to the vagaries of the animation voicing process.

"It's the story of a timid young boy, played by, Macaulay Culkin, who finds the world a frightening and perilous place," Stewart recalled. "As a result of an accident he has in a library, Macaulay enters the world of childrens' fiction as an animated character. In this role, he encounters three generic figures, Fantasy, Horror and Adventure, and I play the voice of Adventure, who is represented as an 18th-century English seafaring man.

"With these three figures, the boy goes on an incredible journey full of perils, danger, excitement and glamour," Stewart continued. "As a result of the experiences, he finds an essential courage in himself and learns that he can stand up and face the world. Most significantly, and this is why I think it's a really important movie, he finds the world of literature and discovers that you can have as many adventures as you wish just by turning the pages of a book. It's a delightful movie, very entertaining."

In Stewart's next movie, *Let It Be Me,* the actor slapped on an American accent and a white wig. ("I have such a strong, dominant presence without my hair, I'd really like to try something else.") In the romantic comedy, Stewart portrayed a New York ballroom-dance instructor and something of a hustler, who encountered a beguiling, mysterious, and unusual woman played by veteran actress Leslie Caron. To prepare for the film, Stewart took crash courses in dancing with his girlfriend Wendy Neuss while they were vacationing aboard the QE2 and learned to convincingly waltz, fox-trot, and quickstep.

"I had the delightful experience of dancing with Leslie down 57th Street to the sound of Frank Sinatra singing *Don't Blame It On My Heart, Blame It On My Youth,*" he enthused. "I thought that should mark the end of my career. I don't think it could ever get any better than that." Unfortunately, most of Stewart's and Caron's parts were edited out of the movie's final cut and Stewart was obviously incensed. "I don't get angry about many things in life, but this *really* angers me," he told a group from one of his fan clubs in New York. To Stewart's relief, however, the producers of the film decided not to release *Let It Be Me* in movie theaters after it proved an "overwhelming major disappointment" at an audience test screening.

Stewart's voice, though, was even better known than his face, thanks to his work in TV commercials as he continued to do voice-overs for RCA, MasterCard, and General Motors. "In the case of the Pontiac commercials, it was a terrific contract financially," he told an interviewer from *Playboy* magazine. "I got more direction as an actor in fifteen minutes in that sound studio, in a satellite hookup to Detroit with people I have never met—detailed, acute, intelligent, sensitive direction—than I might get in six months of doing *Star Trek*. These guys are paying a lot of money and they want it *exactly* right, in twenty different ways. So in a thirty-second commercial they will say, 'We would like you to shave two tenths of a second off this take.' I love that."

Stewart also utilized his rich baritone to narrate documentaries like *From Here to Infinity* and its sister production *The Planets*, the Turner Network's *The MGM Story* and an exposé on serial killers. "The producer, Mark Olshaker, made a documentary about Kenneth Branagh's* *Hamlet* in England, and asked me if I would narrate it, which I did. . . . Then he sent this shocking documentary about serial killers. The best part was that he found out that the guys at the FBI were some of the biggest fans of *Star Trek: The Next Generation,* and that there's a standing invitation to go to Washington and look around the FBI offices, which I will definitely do someday."

In addition to performing his staging of *A Christmas Carol* on Broadway again to sellout audiences and finalizing plans for a television adaptation of the one-man show, Stewart began writing an hour-long drama

---

* Olshaker asked Stewart to narrate the documentary on stage and film star Kenneth Branagh because the former Shakespearean actor had known Branagh ever since his days with the RSC in England. 'I knew Ken when he was first in the business,' Stewart told an interviewer with *Movieline* magazine. 'I auditioned him, and then employed him. He was the most brilliant and most gifted young actor that I had ever seen. Who knew what an epic figure he would become?'

that explored what happened to Pontius Pilate on the day of Christ's crucifixion. "It's an hour-long TV play, an adaptation of a section of a novel called *The Master and the Margarita,*" he told a reporter from *TV Guide*. "It's about the most famous day in the history of the Christian world—the day of the Crucifixion—as seen exclusively from the point of view of Pontius Pilate. In the Bible, Pilate is only seen in the morning when Christ is brought before him. I take it further."

Stewart, in a similar spirit, was offered the role of Hitler in a black comedy but eventually declined after deciding it was just too tasteless. "I never agonized over a project so much," he confessed in an interview in 1995. "It was a brilliant script, an extraordinarily brilliant examining of who this man was. I was very excited by it, and we went so far as doing makeup tests. Finally, I had to turn it down because in this year, when so many anniversaries have been coming up of the pain and suffering of the camps, I could not go to a studio every day and stick on that mustache, put on that wig, put on that uniform, and pretend to be Adolf Hitler. . . . I just felt it would be insensitive. It wasn't finally until I saw myself looking so astonishingly like the man, that I decided I did not have the heart to do it. I still wake up in the middle of the night and ask myself if I made a terrible mistake. But I followed my heart."

Stewart summed up his post-*Generations* future by stating in an interview: "For the first time in my life, I feel that I have a large measure of control over what I'm doing and whom I am doing it with. I've also been very open to what proposals other people make to me. . . . I think one has to stay open to the unexpected—when someone comes to you and says, 'Here, I bet you never thought of doing this but I think you should do it.' "

Within Shouting Distance of an Oscar

In a dramatic departure from his Captain Picard role, Stewart took the advice of his agent and accepted the role of a flamboyant, razor-tongued gay interior designer in *Jeffrey*. "It's the first gay role I've ever played," Stewart said. "I'm thrilled to be doing it. I confess to being a little nervous at the beginning. My agent brought me the script. We'd discussed that the first major part I should undertake when [*Generations*] was complete was something that would take me as far away as possible from Captain Picard, science-fiction and spaceships. So to be playing a contemporary middle-aged gay man in New York was a dream for me, and absolutely perfect. . . . Those who knew my work before *Star Trek*—and I did have a life and career before *Star Trek*—will certainly not be surprised."

Did Stewart expect any backlash from fans who saw him only as the *Enterprise* captain—the man's man and the lady's sex symbol? "I have a feeling there is going to be some consternation in some areas," he acknowledged. "In the public mind there's no confusion—I *am* Captain Picard and that's that. People said to me, 'Is *Jeffrey* a good career move?' When I played Shylock, did anybody say, 'How do you feel about playing a Jew who wants to cut the living heart out of a Christian?' It didn't damage my career at all. I've played Leontes, who tried to kill one of his children. It didn't damage my career. I don't understand how people could think that playing a homosexual could be harmful. That's not an actor. That's somebody who's more concerned about his own image. . . . I don't choose roles wondering whether fans will be shocked or pleased."

Jeffrey, a sexually and politically daring film about a gay man's love life in the age of AIDS, was adapted from an off-Broadway play by gay playwright Paul Rudnick.

The film starred Steven Weber, perhaps best known for his work on TV's *Wings*, as Jeffrey, an actor-waiter afraid of intimacy; Sigourney Weaver as Debra Moorehouse, a New Age evangelist; and Stewart as Sterling, a bourgeois decorator with a mile-high attitude.

Stewart's role in the film was just the sort of uncharted tragic/comic territory he relished. "I've not played many men who appear to be living their lives on a fairly superficial level and who are also witty and entertaining," he said. "The challenge was avoiding stereotypes. I asked [director] Christopher Ashley to slap me if I did anything clichéd. I didn't want the character to be two-dimensional."

Stewart said he took the part because he saw the stage play which saddened him *and* made him laugh. While filming the final scenes in *Generations*, he read the screenplay for *Jeffrey* high atop a rise in the Nevada desert and was once again moved by the story's "candid humor amidst a fatal epidemic." He believed he couldn't *not* take the part, even though friends and colleagues questioned why he chose it to be his next major film role after *Generations*. Stewart felt he had no choice, that he was compelled to become part of the movie, despite others' misgivings.

"I felt an acute sense of responsibility to play Sterling accurately," he said. "I'm not sure to whom I was feeling responsible, but I felt it."

Stewart's character in the film denies impending tragedy, convinced that his HIV-positive lover will never die. When death does comes, it opens up what *USA Today* writer David Patrick Stearns called "dramatic terrain that could put Stewart within shouting distance of an Oscar nomination."

Stewart drew on personal experience to play the part of Sterling. In appearances and interviews promoting *Jeffrey's* release, the actor became noticeably subdued as he recalled the details of losing a close friend to AIDS a few years earlier. But while his friend's death helped him understand Sterling's character more fully, even that loss did not prepare him for New York's dizzying merry-go-round of memorials, funerals, and fund-raisers.

"In this city, as I learned when we began making this movie, people are attending the memorial services several times a week," Stewart said, visibly shaken. "I had no conception of that, not on a personal level. I had my friend's death, and a few other colleagues and acquaintances, but even then I did not have a comprehension of scale and the devastation that it's created."

"Playing gay was not an issue for Patrick," said *Jeffrey* co-star Bryan Batt, who played Stewart's on-screen lover. "I was almost starstruck playing opposite him. But he had no phobias about it, no trouble at all."

Stewart, always the consummate method actor, had fond memories of a photo session he did with Batt on the streets of Manhattan to produce shots of them as a gay couple that would be displayed in the apartment their characters shared. "The photographer went off with Bryan Batt and myself, and Bryan and I walked through the Village as, for all intents and purposes, two lovers out on a sunny Saturday afternoon," Stewart explained. "The photographer, using a long lens, took photographs of us from a distance. I would be dishonest to myself if I did not say that it was a curious feeling—because we were not in front of a camera, we were not on a stage."

Was Stewart afraid of being harassed or being name-called as he walked through the streets of Manhattan arm-in-arm with another man? "I was not at all uneasy about being identified as Patrick Stewart. . . . I was uneasy about being identified as Jean-Luc Picard!"

"That was the most wonderful day, posing in front of houses with our arms around each other," Batt admitted. "When you have so much respect and admiration for someone, it is incredible to have the opportunity to do something like that with him."

Jeffrey playwright and screenwriter, Paul Rudnick, was also equally impressed with Stewart's liberal attitude. "Patrick could care less what kind of rumors or gossip are circulating about him. I think he relishes it."

An interviewer with *The Advocate* told Stewart that many people believed for whatever reasons that the actor was gay. "Maybe there is something that is observable, that I am unaware of, that people are reacting to," Stewart replied. "If there is, I can only say that I feel very good about it. From an evolutionary point of view, the acceptance and embracing of aspects of one's personality is wonderful: To feel areas of vulnerability that I have not in the past associated with being a man. To also be able to admit, as I have been able to in recent years, to deep love and affection— sometimes verging on passion—for some of my male friends and male colleagues. It is wonderful to feel at ease and comfortable with their arms around me and mine around them. To have a kind of delight in that."

Stewart readily admitted in another interview that he learned more about himself by playing a gay character in *Jeffrey.* "It was liberating, playing a man who is sexually oriented toward other men. I found a kind of physical freedom."

Did the role of the gay interior decorator in *Jeffrey* hurt his chances of portraying Captain Picard in another *Star Trek* movie for Paramount? Stewart told a colleague that he expected the producers to understand that "I am an actor and, therefore, expected to act. I took the role because I found it challenging. I feel certain this role will not influence them to make a decision about me one way or another." Stewart also said that there were *Trek* screenwriters "feverishly writing the script for our next movie. And it would be very appropriate right now if this issue of an alternative sexuality could find a place in it."

Within hours of going "on-record" with such comments, rumors were circulating at warp speed that Stewart had "come out of the closet."

Return to Shakespeare

In the summer of 1995 Stewart returned to the stage as Prospero in the New York Shakespeare Festival's production of his beloved *The Tempest* in Central Park's Delacorte Theater. "It makes perfect sense that I'm going from *Jeffrey* to Prospero," he stated in one of many promotional interviews. "Because *The Tempest,* as we're interpreting it, is about ambiguity—realizing that you can love and hate people at the same time, that you can forgive people. And that you needn't be in authority all the time."

The summer production, better known as Shakespeare in the Park, was the fifty-sixth time that Stewart had performed in *The Tempest.* "The first time I played Prospero, I was fifteen years old. The other times, I played the role of Caliban. I had forty years to think of Prospero and my decision to do it this time around was very much based on my life experience."

Ten years had passed since Stewart performed in a formal Shakespearean play and he conceded to the *New York Times* that at fifty-five years old, he had literally grown into the role. "It seems to me there are two perfect times to do Shakespeare. One is when you're very young and utterly inexperienced and massively ignorant and you know nothing. That's one great time to do Shakespeare. Because you don't have any questions at all. And the other time is when you've been around for a while and matured into some of the roles. That's one of the reasons why for me *The Tempest* is so interesting right now. Aging is a blessing. One's just got to hope to live long enough to do all these things."

Stewart recalled that the first time he heard an entire play was in fact *The Tempest*. "I heard it on the radio—I was a child of the radio. I didn't own a television until I was twenty-three, and so it was the sound of the play that appealed to me. And a few months before this, the curate of my local church had given me a *Complete Works of Shakespeare* . . . I must have been about ten . . . and we didn't have many books in my house. But I listened to the play, and I followed along in the published text . . . which was exciting for me to have in my hands the same lines that I could hear the actors speaking."

Stewart admitted, however, that with director George C. Wolfe's blessing, he made changes to *The Tempest* to make it more comprehensible to the audiences in Central Park. "One thing I've done is to cut any line than I had to look up because I didn't understand it. Any line that required me to turn to the editor's comments, or because of obscure use of words . . . I proposed deleting it, because if I don't understand it, what chance does an audience . . . I've radically changed what I think about cutting of Shakespeare in that respect over the last few years because I think comprehension is critical. . . . It's a wonderful production not only because people can understand what's going on, but because it is beautiful to look at it."

After playing to sellout crowds (twenty-four performances with 1,900 people per performance) throughout the summer in Central Park, with hundreds more turned away at the gates, Stewart and *The Tempest* moved indoors to Broadway's Broadhurst Theater in a limited engagement from November 1 through December 31, 1995.

Ben Brantley, writing for the *New York Times,* commented: "Moving indoors has indeed produced a sea change in George C. Wolfe's wild *Tempest.* . . . Nowhere is this more evident than in Stewart's magnificent Prospero. In the Central Park production, he seemed to operate principally in two gears: flaming, anguished resentment and a conscience-stricken sense of moral duty. . . . Now, stripped of the ungainly body mike demanded for outdoor amplification, Stewart uses his multicolored voice to find new emotional and intellectual tones."

A reporter from *US* magazine asked Stewart if Prospero and Picard shared similar characteristics, to which the actor tersely responded, "They're figures of authority." When questioned as to whether the *Enterprise* captain ever crossed over into the Prospero performance, Stewart recalled: "Well, yes. One night, I made the mistake of tugging on the front of my doublet [a gesture he often repeated with his uniform on *Star Trek*]. There was an instantaneous burst of laughter. I was very careful never to do it again."

Stewart was also reminded that Trekkies flooded the Central Park performance, standing overnight in the rain for tickets. "As long as there are bums on the seats, I don't care how they got there," he replied. The interviewer commented that it was "enough to create a new breed of rabid fans—the Willies or Bardies or S'peareans."

Stewart sighed: "Wouldn't it be great if 4,000 people showed up at a Shakespeare convention? That would be nice."

Stewart also acknowledged that it was amazing how many celebrities attended performances of *The Tempest*. After one show, he was on the phone in his dressing room when he heard a soft knock at the door. When his visitor entered, he glanced up to see the face of an actor he had often admired and respected: Paul Newman.

After hurriedly hanging up the phone, Stewart offered Newman some champagne or wine, but the Oscar-winning actor, race car driver, and salad dressing merchant requested a cold beer instead. Stewart gave him a cheap brand, which Newman politely drank but was obviously not up to his personal standards. The next week, a case of more expensive beer was delivered to his dressing room, courtesy of Newman, with a humorous note about his beer being better than what Stewart drank.

Children's Crusade

In early 1996, Stewart returned to television in *The Canterville Ghost*, an atmospheric updating of the Oscar Wilde novella. In the ABC-TV movie Stewart starred as the poltergeist and critically acclaimed *Party of Five's* Neve Campbell played an American teenager who helps him break a centuries-old curse. *TV Guide's* Ray Stackhouse wrote that the children's show was "scary enough to raise goose bumps but never nightmare-inducing."

Stewart was also a guest on two installments of *Sesame Street* in April and May, 1996. Teaching children about the letter "B," the Shakespearean actor performed a rendition of *Hamlet*, in which he talked to the letter rather than the cranium of Hamlet's father. "A 'B' or not a 'B,' that is the question," Stewart said in the booming voice that had launched a thousand space probes in years past. During *Sesame Street's* numeric segment in May, he did a rendition of *The Next Generation's* ever-popular, "Make it so, Number 1."

Continuing his self-proclaimed "children's crusade," Stewart's reading of *Peter and the Wolf* was nominated for a Grammy for Best Spoken Word Album for Children, a relatively low-key category that had recently become a star-studded affair for Hollywood's finest with the likes of Denzel Washington (*John Henry*), Morgan Freeman (*Follow the Drinking Guard*), and even Winona Ryder (*Anne Frank: The Diary of a Young Girl*) as Stewart's competitors.

"It's very exciting to be nominated for a Grammy, albeit in Spoken Word," Stewart admitted. "But given that I'm taking guitar lessons for my next film, Eric Clapton better be prepared to move over." To his amazement, though, Stewart won; unfortunately he was not allowed to make an acceptance speech since the award went to the producer.

After recording a CD ROM called *Nine Worlds* (an interactive journey through the solar system in which his performance won a standing ovation from the crew), Stewart returned to his hometown of Mirfield "to give something back to the area which first stirred my yearnings to become an actor." His old school, Mirfield Free Grammar (or Secondary Modern, as it was called when he was a boy), was planning to build an impressive Performing Arts Center and Stewart agreed to perform his one-man show to raise money for the project at the Lawrence Bately Theatre in the town center of nearby Huddersfield.

"It is an ideal opportunity for me to return to my hometown in a way which can be of some significant value," Stewart admitted. "I still feel very much of a native of this part of Yorkshire and I carry it with me

wherever I go. To now return and support the building of what will be a truly magnificent venture, which
is going to benefit not only the school but also the
entire community, is doubly important to me as it was
to the local authority which found the money to send
me to drama school."

Stewart went on to say that he felt that it was important to return to Mirfield occasionally, to go back
where it all began. "I consider myself very fortunate
to have the career that I have had in the last ten years
and to keep one foot firmly anchored here in Yorkshire has now become very important to me. My home
has become truly a source of regeneration for me in
every possible way. . . . The move to Hollywood was
unexpected and unlooked for and took me as much
by surprise as anyone else. I can remember quite distinctly, about three years ago, one miserable, hot and
smoggy afternoon . . . I was driving on the freeway in
Los Angeles and not feeling very happy. I tried to explain to somebody once how it is when you live
abroad. You wake up every morning and there are a
million things that remind you that you're not at
home."

Batman is Not Forever

After living in hotels in New York for several months
while he filmed *Jeffrey* and performed in both the in-
door and outdoor *Tempest* stage productions, in early
1996 Stewart finally returned to his Hollywood Hills
home and into the loving arms of his girlfriend, *Star
Trek* producer Wendy Neuss ("We kept the phone companies and airlines in business," he confessed to one
interviewer).

Almost as soon as his plane landed at Los Angeles International Airport, however, Stewart began filming the psychological thriller *Safe House*, a role he originally had to turn down because of his Broadway commitment to *The Tempest*. Fortunately, the movie's producers later contacted Stewart and informed him that they would delay filming until January to accommodate his schedule.

Stewart considered *Safe House* the best role he had ever been offered. His character is a former intelligence operative who becomes a recluse in his own impenetrable, high-tech home. His family and doctors suspect he's suffering from an early stage of Alzheimer's disease and has become delusional, when his former boss becomes a leading presidential candidate and threatens his life because of what Stewart's character knows of his past. "It's a brilliant screenplay and an exciting story," the actor enthused during an online interview with several fans.

As Stewart began filming *Safe House*, Warner Brothers readied the fourth *Batman* movie for a September start date and a summer 1997 release (hoping to beat the *Jurassic Park* sequel to the box office). To Stewart's amazement, *Daily Variety* reported that the "inside word" was that director Joel Schumacher was eyeing the former *Star Trek* captain to play the part of ice cold villain Mr. Freeze.

Stewart later said that at the time of *Variety's* article, neither he nor his agent had been contacted by anyone associated with the *Batman* franchise. But after word of the alleged movie offer spread like a virus on the Internet, Director Schumacher did indeed make a phone call to Stewart's representatives. "The director said that he had not even considered me in the role of Mr. Freeze for the next *Batman* movie," Stewart acknowledged during an interview with several of his fans, "but once it appeared in *Variety* and it snowballed on the Internet, he decided I was the perfect choice. Originally, I was never considered for the part. The only truth in the rumor that I would be in the new *Batman* movie is just that—it's a rumor."

So how did the rumor first originate? Within two weeks after the release of *Batman Forever* in the summer of 1995, a news thread began on a comics-related Internet forum calling for the fans' choices for which villains they would like to see appear in the fourth movie, and who would play their roles. Some of the most popular choices included Stewart in the role of Mr. Freeze, Demi Moore and Julia Roberts as comic-book persona Poison Ivy, and John Malkovich and Chevy Chase to play the part of The Scarecrow. Other villains, including Man-Bat, Ras-al-Ghul, and Clayface were also bandied about.

However, by late in the summer, the interesting discussion on the Internet forum suddenly became a rumor among the various news magazines and shows that report the daily buzz in Hollywood. News stories began to appear that *Batman Forever* director Schumacher was being approached to helm the fourth installment, and that the principle actors to play the villains in the new movie would be Stewart as Mr. Freeze with either Demi Moore or Julia Roberts as Poison Ivy.

This incident demonstrates an interesting phenomena now arising as a direct result of the Internet and telecommunications: when does a topic of electronic discussion become legitimate Hollywood buzz to be reported to the general public and not just on the information superhighway? Could the fan speculation occurring on a particular forum actually find its way to the offices of Hollywood film studios such as Warner Brothers? Does the fan base actually make a deciding difference in the direction of a major motion picture?

Interestingly, such action-adventure box-office stars as Arnold Schwarzenegger, Bruce Willis, and Sylvester Stallone, were competing for the part of Mr. Freeze, but the offer was eventually extended to Stewart. Unfortunately, he was forced to decline the coveted role due to the film schedule for the next *Star Trek* movie, which was slated to go before the cameras in early April 1996. Schwarzenegger happily agreed to work around his commitment to another film so he could join the ranks of other high-profile *Batman* villains in past films such as Jack Nicholson (The Joker), Danny DeVito (The Penguin), Jim Carrey (The Riddler), and Tommy Lee Jones (Two Face).

Even though most of Stewart's fans were shocked and disappointed that he turned down the Mr. Freeze role (believing that he committed a monumental career screw-up), Paramount was reportedly positively ecstatic. The studio believed that the actor would likely have refused to participate in any future *Star Trek* films if he had played the villain in the next installment of the hugely popular and profitable *Batman* scenes.

The $5 Million Man

Before agreeing to a whopping $5 million to reprise his role as Captain Picard for the next *Star Trek* movie in 1996, there had been rumors that Stewart's participation in the film was up in the air. After all, when the series grind was gnawing at him physically and emotionally and, in fact, preventing him from pursuing non-*Trek* projects, he was quite reticent about Captain Picard possibly being a vital part of his life and career forever.

"I'm still whining about that," he told an interviewer with a science-fiction magazine. "But it looks like the juggernaut that is *Star Trek* has overwhelmed me. . . . I can imagine doing it, and I would never have *wanted* to imagine that as little as a year ago. I wasn't looking forward to doing *Generations.* I was very tired when the series ended and it looked like a chore to me. Very quickly it became clear that it needn't be a chore at all, that it could be a lot of fun. . . . So far as I am aware, the plan is now to begin filming in April or May for a Thanksgiving release in the United States with a February 1997 date for Britain. So it will actually be two years afterwards. I will have been away from it for 18 months, doing a lot of other work. I'm very interested to see how all of that work will have affected my feelings about the role. . . . I have a feeling that the kind of things that have happened to me in the last 18 months will affect the way I feel about Jean-Luc.

"Besides," Stewart said with a genuine smile on his face, "the best thing about it will be being reunited with the rest of the cast, because I miss them."

Epilogue

Full Circle

I'm sure I'll have to work at it a little harder than I have been doing, because in the past he [Picard] became so much a part of me that once I was in my 'space suit' and walked onto the bridge, I knew who I was and where I was. I'm not sure that will happen again so simply.

—Patrick Stewart on reprising his Captain Picard role in *Star Trek: First Contact* after a two-year hiatus

April 10, 1996

Despite filming outdoors at an abandoned Titan missile silo at a site south of Tucson, additional lighting from spotlights was still required to brighten the scene between Stewart and his co-star, acclaimed actress Alfre Woodard, who played his controversial love interest in the new *Star Trek* movie *First Contact*. As Stewart reached into his Dixon Hill-like civilian overcoat to engage his communicator, streams of sweat began to run down his face, burning his eyes.

"Damn, that hurts!" Stewart swore, almost at the same time as director Jonathan Frakes screamed "Cut!"

"I guess I really shouldn't complain so much," Stewart said to Woodard, as a makeup artist dabbed his face. "It was a hell of a lot hotter in Nevada's Valley of Fire desert where we filmed *Generations* two years ago."

Although Stewart originally told Paramount he would not reprise the role of Captain Picard for the sequel to *Generations,* the studio's offer of $5 million, coupled with a larger and more spacious trailer than his co-stars and the opportunity for him to have some input into the script, were strong enticements for the actor to put the "space suit" back on again.

Stewart eventually signed on the dotted line after Paramount agreed to one final contingent: Jonathan Frakes, his co-star, close friend, and director of numerous *Next Generation, Deep Space Nine* and *Voyager* episodes, would helm *First Contact.* Rick Berman and the studio brass readily agreed, especially in light of the fact that Frakes' salary would be considerably less than two other previous *Star Trek* movie directors they were considering: Nicholas Meyer and Leonard Nimoy. In addition, Frakes would have a much bigger role as Commander Riker in the new film as insurance if Stewart proved uninterested or too expensive.

Even though Stewart's contract permitted him to make creative comments and suggestions on each draft and revision of *First Contact*'s script, the actor was under strict orders from Berman to refrain from convoluting the storyline with any heavy-handed and morose scenes of Picard pining away for his dead nephew as he did in *Generations.*

Although the movie had the best opening weekend of any previous *Star Trek* feature film, *Generations* eventually racked up only $75.5 million in domestic box office receipts, which was exactly the same amount grossed by *The Search for Spock* ten years earlier. Paramount was adamant in its belief that Stewart's subplot concerning his personal loss had distracted from the film's main focus on action with Kirk, Soran, the Duras sisters and the spectacular crash of the *Enterprise*-D.

The studio's Prime Directive to *First Contact*'s screenplay writers Ron Moore and Brannon Braga was to have an action-packed story (more than in *Generations*), a romance for Picard (but don't let Stewart emphasize the B-story) and a return to the fun and camaraderie of *The Next Generation* crew. "Our hopes are high," Moore conceded during an interview. "We have a sense that this one is going to have more of a pace to it [than *Generations*]. It will be a faster movie and an action-packed piece, so it will have a rougher edge. *Generations* had a darker overtone, addressing different views of morality. I don't think we'll go in that direction this time. It will be more adventure, more of a charging-into-action kind of thing."

Stewart glowingly praised *First Contact*'s script as "great" and "a good story that happens to be *Trek*" while appearing at the *Star Trek* 30th Anniversary Grand Slam convention in Pasadena when filming for the new movie was suspended for a few hours on a Saturday. "Please realize that all this talk of action-adventure won't downplay the characters' quieter moments in the movie," he emphasized. "Although it is an ensemble piece, Picard's story arc will be at the center with Data and his emotions coming in second and Riker a close third. *Star Trek* will never be *Star Wars.*"

"We've got a remarkable script," boasted Rick Berman. "It will explore what each of the characters has been doing since the crash of the *Enterprise*-D. And we're also going to see the Borg—which was a very popular *TNG* menace—in a whole new light. *Star Trek: First Contact* has the villainous cyborg race attempting to rewrite the progress of the United Federation of Planets and Starfleet by traveling back in time to sabotage the first test flight of the newly invented warp drive. Captain Picard in command of the new *Enterprise-E* leads *The Next Generation* crew in pursuit and in the 21st century falls in love. . . . From what I've been told, Patrick is eager to show off his newly sculpted body in the movie and will be taking off his shirt to flex his muscles."

Stewart, however, was more anxious to showcase his acting talents in *First Contact* than his physique. "All I know is that I *have* to act. It's a compulsion. I'm driven to it," he acknowledged. "I wouldn't say that I would *die* if it were taken away from me, but a large part of me would shrivel up. That's why it pierces my soul when I hear fans say that I have turned my back on *Star Trek*, that I think I'm *too* good of an actor to continue playing Picard. Just as I have changed some in the past two years, so has the captain, which will allow me as an actor to bring a new dimension to the role, to get reacquainted with an old and dear friend—Jean-Luc Picard."

Notes and Sources

Prologue: All Good Things . . .

1. "Patrick Stewart Lets Down His Hair," by David Rensin. *TV Guide,* July 31, 1993.
2. "The Magnificent Seven," by Michael Logan. *TV Guide,* May 14, 1994.
3. "Inside Trek: Finale Means Mission Cut Short for 'Next Gen,' " by Ian Spelling. *Houston Chronicle,* May 14, 1994.
4. " 'Generation' Ex," by Benjamin Svetkey. *Entertainment Weekly,* May 6, 1994.
5. "Once and Future Captain," by Ian Spelling. *Starlog,* March 1995, no. 212. Starlog Communications International, New York, NY.
6. "A New Enterprise: An Exclusive Interview with *Jeffrey Star,* Patrick Stewart." *The Advocate,* August 22, 1995.
7. "I Can't Believe It's Over! Star Trek: The Next Generation Final Season," by Mark A. Altman. *Sci-Fi Universe,* September 1994.
8. "Patrick Stewart: The Legacy of Captain Picard," by Pamela Roller. *Star Trek: The Official Fan Club,* October/November 1994, no. 99. The Official Fan Club, P.O. Box 111000, Aurora, CO 80011.
9. "Jonathan Frakes: Looking Out for 'Number One,' " interview by Dan Madsen. *Star Trek Communicator*

December/January 1995/96, no. 105. The Official Fan Club, P.O. Box 111000, Aurora, CO 80011.

10. "Patrick Stewart Makes It So," by A. J. Jacobs. *Entertainment Weekly*, October 20, 1995.

11. " 'Trek' Spun Stewart into a New Orbit," by David Patrick Stearns. *USA Today*, August 3, 1995.

12. *Starlog's Science Fiction Heroes and Heroines,* edited by David McDonnell. 1995; Crescent Books, Avenel, NJ.

13. "Q & A: Patrick Stewart," interview by Henry Edwards. *Details,* September 1995.

14. "Star Trek: The Next Generation—Ending the TV Voyages," by Mark A. Altman. *Cinefantastique,* December 1994.

15. *Star Trek: The Next Generation the Official Magazine,* no. 30. '93-'94 Season. Starlog Communications International, New York, NY

Chapter One: Yesterday's Nightmares, Tomorrow's Dreams

1. "The Future of Captain Picard, Part One: An Exclusive Interview with Patrick Stewart," by Dan Madsen. *Star Trek: The Official Fan Club,* September/October 1992, no. 87. The Official Fan Club, P.O. Box 111000, Aurora, CO 80011.

2. "The Future of Captain Picard, Part Two: An Exclusive Interview with Patrick Stewart," by Dan Madsen. *Star Trek: The Official Fan Club,* November/December 1992, no. 88. The Official Fan Club, P.O. Box 111000, Aurora, CO 80011.

3. "A New Enterprise: An Exclusive Interview with *Jeffrey* Star, Patrick Stewart." *The Advocate,* August 22, 1995.

4. Personal conversations with Dr. Kim Oates, October 1995.

5. *Trek the Next Generation Crew Book,* by James Van Hise. 1993; Pioneer Books, Las Vegas, NV.

6. "Patrick Stewart Lets Down His Hair," by David Rensin. *TV Guide,* July 31, 1993.

7. "Star Trek: The Ultimate Trip Through the Galaxies." *Entertainment Weekly,* Special Edition, January 18, 1995. Time, Inc., New York, NY.

8. "Make It So," by Eirik Knutzen. *The Official Star Trek Fan Club of the UK.,* Autumn 1993, no. 2. The Official Star Trek Fan Club of the U.K., Absolute Field Marketing, The Old Barn, Jericho Farm, Worton, Nr. Cassington, Oxon OX8 1EB.

9. *The Dynamite Kid,* by Brian Blessed. 1992; Bloomsbury Publishing Ltd., London, England.

10. "Trekking Onward," by Richard Zoglin. *Time,* November 28, 1994.

11. "Patrick Stewart Makes It So," by A. J. Jacobs. *Entertainment Weekly,* October 20, 1995.

12. "Q & A: Patrick Stewart," interview by Henry Edwards. *Details,* September 1995.

13. "20 Questions: Patrick Stewart," interview by Neil Tesser. *Playboy,* November 1992.

14. "Q & A: Patrick Stewart," interview by Ryan Murphy. *US,* December 1994.

15. "Patrick Stewart: The Next Generation," by Martha Frankel. *Movieline,* November 1994.

16. "Star Trek Captain: Abusive Dad Made My Life a Living Hell," by David Wright. *National Enquirer,* December 1, 1992.

17. " 'Star Trek' Captain: My Nightmare as a Battered Child," interview by Gary A. Schreiber. *National Enquirer,* September 21, 1993.

18. Interview with Patrick Stewart by Steve Wright on BBC Radio 1 FM, April 4, 1993.

19. Commencement Address by Patrick Stewart at Pomona College, May 14, 1995.
20. *Starlog's Science Fiction Heroes & Heroines,* edited by David McDonnell. 1995; Crescent Books, Avenel, NJ.
21. "There's No Place Like Home," by John Mosby. *Sci-Fi Universe,* March 1996.

Chapter Two: From Shakespeare to *Star Trek*

1. "Patrick Stewart: Captain Picard on Shatner, Roddenberry and the Realm of Star Trek," interview by Dan Madsen. *Star Trek Communicator,* December/January 1994/95, no. 100. The Official Fan Club, P.O. Box 111000, Aurora, CO 80011.
2. *Shakespeare in Performance,* edited by Keith Parsons and Pamela Mason. 1995; Salamander Books, Ltd., London, England.
3. "Review: King John," by Ronald Bryden. *London Observer,* June 14, 1970.
4. "Review: Julius Caesar," by Robert Cushman. *London Observer,* October 28, 1973.
5. "Review: Hedda," by Frank Rich. *New York Post,* January 26, 1976.
6. "Review: A Midsummer Night's Dream," by Bernard Levin. *London Sunday Times,* May 15, 1977.
7. "Review: A Midsummer Night's Dream," by Robert Cushman. *London Observer,* May 15, 1977.
8. "Review: Bingo," by John Peter. *London Sunday Times,* August 14, 1977.
9. "Review: Henry IV," by Irving Waddle. *London Times,* June 10, 1982.
10. "Review: Who's Afraid of Virginia Woolf?" by John Peter. *London Sunday Times,* February 22, 1987.

11. "Review: Who's Afraid of Virginia Woolf?" by John Vidal. *Guardian,* February 22, 1987.

12. Interview with Patrick Stewart by Steve Wright on BBC Radio 1 FM, April 4, 1993.

13. *The Next Generation Tribute, Book Two,* edited by James Van Hise. 1994; Pioneer Books, Las Vegas, NV.

Chapter Three: Promotion to Captain

1. America Online with Patrick Stewart, November 3, 1995.

2. "Picard's New Generation," interview by Hilary Oliver. *The List: The Glasgow and Edinburgh Events Guide Magazine,* February 19, 1995.

3. Interview with Patrick Stewart by Steve Wright on BBC Radio 1 FM, April 4, 1993.

4. "Strategic Withdrawal: Patrick Stewart Says Goodbye to Picard and the Enterprise—At Least for Now," by Edward Gross. *Cinescape,* October 1995.

5. "Trekking Onward," by Richard Zoglin. *Time,* November 28, 1994.

6. "The Torch Has Passed Off-Camera, Too," by Michael Walsh and reported by Dan Cray. *Time,* November 28, 1994.

7. *Gene Roddenberry: The Myth and the Man Behind Star Trek,* by Joel Engel. 1994; Hyperion, New York, NY.

8. Interview with Patrick Stewart on KCRA-TV, November 19, 1994.

9. "Biography Shatters Myth of Roddenberry, Not of 'Trek,' " by Bruce Westbrook. *Houston Chronicle,* May 8, 1994.

10. *Starlog's Science Fiction Heroes & Heroines,* edited by David McDonnell. 1995; Crescent Books, Avenel, NJ.

11. "The Future of Captain Picard, Part One: An Exclusive Interview with Patrick Stewart," by Dan Madsen. *Star Trek: The Official Fan Club,* September/October 1992, no. 87. The Official Fan Club, P.O. Box 111000, Aurora, CO 80011.

12. "The Future of Captain Picard, Part Two: An Exclusive Interview with Patrick Stewart," by Dan Madsen. *Star Trek: The Official Fan Club,* November/December 1992, no. 88. The Official Fan Club, P.O. Box 111000, Aurora, CO 80011.

13. "Review: Star Trek: The Next Generation," by Don Merrill. *TV Guide,* February 6, 1988.

14. "Star Trek XXV," by Michael Logan. *TV Guide,* August 31, 1991.

15. *Trek the Next Generation Crew Book,* by James Van Hise. 1993; Pioneer Books, Las Vegas, NV.

16. "20 Questions: Patrick Stewart," interview by Neil Tesser. *Playboy,* November 1992.

17. "Make It So," by Eirik Knutzen. *The Official Star Trek Fan Club of the U.K.,* August 1993, no. 2. The Official Star Trek Fan Club of the U.K., Absolute Field Marketing, The Old Barn, Jericho Farm, Worton, Nr. Cassington, Oxon OX8 1EB.

18. "Patrick Stewart: Captain Picard on Shatner, Roddenberry and the Realm of Star Trek," interview by Dan Madsen. *Star Trek Communicator,* December/January 1994/95, no. 100. The Official Fan Club, P.O. Box 111000, Aurora, CO 80011.

19. "Gnotes: Seen, Heard, Noted & Quoted." *Glamour,* February 1996.

20. *The Next Generation Tribute, Book Two,* edited by James Van Hise. 1994; Pioneer Books, Las Vegas, NV.

21. *The Man Who Created Star Trek: Gene Roddenberry,* by James Van Hise. 1993; Pioneer Books, Las Vegas, NV.

22. *Trek: The Unauthorized Behind-the-Scenes Story of the Next Generation,* by James Van Hise. 1993; Pioneer Books, Las Vegas, NV.

23. *Star Trek: Where No One Has Gone Before,* Text by J. M. Dillard. 1994; Pocket Books, New York, NY.

24. *Star Trek: The Next Generation the Official Magazine,* no. 1. '87-'88 Season. Starlog Communications International, New York, NY.

25. "Inside 'Star Trek: The Next Generations,' " by Mark A. Altman. *Galactic Journal,* no. 23, Winter 1988.

Chapter Four: Power Struggle

1. "Patrick Stewart: The Next Generation," by Martha Frankel. *Movieline,* November 1994.

2. "Patrick Stewart Lets Down His Hair," by David Rensin. *TV Guide,* July 31, 1993.

3. "Q & A: Patrick Stewart," interview by Ryan Murphy. *US,* December 1994.

4. " 'Star Trek' is Born Again . . . Worrying How to Dress a Pig," by Elaine Warten. *TV Guide,* October 24, 1987.

5. "Once and Future Captain," by Ian Spelling. *Starlog,* March 1995, no. 212, Starlog Communications International, New York, NY.

6. *Gene Roddenberry: The Last Conversation,* by Yvonne Fern. 1994: University of California Press, Berkley, CA.

7. *Star Trek Movie Memories,* by William Shatner. 1994; HarperCollins, New York, NY.

8. *Star Trek 25th Anniversary Special.* 1991; Starlog Communications International, New York, NY.

9. *I Am Spock,* by Leonard Nimoy. 1995; Hyperion, New York, NY.

10. *Trek the Next Generation Crew Book,* by James Van Hise. 1993; Pioneer Books, Las Vegas, NV.

11. *The Next Generation Tribute, Book Two,* edited by James Van Hise. 1994; Pioneer Books, Las Vegas, NV.

12. *Trek: The Unauthorized Behind-the-Scenes Story of the Next Generation,* by James Van Hise. 1993; Pioneer Books, Las Vegas, NV.

13. *Star Trek Creator: The Authorized Biography of Gene Roddenberry,* by David Alexander. 1994; Penguin Books, New York, NY.

14. "Nimoy: The Universe Interview," by Sheldon Teitelbaum. *Sci-Fi Universe,* February 1996.

15. *Trek: The Next Generation,* Third Edition, by James Van Hise. 1994; Pioneer Books, Las Vegas, NV.

16. *Gene Roddenberry: The Myth and the Man Behind Star Trek,* by Joel Engel. 1994; Hyperion, New York, NY.

17. *Star Trek: The Next Generation the Official Magazine,* no. 2. '87-'88 Season. Starlog Communications International, New York, NY.

18. *Star Trek: The Next Generation the Official Magazine,* no. 3. '87-'88 Season. Starlog Communications International, New York, NY.

19. America Online with Patrick Stewart, November 3, 1995.

20. *The New Trek Encyclopedia,* by John Peel with Scott Nance. 1994; Pioneer Books, Las Vegas, NV.

21. *Twenty-Fifth Anniversary Trek Tribute,* by James Van Hise. 1991; Pioneer Books, Las Vegas, NV.

22. *Star Trek: The Next Generation the Official Magazine,* no. 4. '87-'88 Season. Starlog Communications International, New York, NY.

23. "Star Trek: Behind the Scenes of the Next Generation," by Mark A. Altman. *Cinefantastique,* March 1989.

24. *Star Trek: Generations the Official Movie Magazine,* November 1994. Starlog Communications International, New York, NY.

Chapter Five: A Piece of the Action

1. "Star Chambers: An Up-Close Trek to the Set of *The Next Generation,"* by Benjamin Svetkey. *Entertainment Weekly,* June 11, 1993.
2. "The Future of Captain Picard, Part One: An Exclusive Interview with Patrick Stewart," by Dan Madsen. *Star Trek: The Official Fan Club,* September/October 1992, no. 87. The Official Fan Club, P.O. Box 111000, Aurora, CO 80011.
3. "The Future of Captain Picard, Part Two: An Exclusive Interview with Patrick Stewart," by Dan Madsen. *Star Trek: The Official Fan Club,* November/December 1992, no. 88. The Official Fan Club, P.O. Box 111000, Aurora, CO 80011.
4. "A New Enterprise: An Exclusive Interview with *Jeffrey* Star, Patrick Stewart," *The Advocate,* August 22, 1995.
5. *Trek The Next Generation Crew Book,* by James Van Hise. 1993; Pioneer Books, Las Vegas, NV.
6. *Beyond Uhura: Star Trek and Other Memories,* by Nichelle Nichols. 1994; Putnam, New York, NY.
7. *Trek: The Next Generation,* Third Edition, by James Van Hise. 1994; Pioneer Books, Las Vegas, NV.
8. *Trek: The Unauthorized Behind-the-Scenes Story of the Next Generation,* by James Van Hise. 1993; Pioneer Books, Las Vegas, NV.
9. *The New Trek Encyclopedia,* by John Peel with Scott Nance. 1994; Pioneer Books, Las Vegas, NV.
10. "Star Trek: Four Generations of Stars, Stories, and Strange New Worlds." *TV Guide* Special Collectors'

Edition, Spring 1995. News America Publications, Inc., Radnor, PA.

11. Personal conversations with David Wright, November 1995.

12. Personal conversations with Marc Cetner, October 1995.

13. *Star Trek: Where No Has Gone Before,* by J. M. Dillard. 1994; Pocket Books, New York, NY.

14. "Patrick Stewart: The Next Generation," by Martha Frankel. *Movieline,* November 1994.

15. *Star Trek: The Next Generation the Official Magazine,* no. 5. '88-'89 Season. Starlog Communications International, New York, NY.

16. *Star Trek: The Next Generation the Official Magazine,* no. 6. '88-'89 Season. Starlog Communications International, New York, NY.

17. Star *Trek: The Next Generation the Official Magazine,* no. 7. '88-'89 Season. Starlog Communications International, New York, NY.

18. *Star Trek: The Next Generation the Official Magazine,* no. 8. '88-'89 Season. Starlog Communications International, New York, NY.

Chapter Six: Dissatisfaction Guaranteed

1. Personal conversations with Michael Glynn, October 1995.

2. *Trek: The Next Generation,* Third Edition, by James Van Hise. 1994; Pioneer Books, Las Vegas, NV.

3. Personal conversations with Mark Lenard, November 1995.

4. "Q & A: Patrick Stewart," interview by Henry Edwards. *Details,* September 1995.

5. "My Appointment with the Enterprise: An Appreciation," by Ursula K. Le Guin. *TV Guide,* May 14, 1994.

6. " 'L.A. Law' Beauty's Love Affair with 'Star Trek' Captain Wrecks His 25-Year Marriage," by Eric Munoz, Michael Glynn, and Lydia Encina. *National Enquirer* February 26, 1991.
7. *Starlog's Science Fiction Heroes & Heroines,* edited by David McDonnell. 1995; Crescent Books, Avenel, NJ.
8. Personal conversations with Jerome George, December 1995.
9. *Trek: The Unauthorized Behind-the-Scenes Story of the Next Generation,* by James Van Hise. 1993; Pioneer Books, Las Vegas, NV.
10. *The Next Generation Tribute, Book Two,* edited by James Van Hise. 1994; Pioneer Books, Las Vegas, NV.
11. *Trek the Next Generation Crew Book,* by James Van Hise. 1993; Pioneer Books, Las Vegas, NV.
12. *The New Trek Encyclopedia,* by John Peel with Scott Nance. 1994; Pioneer Books, Las Vegas, NV.
13. *Twenty-Fifth Anniversary Trek Tribute,* by James Van Hise. 1991; Pioneer Books, Las Vegas, NV.
14. "Star Trek—Behind the Scenes of the Next Generation." *Cinefantastique,* March 1989.
15. "Star Trek: The 25th Anniversary." *Cinefantastique,* December 1991.
16. *Great Birds of the Galaxy,* by Edward Gross and Mark Altman. 1992; Image Publishing, East Meadows, NY.
17. *The History of Trek,* by James Van Hise. 1991; Pioneer Books, Las Vegas, NV.
18. "Once and Future Captain," by Ian Spelling. *Starlog,* March 1995, no. 212. Starlog Communications International, New York, NY.
19. Interview with Patrick Stewart by Steve Wright on BBC Radio 1 FM, April 4, 1993.
20. America Online with Patrick Stewart, November 3, 1995.

21. "20 Questions: Patrick Stewart," interview by Neil Tesser. *Playboy*, November 1992.
22. *Star Trek. The Next Generation the Official Magazine*, no. 9. '89-'90 Season. Starlog Communications International, New York, NY.
23. *Star Trek. The Next Generation the Official Magazine*, no. 10. '89-'90 Season. Starlog Communications International, New York, NY.
24. *Star Trek: The Next Generation the Official Magazine*, no. 11. '89-'90 Season. Starlog Communications International, New York, NY.
25. *Star Trek: The Next Generation the Official Magazine*, no. 12. '89-'90 Season. Starlog Communications International, New York, NY.

Chapter Seven: All the World's a Stage

1. "Q & A: Patrick Stewart," interview by Henry Edwards. *Details*, September 1995.
2. "Patrick Stewart: The Next Generation," by Martha Frankel. *Movieline*, November 1994.
3. " 'L.A. Law' Beauty's Love Affair with 'Star Trek' Captain Wrecks His 25-Year Marriage," by Eric Munoz, Michael Glynn, and Lydia Encina. *National Enquirer*, February 26, 1991.
4. "Behind the Scenes," by Mike Walker. *National Enquirer*, November 19, 1991.
5. "Patrick Stewart Lets Down His Hair," by David Rensin. *TV Guide*, July 31, 1993.
6. *Trek the Next Generation Crew Book*, by James Van Hise. 1993; Pioneer Books, Las Vegas, NV.
7. "20 Questions: Patrick Stewart," interview by Neil Tesser. *Playboy*, November 1992.
8. "A New Enterprise: An Exclusive Interview with *Jeffrey Star*, Patrick Stewart. *The Advocate*, August 22, 1995.

9. "Q & A: Patrick Stewart," interview by Ryan Murphy. *US*, December 1994.

10. "Make It So," by Eirik Knutzen. *The Official Star Trek Fan Club of the U.K.*, Autumn 1993, no. 2. The Official Star Trek Fan Club of the U.K., Absolute Field Marketing, The Old Barn, Jericho Farm, Worton, Nr. Cassington, Oxon OX8 IEB.

11. "The Future of Captain Picard, Part One: An Exclusive Interview with Patrick Stewart," by Dan Madsen. *Star Trek: The Official Fan Club*, September/October 1992, no. 87. The Official Fan Club, P.O. Box 111000, Aurora, CO 80011.

12. "The Future of Captain Picard, Part Two: An Exclusive Interview with Patrick Stewart," by Dan Madsen. *Star Trek: The Official Fan Club*, November/December 1992, no. 88. The Official Fan Club, P.O. Box 111000, Aurora, CO 80011.

13. "TV TALK: Patrick Stewart Prepares for Another 'Trek' Adventure," by Dana Bisbee. The *Boston Herald*, May 28, 1995.

14. "Once and Future Captain," by Ian Spelling. *Starlog*, March 1995, no. 212. Starlog Communications International, New York, NY.

15. Personal conversations with Eric Munoz, January 1996.

16. *Trek: The Next Generation*. Third Edition, by James Van Hise. 1994; Pioneer Books, Las Vegas, NV.

17. *The History of Trek*, by James Van Hise. 1991; Pioneer Books, Las Vegas, NV.

18. America Online with Patrick Stewart, November 3, 1995.

19. *Starlog's Science Fiction Heroes & Heroines*, edited by David McDonnell. 1995; Crescent Books, Avenel, NJ.

20. "Star Trek: Four Generations of Stars, Stories, and Strange New Worlds." *TV Guide*, Special Collectors'

Edition, Spring 1995. News America Publications, Inc., Radnor, PA.

21. *The Next Generation Tribute, Book Two,* edited by James Van Hise. 1994; Pioneer Books, Las Vegas, NV.

22. *Star Trek: The Next Generation the Official Magazine,* no. 13. '90-'91 Season. Starlog Communications International, New York, NY.

23. *Star Trek: The Next Generation the Official Magazine,* no. 14. '90-'91 Season. Starlog Communications International, New York, NY.

24. "Star Trek: The Next Generation Zooming to a Fourth Season," by Mark A. Altman. *Cinefantastique,* September 1990.

Chapter Eight: New Directions

1. *Trek: The Making of the Movies,* by James Van Hise. 1992; Pioneer Books, Las Vegas, NV.

2. "The Undiscovered Kirk," by Dan Yakir. *Starlog,* February 1992, no. 175. Starlog Communications International, New York, NY.

3. Interview with Patrick Stewart on KCRA-TV, November 19, 1994.

4. "The Making of Star Trek VI," by Mark Altman. *Cinefantastique,* April 1992.

5. *Captain Quirk,* by Dennis William Hauck. 1995; Pinnacle Books, New York, NY.

6. *I Am Spock,* by Leonard Nimoy. 1995; Hyperion, New York, NY.

7. *Starlog's Science Fiction Heroes & Heroines,* edited by David McDonnell. 1995; Crescent Books, Avenel, NJ.

8. "Comparing the Captains: Kirk vs. Picard," by Rick Marin. *TV Guide,* August 31, 1991.

9. *Star Trek 25th Anniversary Special.* 1991; Starlog Communications International,New York, NY.

10. *Star Trek Movie Memories,* by William Shatner. 1994; HarperCollins, New York, NY.

11. Personal conversations with Mark Lenard, November 1994.

12. *Trek the Next Generation Crew Book,* by James Van Hise. 1993; Pioneer Books, Las Vegas, NV.

13. *The New Trek Encyclopedia,* by John Peel with Scott Nance. 1994; Pioneer Books, Las Vegas, NV.

14. "Star Trek: The Director's Chair," by Nicholas Meyer. *Omni,* December 1991.

15. "Inside Trek: Stewart Helped Bridge the 'Generations' Gap," by Ian Spelling. *Houston Chronicle,* September 10, 1994.

16. "Picard's New Generation," interview by Hilary Oliver. *The List: The Glasgow and Edinburgh Events Guide Magazine,* February 19, 1995.

17. *NetTrek,* edited by Kelly Maloni, Ben Greenman, Kristin Miller, and Jeff Hearn. 1995; Michael Wolff & Company, New York, NY.

18. *The Next Generation Tribute, Book Two,* edited by James Van Hise. 1994; Pioneer Books, Las Vegas, NV.

19. "Patrick Stewart Lets Down His Hair," by David Rensin. *TV Guide,* July 31, 1993.

20. *Star Trek: The Next Generation the Official Magazine,* no. 15. '90-'91 Season. Starlog Communications International, New York, NY.

21. *Star Trek: The Next Generation the Official Magazine,* no. 16. '90-'91 Season. Starlog Communications International, New York, NY.

Chapter Nine: The Fullest Living

1. *I Am Spock,* by Leonard Nimoy. 1995; Hyperion, New York, NY.

2. "Nimoy: The Universe Interview," by Sheldon Teitelbaum. *Sci-Fi Universe,* February 1996.

3. *Star Trek Movie Memories,* by William Shatner. 1994; HarperCollins, New York, NY.

4. "Star Trek: The Next Generation Zooming to a Fifth Season," by Mark A. Altman. *Cinefantastique,* October 1991.

5. *Unification,* by Jeri Taylor. 1991; Pocket Books, New York, NY.

6. "Star Trek: The 25th Anniversary," interview with Gene Roddenberry by Mark A. Altman. *Cinefantastique,* December 1991.

7. "Star Trek: The Ultimate Trip Through the Galaxies." *Entertainment Weekly,* Special Edition, January 18, 1995. Time Inc., New York, NY.

8. *The History of Trek,* by James Van Hise. 1991; Pioneer Books, Las Vegas, NV.

9. *Trek: The Making of the Movies,* by James Van Hise. 1992; Pioneer Books, Las Vegas, NV.

10. *Captain Quirk,* by Dennis William Hauck. 1995; Pinnacle Books, New York, NY.

11. *Star Trek Creator,* by David Alexander. 1994; Penguin Books, New York, NY.

12. *Gene Roddenberry: The Myth and the Man Behind Star Trek,* by Joel Engel. 1994; Hyperion, New York, NY.

13. *Gene Roddenberry: The Last Conversation,* by Yvonne Fern. 1994; University of California Press, Berkeley, CA.

14. "Patrick Stewart Lets Down His Hair," by David Rensin. *TV Guide,* July 31, 1993.

15. "The Future of Captain Picard, Part One: An Exclusive Interview with Patrick Stewart," by Dan Madsen. *Star Trek: The Official Fan Club,* September/October 1992, no. 87. The Official Fan Club, P.O. Box 111000, Aurora, CO 80011.

16. "The Future of Captain Picard, Part Two: An Exclusive Interview with Patrick Stewart," by Dan Madsen. *Star Trek: The Official Fan Club,* November/December 1992, no. 88. The Official Fan Club, P.O. Box 111000, Aurora, CO 80011.

17. Commencement Address by Patrick Stewart at Pomona College, May 14, 1995.

18. *Starlog's Science Fiction Heroes & Heroines,* edited by David McDonnell. 1995; Crescent Books, Avenel, NJ.

19. "Make It So," by Eirik Knutzen. *The Official Star Trek Fan Club of the U.K.,* August 1993, no. 2. The Official Star Trek Fan Club of the U.K., Absolute Field Marketing, The Old Barn, Jericho Farm, Worton, Nr., Cassington, Oxon OX8 1EB.

20. *Star Trek 25th Anniversary Special.* 1991; Starlog Communications International, New York, NY.

21. *The Next Generation Tribute, Book Two,* edited by James Van Hise. 1994; Pioneer Books, Las Vegas, NV.

22. *The New Trek Encyclopedia,* by John Peel with Scott Nance. 1994; Pioneer Books, Las Vegas, NV.

23. Personal conversations with Mark Lenard, November 1995.

24. "Star Trek: The Director's Chair," by Nicholas Meyer. *Omni,* December 1991.

25. "Inside Trek: With New Book, Nichols Goes 'Beyond Uhura,' " by Ian Spelling. *Houston Chronicle,* October 22, 1994.

26. *Beyond Uhura: Star Trek and Other Memories,* by Nichelle Nichols. 1994; Putman, New York, NY.

27. *Star Trek: The Next Generation the Official Magazine,* no. 17. '91-'92 Season. Starlog Communications International, New York, NY.

28. *Star Trek: The Next Generation the Official Magazine,* no.18. '91-'92 Season. Starlog Communications International, New York, NY.

Chapter Ten: From First Love to Sex Symbol

1. "Theater Review: A Christmas Carol," by Clive Barnes. *New York Post,* December 20, 1991.
2. "Theater Review: A Christmas Carol," by Mel Gussow. *New York Times,* December 20, 1991.
3. "20 Questions: Patrick Stewart," interview by Neil Tesser. *Playboy,* November 1992.
4. America Online with Patrick Stewart, November 3, 1995.
5. "The Future of Captain Picard, Part One: An Exclusive Interview with Patrick Stewart," by Dan Madsen. *Star Trek: The Official Fan Club,* September/October 1992, no. 87. The Official Fan Club, P.O. Box 111000, Aurora, CO 80011.
6. "The Future of Captain Picard, Part Two: An Exclusive Interview with Patrick Stewart," by Dan Madsen. *Star Trek: The Official Fan Club,* November/December 1992, no. 88. The Official Fan Club, P.O. Box 111000, Aurora, CO 80011.
7. Interview with Patrick Stewart on KCRA-TV, November 19, 1994.
8. *Starlog's Science Fiction Heroes & Heroines,* edited by David McDonnell. 1995; Crescent Books, Avenel, NJ.
9. *Trek: The Next Generation,* Third Edition, by James Van Hise. 1994; Pioneer Books, Las Vegas, NV.
10. *The Next Generation Tribute, Book Two,* edited by James Van Hise. 1994; Pioneer Books, Las Vegas, NV.
11. "Q & A: Patrick Stewart," interview by Ryan Murphy. *US,* December 1994.

12. "A New Enterprise: An Exclusive Interview with *Jeffrey* Star, Patrick Stewart." *The Advocate,* August 22, 1995.

13. "Patrick Stewart: The Next Generation," by Martha Frankel. *Movieline,* November 1994.

14. "Patrick Stewart: To the Great Domes of the World." *People,* May 8, 1995.

15. "Q & A: Patrick Stewart," interview by Henry Edwards. *Details,* September 1995.

16. "Our Readers' Choices as TV's Most Bodacious Duo." *TV Guide,* July 18, 1992.

17. "Star Trek: The Ultimate Trip Through the Galaxies." *Entertainment Weekly,* Special Edition, January 18, 1995. Time Inc., New York, NY.

18. "Head of Man Watchers Picks: World's Sexiest Guys Over 50." *National Enquirer,* October 19, 1993.

19. *Trek the Next Generation Crew Book,* by James Van Hise. 1993; Pioneer Books, Las Vegas, NV.

20. "Patrick Stewart Lets Down His Hair," by David Rensin. *TV Guide,* July 31, 1993.

21. "Patrick Stewart: The Legacy of Captain Picard," by Pamela Roller. *Star Trek: The Official Fan Club,* October/November 1994, no. 99. The Official Fan Club, P.O. Box 111000, Aurora, CO 80011.

22. "Star Trek: The Next Generation Zooming to a Fifth Season," by Mark A. Altman. *Cinefantastique,* October 1991.

23. *Captain Quirk,* by Dennis William Hauk. 1995; Pinnacle Books, New York, NY.

24. "Naked City." *Spy,* April 1992.

25. *Star Trek: The Next Generation the Official Magazine* no. 19. '91–'92 Season. Starlog Communications International, New York, NY.

26. *Star Trek: The Next Generation the Official Magazine,* no. 20. '91–'92 Season. Starlog Communications International, New York, NY.

Chapter Eleven: Action and Romance

1. "The Future of Captain Picard, Part One: An Exclusive Interview with Patrick Stewart," by Dan Madsen. *Star Trek: The Official Fan Club*, September/October 1992, no. 87. The Official Fan Club, P.O. Box 111000, Aurora, CO 80011.

2. "The Future of Captain Picard, Part Two: An Exclusive Interview with Patrick Stewart," by Dan Madsen. *Star Trek: The Official Fan Club*, November/December 1992, no. 88. The Official Fan Club, P.O. Box 111000, Aurora, CO 80011.

3. "What's Happening with the Hits: Introducing the Defiant," by Michael Logan. *TV Guide*, September 24, 1994.

4. "Space Race," by Benjamin Svetkey. *Entertainment Weekly*, January 14, 1994.

5. "The Dawn of a New Deep Space Nine," by Michael Logan. *TV Guide*, October 6, 1995.

6. "Deep and Confused: *Can Deep Space Nine* Replace *The Next Generation?*" by Mark A. Altman. *Sci-Fi Universe*, November 1994.

7. "Star Trek's Newest Frontier: Deep Space Nine," by Michael Logan. *TV Guide*, January 2, 1993.

8. " 'Star Trek' Captain to Wed and Whoopi Goldberg Played Matchmaker," by Gary A. Schreiber. *National Enquirer*, March 9, 1993.

9. "Star Trek Captain Finds True Love with a Trek Exec," by Marc Cetner and Jerry George. *National Enquirer*, August 8, 1995.

10. *Starlog's Science Fiction Heroes & Heroines*, edited by David McDonnell. 1995; Crescent Books, Avenel, NJ.

11. "Patrick Stewart: The Next Generation," by Martha Frankel. *Movieline*, November 1994.

12. "Q & A: Patrick Stewart," interview by Ryan Murphy. *US*, December 1994.

13. "A New Enterprise: An Exclusive Interview with *Jeffrey* Star, Patrick Stewart." *The Advocate,* August 22, 1995.

14. "Q & A: Patrick Stewart," interview by Henry Edwards. *Details,* September 1995.

15. "Patrick Stewart Makes It So," by A. J. Jacobs. *Entertainment Weekly,* October 20, 1995.

16. America Online with Patrick Stewart, November 3, 1995.

17. Interview with Patrick Stewart on KCRA-TV, November 19, 1994.

18. "Patrick Stewart Winds Down," by Michael Logan. *TV Guide,* January 15, 1994.

19. "Captain Picard Bridges the Next Generation Gap," by Michael Logan. *TV Guide,* January 2, 1993.

20. *Trek: The Unauthorized Behind-the-Scenes Story of the Next Generation,* by James Van Hise. 1993; Pioneer Books, Las Vegas, NV.

21. *Star Trek: The Next Generation the Official Magazine,* no. 21. '93-93 Season Starlog Communications International, New York, NY.

22. *Star Trek: The Next Generation the Official Magazine,* no. 22. '92-'93 Season. Starlog Communications International, New York, NY.

23. *Star Trek: The Next Generation the Official Magazine,* no. 23. '92-'93 Season. Starlog Communications International, New York, NY.

24. "Heart-Stopping Thrills & Chills in Season Ender of Star Trek: The Next Generation," by Jerome George. *National Enquirer,* March 18, 1993.

25. Interview with Patrick Stewart on *The Tonight Show* with Jay Leno, October 12, 1993.

26. Interview with Patrick Stewart on *The Tonight Show* with Jay Leno, November 1994.

27. *Star Trek: Where No One Has Gone Before,* by J. M. Dillard. 1994; Pocket Books, New York, NY.

Chapter Twelve: The Final TV Voyage

1. "Zooming to a 7th Season," by Mark A. Altman. *Cinefantastique,* October 1993.

2. "Star Trek: The Next Generation—Ending the TV Voyages," by Mark A. Altman. *Cinefantastique,* December 1994.

3. "I Can't Believe It's Over! Star Trek: The Next Generation Final Season," by Mark A. Altman. *Sci-Fi Universe,* September 1994.

4. *Star Trek: The Next Generation the Official Magazine,* no. 26. 93-'94 Season. Starlog Communications International, New York, NY.

5. *Star Trek: The Next Generation the Official Magazine,* no. 27. 93-'94 Season. Starlog Communications International, New York, NY.

6. *Star Trek: The Next Generation the Official Magazine,* no. 28. 93-'94 Season. Starlog Communications International, New York, NY.

7. *Star Trek: The Next Generation the Official Magazine,* no. 29. '93-'94 Season. Starlog Communications International, New York, NY.

8. *Star Trek: The Next Generation the Official Magazine,* no. 30. '93-'94 Season. Starlog Communications International, New York, NY.

9. *The New Trek Encyclopedia,* by John Peel with Scott Nance. 1994; Pioneer Books, Las Vegas, NV.

10. "Patrick Stewart Lets Down His Hair," by David Rensin. *TV Guide,* July 31, 1993.

11. America Online with Patrick Stewart, November 3, 1995.

12. "The Magnificent Seven," by Michael Logan. *TV Guide,* May 14, 1994.

13. "Inside Trek: Finale Means Mission Cut Short for 'Next Gen,'" by Ian Spelling. *Houston Chronicle,* May 14, 1994.

14. "The Future of Captain Picard, Part One: An Exclusive Interview with Patrick Stewart," by Dan Madsen. *Star Trek: The Official Fan Club,* September/October 1992, no. 87. The Official Fan Club, P.O. Box 111000, Aurora, CO 80011.

15. "The Future of Captain Picard, Part Two: An Exclusive Interview with Patrick Stewart," by Dan Madsen. *Star Trek: The Official Fan Club,* November/December 1992, no. 88. The Official Fan Club, P.O. Box 111000, Aurora, CO 80011.

16. "Once and Future Captain," by Ian Spelling. *Starlog,* March 1995, no. 212. Starlog Communications International, New York, NY.

17. "20 Questions: Patrick Stewart," interview by Neil Tesser. *Playboy,* November 1992.

18. "A New Enterprise: An Exclusive Interview with *Jeffrey* Star, Patrick Stewart. *The Advocate,* August 22, 1995.

19. "Patrick Stewart: The Legacy of Captain Picard," by Pamela Roller. *Star Trek: The Official Fan Club,* October/November 1994, no. 99. The Official Fan Club, P.O. Box 111000, Aurora, CO 80011.

20. *Trek the Next Generation Crew Book* by James Van Hise. 1993; Pioneer Books, Las Vegas, NV.

21. *The Next Generation Tribute, Book Two,* edited by James Van Hise. 1994; Pioneer Books, Las Vegas, NV.

22. *Trek: The Next Generation,* Third Edition, by James Van Hise. 1994; Pioneer Books, New York, NY.

23. "Make It So," by Eirik Knutzen. *The Official Star Trek Fan Club of the U.K.,* August 1993, no. 2. The Official Star Trek Fan Club of the U.K., Absolute Field Marketing, The Old Barn, Jericho Farm, Worton, Nr. Cassington, Oxon OX8 IEB.

24. " 'Generation' Ex," by Benjamin Svetkey. *Entertainment Weekly,* May 6, 1994.

25. "Picard Races Through Time to Save the Human Race," by Michael Glynn. *National Enquirer,* May 17, 1994.

26. "Patrick Stewart: The Next Generation," by Martha Frankel. *Movieline,* November 1994.

27. Interview with Patrick Stewart on KCRA-TV, November 19, 1994.

28. "Trekking Onward," by Richard Zoglin. *Time,* November 28, 1994.

29. "Thrills & Chills in 'Star Trek' Spectacular," by Michael Glynn. *National Enquirer,* July 13, 1993.

30. " 'Star Trek' Captain: Cops Grabbed Me as a Terror Suspect," Exclusive interview with Patrick Stewart by Gary A. Schreiber. *National Enquirer,* July 20, 1993.

31. Patrick Stewart on *Saturday Night Live,* February 5, 1994.

Chapter Thirteen: *Generations* Gap

1. "The Making of Star Trek: Generations—Behind-the-Scenes Secrets," by Edward Gross. *Cinescape,* December 1994.

2. "Generations: Picard's New Trek," by Mark A. Altman. *Sci-Fi Universe,* November 1994.

3. Interview with Patrick Stewart on *The Late Show* with David Letterman, July 5, 1994.

4. *Star Trek: Generations the Official Movie Magazine,* November 1994. Starlog Communications International, New York, NY.

5. "Trekking Onward," by Richard Zoglin. *Time,* November 28, 1994.

6. "William Shatner: The Universe Interview," by David Giammarco. *Sci-Fi Universe,* November 1995.

7. " 'Generation' Ex," by Benjamin Svetkey. *Entertainment Weekly,* May 6, 1994.

8. "Once and Future Captain," by Ian Spelling. *Starlog,* March 1995, no. 212. Starlog Communications International, New York, NY.

9. "Patrick Stewart: The Legacy of Captain Picard," by Pamela Roller. *Star Trek: The Official Fan Club,* October/November 1994, no. 99. The Official Fan Club, P.O. Box 111000, Aurora, CO 80011.

10. *The New Trek Encyclopedia,* by John Peel with Scott Nance. 1994; Pioneer Books, Las Vegas, NV.

11. "Patrick Stewart: The Next Generation," by Martha Frankel. *Movieline,* November 1994.

12. *Starlog's Science Fiction Heroes & Heroines,* edited by David McDonnell. 1995; Crescent Books, Avenel, NJ.

13. "Strategic Withdrawal: Patrick Stewart Says Goodbye to Picard and the Enterprise—At Least For Now," by Edward Gross. *Cinescape,* October 1995.

14. Interview with Patrick Stewart on KCRA-TV, November 19, 1994.

15. "Patrick Stewart: Captain Picard on Shatner, Roddenberry and the Realm of Star Trek," interview by Dan Madsen. *Star Trek Communicator,* December/January 1994/95, no. 100. The Official Fan Club, P.O. Box 111000, Aurora, CO 80011.

16. "Keep on Trekkin': On the Set of the New Star Trek," by John Housley. *Premiere,* December 1994.

17. "Nimoy: The Universe Interview," by Sheldon Teitelbaum. *Sci-Fi Universe,* February 1996.

18. " 'Generations' Rules the Galaxy at Box Office," by Robin DeRosa. *USA Today,* November 21, 1994.

19. *Star Trek Generations,* by J.M. Dillard. 1994; Pocket Books, New York, NY.

20. *Trek: The Next Generation,* Third Edition, by James Van Hise. 1994; Pioneer Books, Las Vegas, NV.

21. *Star Trek Movie Memories,* by William Shatner. 1994; HarperCollins, New York, NY.

22. "Jonathan Frakes: Looking Out for 'Number One,' " interview by Dan Madsen. *Star Trek Communicator,* December/January 1995/96, no. 105. The Official Fan Club, P.O. Box 111000, Aurora, CO 80011.

23. "Star Trek: The Ultimate Trip Through the Galaxies," *Entertainment Weekly,* Special Edition, January 18, 1995. Time, Inc., New York, NY.

24. "Kirk Teams Up with Picard—& Dies in His Arms," by Mac Cetner. *National Enquirer,* May 17, 1994.

25. "Beam Him Down," by Cynthia Sanz. *People,* November 28, 1994.

26. "Inside Trek: 'Generations' Heavy Kills Kirk—Sort of" by Ian Spelling. *Houston Chronicle,* December 3, 1994.

27. "Inside Trek: Shatner Hasn't Missed Much in His 30-Year Trek," by Ian Spelling. *Houston Chronicle,* August 27, 1994.

28. "Absolutely Nebulous: Exploring the 'Generations' Flap," by Albert Kim and Frank Spotnitz, *Entertainment Weekly,* October 7, 1994.

29. "Kirk Out? Puzzling Over Captain's Fate in *Star Trek Generations,* "by Ann Oldenburg, *USA Today,* October 26, 1994.

30. "Beams Away: 'The Next Generation' Boldly Goes Where Few Series Have Gone Before—the Big Screen," by Rebecca Ascher-Walsh. *Entertainment Weekly,* March 25, 1994.

31. *I Am Spock,* by Leonard Nimoy. 1995; Hyperion, New York, NY.

32. "Q & A: Patrick Stewart," interview by Ryan Murphy. *US,* December 1994.

33. "Picard's New Generation," interview by Hilary Oliver. *The List: Glasgow and Edinburgh Events Guide,* February 19, 1995.

34. Interview with Patrick Stewart by Steve Wright on BBC Radio 1 FM, April 4, 1993.

35. "William Shatner: A Farewell to Kirk," interview by David Rensin. *TV Guide*, October 8, 1994.
36. " 'Generations' Rap," interview with Patrick Stewart by Craig Modderno. *TV Guide*, October 8, 1994.
37. *Beyond Uhura: Star Trek and Other Memories*, by Nichelle Nichols. 1994; Putnam, New York, NY.
38. *To the Stars: The Autobiography of George Takei*, by George Takei. 1994; Pocket Books, New York, NY.
39. Personal conversations with George Takei, February 1996.
40. "Generations," by Michael Beeler and Sue Uram. *Cinefantastique*, December 1994.
41. *Captain Quirk*, by Dennis William Hauck. Pinnacle Books, New York, NY.
42. "Trekker Treat," by Michael Logan. *TV Guide*, January 20, 1996.
43. "Inside Trek: Just-Released Bio Gets Real on Roddenberry, " by Ian Spelling. *Houston Chronicle*, June 11, 1994.

Chapter Fourteen: Finally Out of Uniform

1. "News & Notes: Flashes," by Stephen Schaefer. *Entertainment Weekly*, August 4, 1995.
2. " 'Trek' Spun Stewart into a New Orbit," by David Patrick Stearns. *USA Today*, August 8, 1995.
3. "Patrick Stewart Lets Down His Hair," by David Rensin. *TV Guide*, July 31, 1993.
4. "Patrick Stewart Makes It So," by A. J. Jacobs. *Entertainment Weekly*, October 20, 1995.
5. "The Week's Best Bets for Kids," by Ray Stackhouse. *TV Guide*, January 27, 1996.
6. "On Stage, and Off," by Donald G. McNeil, Jr. *New York Times*, April 28, 1995.

7. "A Question for Patrick Stewart." *New York Times Magazine,* June 25, 1995.
8. "Star Tracks." *People,* July 24, 1995.
9. "Talk is Chic," by Tiarra Mukherjee. *Entertainment Weekly,* February 9, 1996.
10. America Online with Patrick Stewart, November 3, 1995.
11. "Briefly . . ." *USA Today,* March 8, 1996.
12. "Low-Budget Drama is Sly's Next Move," by Jeannie Williams. *USA Today,* March 14, 1996.
13. "Warner Preps New *Batman." Cinescape,* November 1995.
14. "A Tights Squeeze," by Steve Daly and Anne Thompson. *Entertainment Weekly,* March 8, 1996.
15. "Hollywood Banks on the Bard: Producing Shakespeare as They Like It," by David Patrick Stearns. *USA Today,* December 18, 1995.
16. "Inside Trek: 'Grandma Trek' Runs Network of Volunteers," by Ian Spelling. *Houston Chronicle,* October 30, 1995.
17. "Inside Trek: Guest Stars Make Tracks After Being on 'Trek,' " by Ian Spelling. *Houston Chronicle,* September 4, 1993.
18. "The Future of Captain Picard, Part One: An Exclusive Interview with Patrick Stewart," by Dan Madsen. *Star Trek: The Official Fan Club,* September/October 1992, no. 87. The Official Fan Club, P.O. Box 111000, Aurora, CO 80011.
19. "The Future of Captain Picard, Part Two: An Exclusive Interview with Patrick Stewart, " by Dan Madsen. *Star Trek: The Official Fan Club,* November/December 1992, no. 88. The Official Fan Club, P.O. Box 111000, Aurora, CO 80011.
20. Commencement Address by Patrick Stewart at Pomona College, May 14, 1995.
21. Interview with Patrick Stewart by Steve Wright on BBC Radio 1 FM, April 4, 1993.

22. "Strategic Withdrawal: Patrick Stewart Says Good-bye to Picard and the Enterprise—At Least for Now," by Edward Gross. *Cinescape,* October 1995.

23. "The Movie's the Thing: Set Diary," by Paul Rudnick. *Premiere,* September 1995.

24. Interview with Patrick Stewart by Wayne Hoffman for *Seattle Gay News,* August 4, 1995.

25. "A New Enterprise: An Exclusive Interview with *Jeffrey* Star, Patrick Stewart," *The Advocate,* August 22, 1995.

26. "Entertainment Extra," by Evelyn Ludvigson. King Features Syndication, January 14, 1996.

27. "What's the Deal with *Star Trek VIII?*" by Mark A. Altman. *Sci-Fi Universe,* March 1996.

28. "There's No Place Like Home: Patrick Stewart Goes Back to Where it All Began," by John Mosby. *Sci-Fi Universe,* March 1996.

29. "Once and Future Captain," by Ian Spelling. *Starlog,* March 1995, no. 212. Starlog Communications International, New York, NY.

30. "Star Trek: The Ultimate Trip Through the Galaxies." *Entertainment Weekly,* Special Edition, January 18, 1995. Time, Inc. New York, NY.

31. "Q & A: Patrick Stewart," interview by Henry Edwards. *Details,* September 1995.

32. "20 Questions: Patrick Stewart," interview by Neil Tesser. *Playboy,* November 1992.

33. "Q & A: Patrick Stewart," interview by Ryan Murphy. *US,* December 1994.

34. "Patrick Stewart: The Next Generation," by Martha Frankel. *Movieline,* November 1994.

Epilogue: Full Circle

1. "What's the Deal with *Star Trek VIII?*" by Mark A. Altman. *Sci-Fi Universe,* March 1996.

2. "Star Trek: Ready for Action," by Edward Gross. *Cinescape,* May 1996.

3. "State of the Trek Report," by Mark A. Altman. *Sci-Fi Universe,* June 1996.

4. "Star Trek: It's Not Easy Being Frakes," by N'Gai Croal and Brad Stone. *Newsweek,* May 20, 1996.

5. "Inside Trek: Producer Charts Course Through 'Trek' Universe," by Ian Spelling. *Houston Chronicle,* November 4, 1995.

6. "Red Alert," by Chris Nashawaty. *Entertainment Weekly,* May 3, 1996.

7. "The Next 'Generation' Movie," by Michael Logan. *TV Guide,* October 7, 1995.

8. "Boldly Going to Broadway: A Tale of Two Captains," by Michael Logan. *TV Guide,* December 16, 1995.

9. "Jonathan Frakes to Direct Next Feature Film," interview by Dan Madsen. *Star Trek Communicator,* March/April 1996, no. 106. The Official Fan Club, P.O. Box 111000, Aurora, CO 80011.

10. "The Next Feature Film to Explore the Beginnings of Starfleet!" interview by Dan Madsen. *Star Trek Communicator,* October/November 1995, no. 104. The Official Fan Club, P.O. Box 111000, Aurora, CO 80011.

11. "Patrick Stewart Reports for Duty Aboard the Enterprise in Next 'Trek'." *The Detroit News,* November 24, 1995.

About the Authors

James Hatfield is the former film critic for *The Texas Women's News* and a frequent contributor to other Lone Star State regional publications. Having returned to his native Arkansas from Dallas in 1994, where he was for many years the vice-president of a large real estate management company, he now lives in a small town at the foothills of the Ozarks. He divides his time between writing books, computer troubleshooting, reviewing movies, hunting for antiques, and fishing on Beaver Lake for "that trophy Bass."

George Burt, Ph.D. (affectionately known as "Doc") is a computer consultant to major businesses and industries in Texas, specializing in software application development. Doc met his co-author while working on a major computer project for one of America's largest retail companies and, after discovering they were both diehard X-Philes and Trekkers, have been writing partners ever since. Doc makes his home in Dallas, Texas, where he spends his leisure time reading law books (he's also a paralegal) or indulging in his real passion—cheering for the Super Bowl champion Dallas Cowboys!

Also by the Authors

The Ultimate Trek Trivia Challenge for the Next Generation

INFORMATIVE—
COMPELLING—
SCINTILLATING—
NON-FICTION FROM PINNACLE TELLS THE TRUTH:

BORN TOO SOON   (751, $4.50)
by Elizabeth Mehren
This is the poignant story of Elizabeth's daughter Emily's premature birth. As the parents of one of the 275,000 babies born prematurely each year in this country, she and her husband were plunged into the world of the Neonatal Intensive Care unit. With stunning candor, Elizabeth Mehren relates her gripping story of unshakable faith and hope—and of courage that comes in tiny little packages.

THE PROSTATE PROBLEM   (745, $4.50)
by Chet Cunningham
An essential, easy-to-use guide to the treatment and prevention of the illness that's in the headlines. This book explains in clear, practical terms all the facts. Complete with a glossary of medical terms, and a comprehensive list of health organizations and support groups, this illustrated handbook will help men combat prostate disorder and lead longer, healthier lives.

THE ACADEMY AWARDS HANDBOOK   (887, $4.50)
An interesting and easy-to-use guide for movie fans everywhere, the book features a year-to-year listing of all the Oscar nominations in every category, all the winners, an expert analysis of who wins and why, a complete index to get information quickly, and even a 99% foolproof method to pick this year's winners!

WHAT WAS HOT   (894, $4.50)
by Julian Biddle
Journey through 40 years of the trends and fads, famous and infamous figures, and momentous milestones in American history. From hoola hoops to rap music, greasers to yuppies, Elvis to Madonna—it's all here, trivia for all ages. An entertaining and evocative overview of the milestones in America from the 1950's to the 1990's!

Available wherever paperbacks are sold, or order direct from the Publisher. Send cover price plus 50¢ per copy for mailing and handling to Penguin USA, P.O. Box 999, c/o Dept. 17109, Bergenfield, NJ 07621. Residents of New York and Tennessee must include sales tax. DO NOT SEND CASH.

FUN AND LOVE!

THE DUMBEST DUMB BLONDE JOKE BOOK (889, $4.50)
by Joey West

They say that blondes have more fun . . . but we can all have a hoot with THE DUMBEST DUMB BLONDE JOKE BOOK. Here's a hilarious collection of hundreds of dumb blonde jokes—including dumb blonde GUY jokes—that are certain to send you over the edge!

THE I HATE MADONNA JOKE BOOK (798, $4.50)
by Joey West

She's Hollywood's most controversial star. Her raunchy reputation's brought her fame and fortune. Now here is a sensational collection of hilarious material on America's most talked about MATERIAL GIRL!

LOVE'S LITTLE INSTRUCTION BOOK (774, $4.99)
by Annie Pigeon

Filled from cover to cover with romantic hints—one for every day of the year—this delightful book will liven up your life and make you and your lover smile. Discover these amusing tips for making your lover happy . . . tips like—ask her mother to dance—have his car washed—take turns being irrational . . . and many, many more!

MOM'S LITTLE INSTRUCTION BOOK (0009, $4.99)
by Annie Pigeon

Mom needs as much help as she can get, what with chaotic schedules, wedding fiascos, Barneymania and all. Now, here comes the best mother's helper yet. Filled with funny comforting advice for moms of all ages. What better way to show mother how very much you love her by giving her a gift guaranteed to make her smile everyday of the year.

Available wherever paperbacks are sold, or order direct from the Publisher. Send cover price plus 50¢ per copy for mailing and handling to Penguin USA, P.O. Box 999, c/o Dept. 17109, Bergenfield, NJ 07621. Residents of New York and Tennessee must include sales tax. DO NOT SEND CASH.